IRELAND'S LITERATURE
SELECTED ESSAYS

Terence Brown was born in Loping, China, in 1944, raised in Holywood, Co. Down, and educated at Trinity College, Dublin, where he is Fellow and Associate Professor of English. His books include *Louis MacNeice: Sceptical Vision* (1975), *Northern Voices: Poets from Ulster* (1975) and *Ireland: A Social and Cultural History 1922-1985* (1985); he has co-edited *The Irish Short Story* (1979) and *Tradition and Influence in Anglo-Irish Poetry* (1988). He has lectured on Anglo-Irish literature in many parts of the world.

. FEB

MAY 95

04. NOV

D1494158

IN MEMORY OF MY MOTHER

IRELAND'S
LITERATURE
SELECTED ESSAYS

NES
CURREL
HARG

WITHDRAWN FROM STOCK

Inv/94 : 158S   Price IR£9.95
Title: IRELAND'S LITERATURE
Class: 820.99415

THE LILLIPUT PRESS
MULLINGAR
and
BARNES & NOBLE BOOKS
TOTOWA, NEW JERSEY

Copyright © Terence Brown 1988

All rights reserved. No part of this publication
may be reproduced in any form or by any means
without the prior permission of the publisher.

First published in 1988 by
THE LILLIPUT PRESS LTD
Gigginstown, Mullingar
Co. Westmeath, Ireland

British Library Cataloguing in Publication Data

Brown, Terence, *1944–*
Ireland's literature : selected essays
1. Irish literature – Critical studies
I. Title
891.6'2'09

ISBN 0-946640-24-6
ISBN 0-946640-25-4 Pbk

First published in the USA 1988 by
BARNES & NOBLE BOOKS
81 Adams Drive, Totowa, New Jersey 07512

Library of Congress Cataloging in Publication Data

Brown, Terence.
Ireland's literature.
Includes index.
1. English literature—Irish authors—History and criticism.
2. Ireland in literature. 3. Literature and history.
4. Ireland—Intellectual life—20th century.
5. Ireland—Intellectual life—19th century. I. Title.
PR8718.B76 1988   820'.9'89162   88-16638

ISBN 0-389-20802-7

Jacket design by Jole Bortoli
Set in 10 on 12 Palatino by
Koinonia Ltd of Manchester
and printed in England by
Billings & Sons Ltd of Worcester

CONTENTS

Preface   ix

1   Saxon and Celt: The Stereotypes   3
2   Thomas Moore: A Reputation   14
3   Edward Dowden: Irish Victorian   29
4   The Church of Ireland and
        the Climax of the Ages   49
5   Canon Sheehan and the Catholic Intellectual   65
6   Yeats, Joyce and the Irish Critical Debate   77
7   After the Revival: Seán Ó Faoláin
        and Patrick Kavanagh   91
8   Some Young Doom: Beckett and the Child   117
9   Austin Clarke: Satirist   127
10 Geoffrey Taylor: A Portrait   141
11 C. S. Lewis: Irishman?   152
12 Donoghue and Us Irish   166
13 Show Me a Sign: Brian Moore and
        Religious Faith   174
14 Poets and Patrimony: Richard Murphy
        and James Simmons   189
15 A Northern Renaissance: Poets from
        the North of Ireland 1965-1980   203
16 Remembering Who We Are   223
17 Awakening from the Nightmare:
        History and Contemporary Literature   243

Acknowledgments   257
Index   259

PREFACE

In 1986 a new Irish literary and cultural journal, *The Irish Review*, chose to announce its presence to the world, not with an inaugural editorial but by printing an essay by the historian Roy Foster entitled 'We Are All Revisionists Now', which sought to align the journal with the spirit of sceptical critical enquiry. In so doing, its editors were recognizing, I believe, the pre-eminence of history among the humanistic disciplines practised in Irish academe. From at least the 1960s a steady stream of Irish historical scholarship has subjected the whole canon of Irish political and economic history to scrupulous scrutiny. That work has been responsible for challenging received wisdom on such matters as the consequences of the Penal Laws, landlord and tenant rela-tions in the nineteenth century, the causes of the Famine, the significance of the Land War, the nature of the revolution which gave Ireland its modern independence, and the social and economic basis of Ulster Unionism. And, most strikingly, it was historians like the late F. S. L. Lyons, Conor Cruise O'Brien and Louis Cullen who took the first steps into the complex world of Irish cultural history: Lyons in his masterly chapter 'The battle of two civilisations' in *Ireland Since the Famine*, O'Brien in his revisionist essay 'Passion and Cunning: An Essay on the Politics of W. B. Yeats', and Cullen in a pioneering critique of a key literary historical work, Daniel Corkery's *The Hidden Ireland*. The historians' contribution to the intellectual life of modern Ireland is perhaps measured by the facts that Leland Lyons was at work on the official biography of W. B. Yeats when he died in 1983, and that his successor in the task is the same Roy Foster who launched *The Irish Review*.

In this context the literary and cultural historian who wishes to reflect on the history of Irish writing in English since the eighteenth and nineteenth centuries, and on the inter-relation-ship between that literature and the society in which it came to life and finds a readership, is conscious that his interrogation of the past and present must be conducted in ways that take account of the changing maps of modern Irish history as a whole. For literary and cultural history cannot be conducted as if these can convincingly exist in isolation from other modes of historical imagining.

Accordingly, this collection of essays, which constitutes a series of soundings in Irish literary and cultural history, seeks to bear in mind as it engages in various forms of enquiry (literary critical, biographical, sociological) the contexts which modern Irish historiography has made available to us. In this respect further knowledge about nineteenth-century Ireland must enforce re-examination of the origins and nature of the Irish Literary Revival. The degree to which that movement was a part of the history of Victorian Britain in which Ireland played a part must increasingly, I think, stimulate 'revisionist' enquiry. The essays here on such figures as Tom Moore, Edward Dowden and Canon Sheehan, and on the Church of Ireland and the origins of the Literary Revival, should tentatively open the path to study of the rich and scarcely harvested field of Irish Victorian life and thought.

The grandeur and durability of Yeats's poetic and dramatic achievement, together with the power of his mythologizing, polemical skill, is of course the principal reason why it has been so easy in the past to read most nineteenth-century Irish literature as a prologue to the main text inscribed on Irish history by Yeats and his confederates. That the culmination of the Literary Revival was contemporaneous with the historical climax of the nationalist revival and the rise of Sinn Fein, must give added force to a view of Ireland's cultural and literary history in which the nineteenth century is read as at best merely a germinating soil and at worst a kind of depressed trough in which post-Famine Victorian Ireland was the lowest point. Similarly, the remarkable achievements of the generation of writers associated with the Revival movement have almost inevitably meant that subsequent writing has been reflected upon as in some way belated, necessarily over-shadowed. And the fact that such writing was associated with a period of post-revolutionary disillusionment, and with the historical inconclusiveness of Partition and the Free State, deepened the sense of anti-climax. Throughout that period, until very recent times, the achievements of Yeats, and then increasingly of Joyce, dominated the critical field and the works of post-Revival writers (the very term indicative of the context in which they must be viewed). Several essays in this volume consider therefore how such writers have responded to their belated condition, while another examines how the respective careers of Yeats and Joyce have served as poles in the dialectics of a repetitive critical debate.

Some of the impetus for the historical revisionism of recent times in Ireland, where it has not simply had its origins in disinterested critical enquiry, has been the conflict in Northern Ireland. Conventional Irish nationalist self-understanding has been challenged by the awful events of the last twenty years. The challenge to a conventional Irish literary history which regards the Revival as culmination and the post-Revival period as a kind of coming to terms with an overwhelming inheritance, has stemmed from the North itself. For at the very least the emergence of so many poets, playwrights and, more recently, novelists, from the province poses the question as to how the literary and cultural map of Ireland must be re-drawn to take account of this new imaginative territory, one where the Revival legacy weighs less heavily and where the colonial links with the United Kingdom akin to those which where forged in the nineteenth century between the literary cultures of Great Britian and Ireland, still obtain.

Throughout the century individual talents have had differing relations to what might be conceived of as the tradition. These figures, genetic sports, eccentrics or abberations as they might be reckoned, also serve to alert us to the fact that literary history, like other modes of historical thought, has to take account of contingency and matter which cannot readily be assimilated to a shapely thesis. The varying careers of C. S. Lewis, Geoffrey Taylor, Denis Donoghue and Brian Moore, in my evocations of them and their work, give, I hope, a sense of the irreducible variety of literary development in the period.

The final section of this book explores how, in relation to the North, history itself becomes a focus of imaginative energy at the point where the concerns of artist, historian and citizen converge.

Terence Brown
Trinity College, Dublin
September 1988

IRELAND'S LITERATURE
SELECTED ESSAYS

1

SAXON AND CELT: THE STEREOTYPES

In a paper given in 1983 Nicholas Canny directed our attention to Edmund Spenser's *A View of the Present State of Ireland*, identifying it as a key document in the history of the development of an Anglo-Irish identity.[1] Encapsulating as it does, in Canny's judgement, many of the staples of colonialist comment on Irish life since at least the time of Geraldus Cambrensis, it provides in its 'elegant and coherent'[2] form a justification for the English presence in Ireland beyond that of mere conquest. Colonialism in Spenser's treatise is invested with a moral dimension, since it has as one of its elements the intent of a social improvement that will so change the Irish environment that it will become an appropriate context for the application of that inestimable good, the English Common Law. As conditions pertained in Elizabethan Ireland the Common Law could not be appropriately applied, so Spenser believed, because of the inveterate barbarism of the people, bound by loyalty to their septs and clans. In such conditions it could not but be subverted. Following the military defeat and subjugation of the Irish, their resettlement and introduction to town life, education and eventual conversion, then and then only could English Common Law bestow all its benefits in a country that had hitherto been in all essential matters beyond law. Change the environment to change the man, is Spenser's theme.

The image of barbarism that Spenser presents in his treatise is worth some study. Canny alerts us to the fact that it is a fairly conventional one, depending, as others had done, on 'resort to surgical or horticultural metaphors'.[3] The following is characteristic of the latter:

all these evils must be first cut away by a strong hand, before any good can be planted, like as corrupt branches and unwholesome boughs are first to be pruned, and the foule mosse cleansed and scraped away, before the tree can bring forth any good fruite.[4]

But perhaps the image here escapes the merely conventional in its vivid particularity, the phrase 'foule mosse' subtly reminding one of that other conventional metaphoric strand in the work which associates the barbarous life of the Irish with contagion, infection, disease. And throughout there is an impression of Ireland and the Irish which has a compelling power. The country seems a land of woods and glens in which lawless, ignorant (Spenser's repeated word is 'lewd', as in St Paul's 'lewd fellows of the baser sort') and licentious people skulk in their obstinate attachment to superstitious and ancestral loyalties; the hair worn as a glib and the enveloping mantle seem the outward signs of inward deceit, suited as they are to disguise and concealment. The sword and famine will bring them to the point of submission, as it had once done in Munster which the poet remembers in a haunting passage compact both of pity and anticipation of the final solution proposed in his own pages:

Out of every corner of the woods and glynnes they came creeping forth upon their hands, for their legges could not beare them; they looked like anatomies of death, they spake like ghosts crying out of their graves; they did eate the dead carrions, happy where they could finde them, yea, and one another soone after, insomuch as the very carcasses they spared not to scrape out of their graves; and, if they found a plot of watercresses or shamrocks, there they flocked as to a feast for the time, yet not able long to continue therewithall [. . .].[5]

Canny suggests that the English or Anglo-Irish in Ireland were sustained by this vision of themselves as the bearers of law to the regions of barbarism until the end of the seventeenth century. It seems unlikely that the eighteenth century radically altered their perception. Bishop Berkeley's famous assault, for example, on the work-shy Irish in his tract 'A Word to the Wise' seems but a simple variant in the theme.

It was of course the Romantic movement of the late eighteenth and early nineteenth centuries that transformed the way in which men and women from apparently advanced societies perceived those societies which had in the past been considered simply barbaric. And some English and Anglo-Irish perception of Ireland was to be influenced by this general shift in European awareness. Furthermore, concurrent with the Romantic revival and in some respects an aspect of it, the rise of nationalism encouraged the elevation of national stereotypes to the level of racial characteristics, as the semi-sacred possession of an authentic 'people'. In this new philosophic context what had once been regarded as mere barbarism could be esteemed in Romantic terms as uncorrupted, unsophisticated innocence and in nationalist terms as racial characteristics. The nineteenth century affords a number of interesting examples of English and Anglo-Irish writers reflecting on English and Irish identity in these novel terms (as well as any number who merely restated in racial and class terms the old categories of civilization and barbarism). What is striking is that the Romantic perspective allows only for a softening or blurring of Spenser's stark sense of English order and Irish lawlessness. This nineteenth century Romantic version of Spenser's dualism is of course the contrast between the capable, sober, solid Saxon and the poetic, sentimental, otherworldly Celt.

An early example of such thinking in which we actually are afforded the opportunity to observe Spenser's work undergoing a sea change in the waters of Romantic feeling is provided by the Ulster poet William Hamilton Drummond. Drummond published his poem *The Giant's Causeway* in 1811. In this curious blend of scientific and topographical verse with Ossianic feeling, Drummond finds time to celebrate the union of Great Britain and Ireland in terms that make clear that a sentimental regard for the Gaelic past is not to be allowed to interfere with his more rationally based respect for imperial progress. In his notes to the poem we come on the following interesting passages. He compares the peasantry of the low glens in County Antrim with more recent Scots settlers:

In the peasantry of the low glens we behold a [. . .] race open, obliging, communicative without hope of reward, acquainted with the traditionary history of their country, and retaining the native language and characteristic inquisitiveness of the Irish.

The address with which a peasant puts his questions to discover from a stranger his country, profession, circumstances, in short his whole history, and the perseverance with which he resumes his inquiries, when baffled by an evasive answer, are surprising. Gain his confidence, and it is easily gained by a little familiar conversation, and he will unbosom his whole soul to you [. . .] and take a pride in *insensing* you (the Irish peasant is never at a loss for an expression) into the subject of any of your enquiries.

The inhabitants of the rest of the coast are chiefly of recent Scotch origin, and have less suppleness, simplicity, and courtesy, but more solidity, industry, and domestic comforts, united to a high spirit of Presbyterian independence.[6]

Here we have the contrast between the solid and the sensitive (expressed by Drummond in Ulster as a contrast between Scots settler and native peasant) that became one variant of nineteenth century racial type-casting. The Irish are cast as sensitive, poetic, sentimental, the English (or Scots) are steady, sober, fitted to rule.

Elsewhere in his notes Drummond refers directly to Spenser's *View*, expatiating on the famous passage where the Elizabethan poet censures the Irish bards for their licentious disregard for the moral virtues in the compositions. But where Spenser had not allowed the fact that their works 'savoured of sweet wit, and good invention, and were sprinkled with some pretty flowers of their naturall device which gave good grace and comelinesse unto them'[7] to deter him from severe moral condemnation, Drummond, indulging Romantic feeling, invests his description of the bards with a lyrical poignancy. And he makes them, indeed, poetic representatives of the Irish peasantry he has observed in the Antrim glens. Both possess sensibility, but lack the sense which makes progress an imperial prerogative:

Like the bards of Wales, they took a decided part in opposing the English power, and by their animated strains in which they dwelt on the exploits of their ancestors, and the sweets of liberty, the ruin of their country, and the rapacity of her invaders, fomented a spirit of rebellion which could be allayed, only by the extinction of their order. To effect this, several rigorous laws were enacted against them, in the reigns of Edward III, Henry VIII, and Elizabeth. They were obliged to seek the protection of solitude and concealment. Surrounded by the wild scenery of their rocks and mountains, they poured out their expiring notes with exquisite and inimitable pathos. Their numbers gradually diminished, and their profession, yielding to the progress of civilization and refinement, at length became extinct.[8]

A sensitive, sentimental, backward-looking people, it is implied, excel as artists only in the poetry of lost causes.

The early decades of the nineteenth century saw the idea of racial characteristics and the contrast between Saxon and Celt become solidly entrenched, so that by 1834 the young Samuel Ferguson could write, with a clear sense that he is dealing in accepted[9] categories:

We believe that [. . .] there are as essential differences between the genius's as between the physical appearances of nations. We believe that [. . .] no stultifying operation of mere security, plenty or laborious regularity could ever, without actual physical transubstantiation, reduce the native Irishman to the stolid standard of the sober Saxon.[10]

But it is of course in Matthew Arnold's *On the Study of Celtic Literature* (1867) that the contrast between stolidity and poetry is employed with most subtlety and rhetorical elegance. In that essay an association of racial differences with artistic deficiency, bluntly stated by Spenser, seen in proto-typical, Romantic form in Drummond's gloss on Spenser, becomes fully developed.

Arnold's essay, as John V. Kelleher has definitively shown,[11] plays unintentionally a very backhanded compliment to the Celts and their literature. The Celtic genius with 'sentiment as its main basis, with love of beauty, charm, and spirituality for its excellence, ineffectualness and self-will for its defect',[12] lacks in Arnold's view the capacity for political self-government: 'the skillful and resolute appliance of means to end which is needed both to make progress in material civilization, and also to form powerful states, is just what the Celt has least turn for.'[13] And his art is of a piece with the deficiency, lacking in architectural power: 'he has only produced poetry with an air of greatness investing it all, and sometimes giving. . . to short pieces, or to passages. . . singular beauty and power.'[14] And that beauty and power is often part of the melancholy wrought of the Celtic peoples' 'adverse destiny, their immense calamity'[15] where it is not a kind of 'magic', product of 'a vivid and near interpretation of nature',[16] of which a primitive people are more capable than an advanced.

Kelleher makes a very persuasive case for considering much poetry written by Irishmen and women in the years between the fall of Parnell and the War of Independence as work which seems to prove the aptness of Arnold's categories and the accuracy of his assessment of the Celtic genius. Celtic Twilight poetry might almost have been written, so Kelleher implies, to Arnold's prescription. And Arnold may indeed have been partly responsible for creating a critical climate in which work of a particular kind could gain currency as representing the Celtic imagination. That it did so in a context which was in part created by a redefinition in aesthetic terms of the colonial imperative is an idea all practitioners in the mode would undoubtedly have rejected with outrage. But the colonial condescension is clearly present in even so well intentioned a commentator as Arnold. How ideas of the Arnoldian kind could be exploited, not on behalf of a cultural nationalism as many writers of the Irish Literary Revival hopefully assayed, but on behalf of a brutal imperialistic interpretation of Irish history, is evidenced by James Anthony Froude's work, *The English in Ireland in the Eighteenth Century*.

This work, first published in 1874 with a second edition appearing in 1881, includes in its preface a metaphor that takes us back to Spenser, when Froude writes: 'The type of Irish agitation is so unchanging that the disease is at all times obviously the same.'[17] The author's general thesis is that the Irish are a people who, lacking personal restraint, would have welcomed strong, just rule (Froude was a devoted exponent of Carlyle's ideal of the heroic). A people capable of great loyalty to such leadership had been in fact betrayed by the fitful, desultory colonialism of the English, which became especially so after the Union (the second edition contained a supplementary chapter on the effects of that Union). From this melancholy state of affairs Froude finally derives his conclusion that Ireland should be left to the Irish. But his earlier assessment of their racial character could not have given him much hope that independence would bring them national well-being. The passage, in terms Arnold had earlier employed, discerns even in Irish art and letters symptoms of racial disequilibrium:

Lighthearted, humorous, imaginative, susceptible through the entire range of feeling, from the profoundest pathos to the most playful jest, if they possess some real virtues they possess the counterfeits of a hundred more. Passionate in everything – passionate in their patriotism, passionate in their religion, passionately courageous, passionately loyal and affectionate, they are without the manliness which will give strength and solidity to the sentimental part of their dispositions, while the surface and show is so seductive and so winning that only experience of its instability can resist the charm.

8

The incompleteness of character is conspicuous in all they do and have done; in their history, in their practical habits, in their arts and in their literature. Their lyrical melodies are exquisite, their epic poetry is ridiculous bombast. In their lives of their saints there is a wild if fantastic spendour; but they have no history, for as a nation they have done nothing which posterity will not be anxious to forget; and if they never have produced a tolerable drama, it is because imagination cannot overstrip reality. In the annals of ten centuries there is not a character, male or female, to be found belonging to them with sufficient firmness of texture to be carved into a dramatic outline [. . .]. The Irish are the spendthrift sister of the Arian race.[18]

One would like to believe that such categorical thinking received its quietus from *John Bull's Other Island*, was overwhelmed by the obviously heroic outlines of Yeats's Cuchulain cycle, and was laid finally to rest by the manifestly epic, architectural achievement of Joyce's *Ulysses*. Edward VII may have broken his chair laughing at a command performance of Shaw's play in 1905 (the play of which Shaw wrote 'I never achieved such a feat of construction in my life'[19] as if to give the lie to Arnold and those who thought like him); Yeats's drama and Joyce's fiction may have indisputably entered the modernist canon, but the diminution of efforts to stereotype racially the Irish in contrast with the English probably owes much more to the loss of English interest in Ireland after independence than to any of those works.[20] For where that interest had perforce to be maintained, in the six counties of Ulster that continued to enjoy British rule by proxy after 1922, the categories remained very much alive and usually without any nineteenth-century Romantic gloss.

As in the passage quoted earlier from the poet of *The Giant's Causeway*, William Hamilton Drummond, the categories of Saxon and Celt in Ulster are frequently transmitted into a contrast between Scots-Irish and Celt. A classic example of this is to be found in James Barkley Woodburn's book of 1914, *The Ulster Scot: His History and Religion* (a work which set the tone for much subsequent Ulster Protestant propaganda). This volume, forged in the heat of the Home Rule crisis, is a deeply felt attempt to justify Protestant Ulster's rejection of the Home Rule Bill. So the Ulster Scot, although Celtic blood does flow in his veins, is 'stern, dogged and strong of purpose; independent, self-contained and self-reliant, able to stand on his own feet, and

intensely proud of the fact [. . .]. But perhaps the main out-
standing fact about him is his power to command.'[21] In familiar
contrast, 'the Catholics of the South are more courteous and
versatile, with a singular attractiveness of manner. They are
brave and patient and endure privations without a murmur
[. . .]. But their qualities though attractive are not those which
fit men for ruling.'[22]

Two Ulster poets have explored in recent times the contrast
between settler and native examined here: John Hewitt and
Seamus Heaney. What is most interesting in their treatment of
the theme, coming as it does from differing sides of the house,
as it were, is that they take us back to Spenser – both in the
imaginative constituents of their vision of the dualism and in
their shared assumption that the differences observable between
peoples have their origin not in race (nor in any other single
cause, like religion or class) but in the environment in the full
sense, physical, geographic, social, historic and political.

John Hewitt's poem 'The Colony' (written in 1949), as he
states himself, allegorizes 'the regional circumstance as that of
a Roman colony at the Empire's waning'[23] but it does so in
imagery reminiscent of Spenser's haunted fear of Irish barbarism
that stirs beneath the reasoned, elegant surface of his treatise.
Hewitt has his colonist, no Roman but an Irish planter, fearful
of the septs with their mysterious rites and loyalties plotting in
the hidden places; but he is also certain that he has brought order
and civility to the land: 'We planted little towns to garrison/the
heaving country, heaping walls of earth.'[24] The colony 'laboured
hard and stubborn, draining, planting,/till half the country took
its shape from us'. But

> back of all our thought
> the threat behind the dream, those beacons flare,
> and we run headlong screaming in our fear [. . .]
> We took their temples from them and forbade them,
> for many years, to worship their strange idols.
> They gathered secret, deep in the dripping glens,
> chanting their prayers before a lichened rock.[25]

The concluding passages of Hewitt's poem discursively dwell
on the differences between the two peoples, colonists and
colonized, recognizing, as he does in many poems, how such
characteristics are historically, socially and physically deter-

mined. But another poem, 'An Irishman in Coventry', suggests how deeply that sense we met in Spenser of a colony threatened by a barbarous people troubles his imagination. Glad to be free of Ireland in a tolerant English city, this poem has the poet come upon an 'enclave of my nation',[26] an exile's céilidhe. The occasion prompts reflection on a people with whom he chooses to identify, but in terms that clearly betray his critical fear of them:

> The faces and voices blurring round me [. . .]
> called up a people endlessly betrayed
> by our own weakness, by the wrongs we suffered
> in that long twilight over bog and glen,
> by force, by famine and by glittering fables
> which gave us martyrs when we needed men,
> by faith which had no charity to offer,
> by poisoned memory, and by ready wit
> with poverty corroded into malice,
> to hit and run and howl when it is hit.[27]

In a series of poems in *Wintering Out* (1972) and *North* (1975) Seamus Heaney broods on the sixteenth-century colonization of Ireland. In some of them the familiar contrast between imperial England and untamed Ireland is re-cast as a contrast between male and female, the contemporary calamity being understood as the inevitable outcome of an historic sexual assault. The effect of this, as is the case with all deterministic forms of historical interpretation, is to exonerate. In 'Ocean's Love to Ireland'[28] England as male placed by geography in proximity to Ireland as female can have only the one result:

> Speaking broad Devonshire,
> Ralegh has backed the maid to a tree
> As Ireland is backed to England.
> And drives inland [. . .].

Heaney's re-interpretation of the contrasting categories in terms of sexual relationships between an imperial male and an only partially subdued female implies, therefore, that national racial stereotypes have their origins in a determining historic accident, in just the way Hewitt's vision of colonist and colonized does. But where Hewitt, for all his unexceptionable liberalism, is still haunted by the imagery of a land of wood and glen which allows a people 'to hit and run and howl when it is hit', Heaney, despite the melancholy, contemplative passivity of his work as a whole, is committed to those people, is one with them, In 'Bog Oak' we see a subjugated Munster of the sixteenth century through the eyes of a poet who in another poem ('Exposure') identifies himself as 'a wood-kerne/Escaped from the massacre'[29]:

> I might tarry
> with the moustached
> dead, the creel-fillers,
>
> or eavesdrop on
> their hopeless wisdom
> as a blow-down of smoke
> struggles over the half-door
>
> and mizzling rain
> blurs the far end
> of the cart track
> [. . .]
> Perhaps I just make out
> Edmund Spenser,
> dreaming sunlight,
> encroached upon by
>
> geniuses who creep
> 'out of every corner
> of the woodes and glennes'
> towards watercress and carrion.[30]

NOTES

1. Nicholas Canny, 'Edmund Spenser and the Development of an Anglo-Irish Identity' in *The Yearbook of English Studies*, 13 (1983), pp. 1-19.
2. *Ibid.*, p. 2.
3. *Ibid.*, p. 7.
4. Quoted from *Ancient Irish Histories. The Works of Spenser, Campion, Hanmer* (Port Washington, New York, London, 1970), I, p. 152.
5. *Ibid.*, pp. 166f.
6. William Hamilton Drummond, *The Giant's Causeway. A Poem* (Belfast, 1811), p. 152.
7. *Ibid.*, Drummond slightly misquotes Spenser here.
8. *Ibid.*
9. L. P. Curtis, Jr., has argued that the categories only became fully stereotypical and racial in the middle decades of the century and became most

widely employed as such in the years 1860-90 when British Imperial power was at its height. See L. P. Curtis Jr., *Anglo-Saxons and Celts* (Connecticut 1968). The categories were however already reasonably well-known and racially expressed even by the 1830s, as the Ferguson quotation suggests.

10. Samuel Ferguson, 'Hardiman's Irish Minstrelsy', *The Dublin University Magazine*, 4/20 (August 1834), pp. 154f.

11. John V. Kelleher, 'Matthew Arnold and the Celtic Revival' in *Perspectives of Criticism*, ed. H. Levin (1950; repr. Chicago 1971), pp. 197-221.

12. Quoted from Kelleher, p. 210.

13. *Ibid.*

14. *Ibid.*

15. *Ibid.*, p. 211.

16. *Ibid.*

17. J. A. Froude, 'Preface' to *The English in Ireland in the Eighteenth Century* (London 1881).

18. *Ibid.*, pp. 22-4.

19. Quoted in the introduction to *John Bull's Other Island* in *The Genius of the Irish Theatre*, eds Sylvan Barnet, Morton Berman, William Burto (New York 1960), p. 14.

20. L. P. Curtis, Jr., *op. cit.*, suggests that the death of some of the most famous propagators of the racial theory of national characteristics may have tended to diminish the frequency with which the categories were employed. That they retained their force, often in the crudest form, in Ulster in the twentieth century where the colonial conditions of nineteenth-century Ireland as a whole were sustained, suggests that the matter is more complex. Comparison with the history of other national stereotypes, as, for example, the Indian and African, in continents where colonial power was maintained through much of the twentieth century, could be most instructive here.

21. James Barkley Woodburn, *The Ulster Scot: His History and Religion* (London 1914), p. 396.

22. *Ibid.*, pp. 396f.

23. John Hewitt, 'No Rootless Colonist', *Aquarius*, 5 (1972), p. 94.

24. John Hewitt, *Collected Poems, 1932-1967* (London 1968), p. 75.

25. *Ibid.*, p. 76.

26. *Ibid.*, p. 111.

27. *Ibid.*

28. Seamus Heaney, *North* (London 1975), p. 46.

29. *Ibid.*, p. 73.

30. Seamus Heaney, *Wintering Out* (London 1972), pp. 14f.

2

THOMAS MOORE: A REPUTATION

'Mr Moore, I have not read your Larry O'Rourke. I don't
like Irish stories.' (Lady Holland)

In 1934, one hundred years after the last instalment of Moore's
Irish Melodies had just been published, Trinity College, Dublin,
chose to honour its alumnus in the form of a Trinity Monday
discourse. On the day on which the Board of that college elects
members of the university to offices to which Tom Moore would
in his day have been ineligible on the grounds of his religion, a
celebratory discourse is delivered on one or other of the college's
distinguished sons or daughters. In 1934 Wilbraham Fitzsimon
Trench, Professor of English Literature in the University of Dublin and immediate successor to Edward Dowden[1] in that chair,
was appointed to address a college audience on Thomas Moore.
The college, in its wisdom, determined that the tradition that
the discourse should be delivered in the college chapel would
be set aside. It was felt, I understand, that the poet of such
dubious, even licentious works as *The Odes of Anacreon*, not to
speak of the poems of Thomas Little Esq., was unsuitable matter
for the chastely Anglican decorum of that chamber.[2] Moore's
reputation it seems was not so secure, even in the matter of
morals, as to satisfy the Board which granted him his Bachelor
of Arts degree 135 years previously. But we know Moore's
opinion of the Board of Trinity College and its Fellows: they were
'scoundrelly monks' only two of whom (the Provost and his
tutor) had subscribed to his first volume. They were 'a cursed
corporation of boobies'.[3]
Trench took the opportunity of his discourse to plead the
cause of Moore's 'Let Erin Remember' as a substitute anthem
for the Irish Free State and in its published form to project a

vision of Irishness that in its facile inanity would not have seemed out of place in Moore's Regency drawing-rooms:

The figure of Hibernia on the cover front is a copy of the woodcut which appeared on the first instalment of Moore's *Irish Melodies* and which had been previously utilized (in 1803) in a Dublin street ballad done on the death of Robert Emmet. The other one, shown on back of cover, was what someone called a 'sublimation' of the original figure, a 're-fined' design done by Stothard for later issues on the *Melodies*. The billing and cooing of doves at Hibernia's feet should be taken to represent in sublimated form the present relations betweem the Six Counties and the Twenty-six.[4]

The poet of bland wish-fulfilments was still, it seems, having his effect.

Trench's lecture is, more interestingly, an attempt to assess Moore's contemporary reputation, to account for the vicissitudes it had endured and to comprehend how it once stood so high in European estimation. He summarizes the case with precision: 'he enjoyed such widespread contemporary fame as was seldom the lot of any poet, and then, having risen ever so high, he was afterwards to fall ever so low in the regard of later generations.'[5] He notes how Edmund Gosse in 1884 complained that there were 'critics who "dared" to deny to Moore any poetic merit, and treated him as an outcast'[6] and he somewhat dispiritedly seeks out those who have had a good word to say for Moore in the face of almost unceasing detraction. This of course included most Irish writers and critics, and subsequent voices were to swell the flood. In 1900 Stopford A. Brooke had in identifying Moore's virtues diagnosed the fatal weakness of his verse when he wrote of his 'shallow, brilliant, and sometimes tinsel poetry'[7] and had done so in a period when Moore still could just about lay claim to the title of national bard. He reckoned his patriotism 'more dainty than passionate, nurtured more by soft music than by salt tears'.[8] Later generations were to be even more acerbic. Yeats, with that casual mastery of denigration which is the obverse of his gift for the mythology of friendship, damned him as 'merely an incarnate social ambition'.[9] Kavanagh was to write with less economy but more venom when he noted the 'cowardice of Ireland' in his statue and observed:

> No poet's honoured when they wreathe this stone
> An old shopkeeper who has dealt in the marrow-bone

Of his neighbour looks at you[10]

identifying Moore, in an odd set of social permutations, with Yeats's Paudeen in his shop. And recently, in a brilliant hatchet-job, Tom Paulin has damned Moore as a professional Irishman: 'He seems to have been one of those deeply selfish people whose radiant self-love casts a brief, delighted spell on everyone they meet.' For Paulin, 'his personality was such a flimsy, frothy bundle of visiting cards and song sheets that it is vitually impossible to percieve any natural integrity in the man'.[11]

The Irish critics who have attempted more measured assessment have scarcely been able to defend Moore from such assaults in any really convincing way. They must depend, as did Stephen Gwynn and his biographer L. A. G. Strong, on reckoning Moore more rhetorician than poet whose mellifluous numbers were meet matter for musical performance. They can point to one or two of the *Melodies* as inaugural of the Irish mode in English (Thomas MacDonagh in 1916 printed 'At the Mid Hour of Night' and 'The Irish Peasant to His Mistress' in the section of his book *Literature in Ireland* entitled 'Poems of the Irish Mode') and can remind their readers that Yeats, despite his lethal phrase, remembered, as he told L. A. G. Strong in 1937,[12] that there were two of Moore's poems that he admired immensely (probably 'The Light of Other Days' and 'At the Mid Hour of Night') which he had included in his turn-of-the-century anthology, *A Book of Irish Verse*. They can furthermore remind readers how much James Joyce, the singer as well as the writer, appreciated *The Irish Melodies*, allowing them to sound through almost all of his works like ghosts from the past, referring knowledgably to them in his letters. And the Irish critic can, as does Anthony Cronin, acknowledge that Moore gave the Irish people a sense of their own history, however limited and deformed, when they had no other:

The Irish no longer need Tom Moore, in the way they needed him when he was, very nearly, their all in all. But in saying that we should have the grace to remember what he meant when he was, single-handed, repository, re-vivifier and reviver; when to the facile sadness and sense of loss of the minor romantics he brought, as a darker colouration, the greater and somewhat more serious sense of loss of an entire people.[13]

An estimate which concurs with Terence de Vere White's judgement of 1977 in the most recent biography, where Moore is granted his own unassertive patriotism, a patriotism which depends on the singing voice and a nicely judged social tact:

Hazlitt would have had Moore compose something as stirring as 'The Marseillaise'. But he was not intent on raising street barricades; his purpose was other; he sought to charm. The tocsin does not sound in 'The Minstrel Boy', or if it does, not so loud as to shake the teacups; but it was a considerable achievement to have brought Ireland's story into those London lives. Again we are at sea as to the impression made by the words unless we can imagine Moore singing them.[14]

And Seamus Heaney in 1979, the bi-centennial year, bore witness to the power of that version of Ireland to one whose cultural inheritance was as yet undeveloped: 'Before I read my Corkery at St Columb's College, I believe that my own sense of an Irish past was woven from the iconography of AOH banners and phantoms out of Moore's melodies.'[15]

Considering the Irish critical estimate of Thomas Moore it would be possible to repeat Saintsbury's report of 1914 about his critical reputation in general: 'For something like half a century it has been rare to find an estimate of Moore which, if not positively contemptuous has not been at least apologetic.'[16] But no Irish critic has quite managed (though Robert Welch comes close in his *Irish Poetry from Moore to Yeats*) to achieve Saintsbury's balanced, sane measure of the man and his art. Saintsbury states the case against Moore with exact comprehensiveness: 'always trivial', 'never intense', 'never reaches passion, but only sentiment and that sentiment is too often mawkish if not even rancid', 'a clever craftsman, but never a real artist'. 'He plays with patriotism, with politics, with everything.'[17] In defence, Saintsbury, who demands we read Moore entire before we rush to judgment, reminds us of the 'curiously pervading and adequate character of such goodness as he possesses'[18] and advises that it is possible 'to find a pastime of pleasure, now and then, in Moore's abundant store of sentiment'.[19]

This assessment of Moore as endlessly dependable, as a poet who could always be trusted to provide modest if sometimes artifical pleasures, seems to me very sound and could account for a real public success and a minor critical reputation. What it doesn't of course do is explain Moore's quite remarkable commercial triumphs and his altogether inflated critical reputation during his lifetime. It does not answer Professor Trench's puzzled question which in any chapter on the history of early nineteenth-century literary taste must find an answer.

Perhaps we should remind ourselves of some of the facts of the matter. In thirty-five years of writing poetry, as Wordsworth told Moore, his total proceeds were less than £1000. Moore reflects in his diary that in the same period of time he had brought in £20,000. The *Melodies* were steady earners – for many years his publisher gave him £500 as a retainer for these works and the contract Moore signed with Longman for his oriental romance *Lalla Rookh*, published in 1817, assured him £3000, and is a milestone in the economics and sociology of literature. Comparative money values between the present and the early nineteenth century are harder to make than between the present and the eighteenth century. The rapid inflation from the 1790s onwards made values fluent. But in the London of Moore's success, as one social historian notes[20] in an attempt to fix the value of money, a constable could be recruited for a guinea a week. Moore, though never a propertied and secure literary man, like Scott for example, before his ruin, was nevertheless doing remarkably well when Longman made that offer. And his publisher was not to be disappointed. *Lalla Rookh* went almost immediately into six editions. By 1841 it had run through an extraordinary twenty editions. Understandably, Thomas Longman in 1836 christened *Lalla Rookh* 'the cream of the copyrights'.[21] Moore's *Melodies* had had a fairly good critical reception. Apart from some predictable captiousness in the Tory journals, who knew Moore for a Whig, even when bedecked in a turban, the critical reception of *Lalla Rookh* in Britain was just the sort of thing an author hopes for. Notable reviewers in notable places, *The Edinburgh Review*, *Blackwood's*,[22] were high in their praises, even taking the trouble to exonerate Moore from the charge of licentiousness which had dogged his earlier reputation. And Moore could console himself that if some of his English contemporaries were less than enthusiastic about his poetic exploits in the Orient (Leigh Hunt for one declining to review it lest his published opinions mar a valued friendship), then European literary luminaries were not slow in their high commendation. Goethe, it seems, was an admirer of Moore and of *Lalla Rookh*. Stendhal read the work five times, the young Victor

Hugo was impressed. It was translated into many languages and became the inspiration for paintings and musical compositions, attracting the attention of among others Daniel Maclise and Robert Schumann. And, in 1821, Moore had the satisfaction (akin to selling the film rights, one presumes) of knowing his work made the basis of an extraordinary entertainment in Berlin at the Court of Frederick William IV of Prussia, where several orchestras and 186 people participated in a series of 'tableaux vivants'. Four thousand guests attended this sumptious occasion and the subsequent supper. The grocer's son had arrived.[23]

If mere dependability cannot account for such astonishing success, how shall we answer Professor Trench's question? 'What were the causes of his scarce merited contemporary reputation?' Trench's own reply, that Moore was ideally suited to supply a Romantic age with ready sentiment as 'a delicate receiver and transmitter of the messages of and for the age'[24] is inadequate, for it does not identify those messages in any detailed way. He just assures us that they were the same kinds of things as those with which both Scott and Byron were wooing a receptive public.

The messages of the *Melodies* were the poignancy of loss, the charm of ruination, of buildings, a people's youth, and the poetic appeal of the buried life. The *Melodies* treat of Irish history as if its true significance was to provide a drawing-room audience with metaphors of its own indulgent sense of personal mutability. So poems which evoke an Ireland of lost battles, silenced harps, the silent tear, the muted bard, are interspersed with poems which evoke the personal sorrows of a poet whose present gaiety disguises the depths of his own sorrows. Poems of this latter type are subtly suited to drawing-room performance. They suggest how the joys of sociable good fellowship of the kind their auditors are in fact enjoying as they listen to the affecting Mr Moore, are passing joys, are an alleviation of the customary lot:

> Oh think not my spirits are always as light
> And as free from a pang as they seem to you now

he sings.

> No, life is a waste of wearisome hours

> Which seldom the rose of enjoyment adorns
> [. . .]
> But send round the bowl and be happy awhile
>   May we never meet worse in our pilgrimage here
> Than the tear that enjoyment can gild with a smile,
>   And the smile that compassion can turn to a tear.

The audience's own awareness of buried sorrow, sweetened in a moment of convivial sentiment, is then directed to images of a country whose past is as sorrowful as anything they might wish to feel of themselves – Ireland is a land of last glimpses, exiles' regrets, of a poet's songs, where sorrow from the depths is always breaking through:

> But though glory be gone, and though hope fade away
>   Thy name, loved Erin, shall live in his songs,
> Not even in the hour when his heart is most gay
>   Will he lose the remembrance of thee and thy wrongs.

Sorrow for Ireland is indistinguishable from sorrow for oneself, so send round the bowl and be happy awhile.

The frequent metaphors of personal sorrow buried in the past also have a direct equivalent in images of Ireland's buried historical disaster. 'Let Erin Remember' has Ireland's former glory under water:

> On Lough Neagh's bank as the fisherman strays,
>   When the clear cold eve's declining,
> He sees the round towers of other days
>   In the wave beneath him shining.

'The Song of Fionnualla' has Erin asleep 'in her darkness'. In 'Erin, O Erin' 'The lily lies sleeping through winter's cold hour', and 'The Origin of the Harp' tells how the Irish harp was once 'A siren of old who sang under the sea'. In evoking an undersea or buried world, Moore was touching in a prettified way what was to become a nineteenth-century poetic and literary motif. Tennyson's 'The Kraken', Arnold's 'The Forsaken Merman', William Allingham's 'The Lady of the Sea', even Charles Kingsley's 'The Water Babies', all were to reflect a fascination with the underwater world as a metaphor of the strange, the exotic, of invisible realms.

Moore's poetic exploitation of the Irish past as an exotic dimension of experience which, as Seamus Deane has stated, is

'so deeply buried that it was not recoverable except as sentiment',[25] was, of course, an aspect of the Celticism that had
flowered in the fertile soil of the Ossianic enthusiasm. Orientalism, as Edward Said argues in his book of that name, was a
cognate preoccupation to many contemporary concerns. He
writes, reflecting on Mozart's eastern sympathies in *The Magic
Flute* and *The Abduction from the Seraglio:*

It is very difficult nonetheless to separate such intuitions of the Orient
as Mozart's from the entire range of pre-Romantic and Romantic re-
presentations of the Orient as exotic locale. Popular Orientalism during
the late eighteenth century and the early nineteenth attained a vogue
of considerable intensity. But even this vogue, easily identifiable in
William Beckford, Byron, Thomas Moore and Goethe, cannot be simply
detached from the interest taken in Gothic tales, pseudomedieval idylls,
visions of barbaric splendour and cruelty.[26]

Said might have included Celticism as a vogue from which
Orientalism cannot easily be detached, along with the Gothic
tales and the rest which he lists. For the Orient and Ireland, as
treated by the European literary imagination, were expected to
display similarities, as Byron, when he dedicated his poem *The
Corsair* to Tom Moore, made clear:

It is said among friends. . . I trust truly, that you are engaged in the
composition of a poem whose scene will be set in the East; none can
do those scenes so much justice. The wrongs of your own country, the
magnificent and fiery spirit of her sons, the beauty and feeling of her
daughters, may there be found; and Collins, when he denominated his
Oriental his Irish Eclogues, was not aware how true, at least, was part
of his parallel. Your imagination will create a warmer sun, and less
clouded sky; but wildness, tenderness and originality are part of your
claim of oriental descent, to which you have already thus far proved
your title more clearly than the most zealous of your countryman's
antiquarians.[27]

Byron, in the reference to Collins here, is recalling Dr
Johnson's *Life* of the poet of the *Persian Eclogues*, where he
reported, 'In his maturer years he was accustomed to speak very
contemptuously of them, calling them his Irish Eclogues, and
saying they had not in them one spark of Orientalism. . . .'[28]
Byron believes that Moore's Irishness will allow him to light
oriental fires in his work since Ireland and the Orient share
characteristics – wildness, tenderness and originality. Byron's

dedication suggests therefore that Moore's successes with *Lalla Rookh* were because he satisfied simultaneously Irish and oriental stereotypical expectations.

This analogy between an Irish and an oriental sensibility was returned to by reviewers of *Lalla Rookh*. John Wilson in *Blackwood's* celebrated Moore as the poet of 'whatever is wild, impassioned, chivalrous and romantic, in the history of his country and the character of his countrymen'.[29] This obviously equipped him for a poetic journey to the Orient. But it was Francis Jeffrey in *The Edinburgh Review* who drew the parallel most interestingly:

There is a great deal of our recent poetry derived from the East. But this is the finest Orientalism we have had yet. The land of the Sun has never shone out so brightly on the children of the North – nor the sweets of Asia been poured forth, nor her gorgeousness displayed so profusely to the delighted senses of Europe. The beauteous forms, the dazzling splendour, the breathing odours of the East, seem at last to have found a kindred poet in that Green Isle of the West, whose genius has long been suspected to be derived from a warm clime, and now wantons and luxuriates in these voluptious regions, as if it felt that it had at length required its native element.[30]

So the Irish are oriental exiles who find their 'native element' in 'voluptious regions' east of the Bosphorus. In writing an oriental romance, therefore, Moore confirmed British stereotypes of Ireland. But, he also wrote of the Orient in ways that made quite certain that any politically suspect potential in his material would have no opportunity to inhibit his critical and commercial success. Jeffrey could commend Moore (as did *Blackwood's* as well) for the pervasive orientalism of his imagery in *Lalla Rookh*, but could assure prospective readers:

We would confine this remark, however, to descriptions of external objects, and the allusions to literature and history – to what may be termed the *materiel* of the poetry before us. The characters and sentiments are of a different order. They cannot, indeed, be said to be copies of European nature; but they are still less like that of any other region. They are in truth, poetical imaginations – but it is to the poetry of rational, honourable, considerate and humane Europe, that they belong – and not to the childishness, cruelty and profligacy of Asia. So far as we have yet seen there is no sound sense, firmness of purpose or principled goodness, except among the nations of Europe and their genuine descendants.[31]

So Moore, although possibly descended from the peoples of 'childishness, cruelty and profligacy' and, as an Irishman, one who finds himself at home in the 'voluptious' East, can be reckoned sufficiently European to receive Jeffrey's commendation. For his work contains characters who exhibit European virtues and the sentiments as a whole belong to 'rational, honourable, considerate and humane Europe'.

Moore confirms prejudices about Ireland and the Orient in *Lalla Rookh* in at least two ways. He portrays the Orient as a cockpit of religious fanaticism and he exhibits its vast variety within which that fanaticism can have free play. The Orient clearly awaits the rationalizing influence of European empire. At the opening of the first of the four poems which make up *Lalla Rookh*, 'The Veiled Prophet of Khorassan', we see the variegated oriental world in thrall to the fanatical and evil false prophet Mokanna:

> every beauteous race beneath the sun,
> From those who kneel at Brahma's burning founts
> To the fresh nymphs bounding o'er Yemen's mounts,
> From Persia's eyes of full and fawn-like ray
> To the small, half-shut glances of Kathay
> And Georgia's bloom, and Azab's darker smiles
> And the golden ringlets of the Western Isles;
> All, all are there [. . .]

Mokanna is a death-worshipping imposter, who has fomented a popular uprising in which religious resentment and fanaticism play a crucial role:

> Such was the wild and miscellaneous host
> That high in air their motley banners tossed
> Around the Prophet-chief – all eyes still bent
> Upon that glittering veil, where'er it went
> That beacon through the battle's stormy flood,
> That rainbow of the field, whose showers are blood.

Against this threatening turbulence Moore sets an image of imperial order in the description of the all-conquering Caliph's army. The motley revolutionary crew of Mokanna is to be overwhelmed by the unifying power of Empire:

> Ne'er did the march of Mahadi display
> Such pomp before; – not even when on his way

> To Mecca's temple, when both land and sea
> Were spoiled to feed the pilgrim's luxury;
> When round him, 'mid the burning sands, he saw
> Fruits of the North in icy freshness thaw,
> And cooled his thirsty lip, beneath the glow
> Of Mecca's sun, with urns of Persian snow –
> Nor e'er did armament more grand than that
> Pour from the kingdoms of the Caliphat.
> First in the van the People of the Rock,
> On their light mountain steeds of royal stock;
> Then chieftans of Damascus, proud to see
> The flashing of their swords' rich marquetry
> Men from the regions near the Volga's mouth
> Mixed with the rude, black archers of the South
> And Indian lancers, in white turban'd ranks
> From the far Sinde, or Attocks sacred banks
> With dusky legions from the Land of Myrrh,
> And many a mace-arm'd Moore and Mid-Sea Islander.

Europe's imperial dreams are justified in these elaborate fantasies[32] – but so is Great Britain's sound government of an Ireland that is prey to fanaticisms and irrationalities of the kind Mokanna represents. Indeed Mokanna may carry some of Moore's own feeling about his dangerous fellow-countryman, Daniel O'Connell. While working on *Lalla Rookh* he wrote to his life-long friend Lady Donegal, who had written to advise him against associating with 'Irish Democrats' on a forthcoming visit to Dublin. His reply may have been to provide his aristocratic friend with what she wished to hear, but a note of personal distaste was also struck:

. . . if there is anything in the world that I have been detesting and despising more than another for this long time past, it has been those very Dublin politicians who you so fear I should associate with. I do not think a good cause was ever ruined by a more bigoted, brawling and disgusting set of demagogues; and though it be the religion of my fathers, I *must* say that much of this vile vulgar spirit is to be traced to that wretched faith, which is again polluting Europe with Jesuitism and inquisitions, and which of all the humbugs that have stultified mankind is the most narrow-minded and mischievous; so much for the danger of my joining Messrs O'Connell, O'Donnel etc.[33]

And, as if to disarm critics who might have found his story in 'The Fire-Worshippers' of a Zoroastrian last-ditch stand in

24

Iran (punning on Erin) against the Moslem invader too sediti-
ously akin to the tragic tale of Robert Emmet and Sarah Curran,
Moore subverts his own poem. In one of the prose passages
(which frame the four poetic tales) Moore includes a satiric portrait of a critic who determines on reporting the young poet who
entertains the company on their journeying for the very crime
of sedition. It's a signal – don't take this too seriously – even
though as he admitted in a preface to an 1841 edition that it was
'The Fire-Worshippers' that had most stimulated his interest as
he worked on the poem. From that moment when he conceived
of the idea of writing of the fire-worshippers of Persia, he tells
us, 'a new and deep interest in my whole task took possession
of me. The cause of tolerance was again my inspiring theme;
and the spirit that had spoken in the melodies of Ireland soon
found itself at home in the East.'[34]

So Moore's *Melodies* exploited a relationship between an audience's personal feelings and Irish history as a metaphor of loss
and buried emotion. *Lalla Rookh* exploited European and British
expectations and prejudices about the Orient and Ireland in
ways that allowed it a critical and commerical triumph.

There is one further aspect of Moore's poetry which may
account for its contemporary success. In a period of economic
insecurity and uncertainty in Britain he was a poet skilled in
evoking the romance of poverty *and* of riches. The charm of
penury is an affecting theme in the *Melodies*, while *Lalla Rookh*
indulges visions of opulent wealth of a quite unembarrassed
vulgarity. While he was writing this work, in the wake of the
Napoleonic War, England was enduring very straitened circumstances. Taxation rates in 1814 and 1815 were higher than at any
period before 1885. In 1815, 300,000 men were thrown on the
labour market because of demobilization. Wheat prices were
high in 1816 and 1817, causing much misery and economic
depression.[35] And Moore sensed the general distress. Furthermore, in January 1817 Moore's father lost his post as Barrack-
master of Island Bridge, drawing from the poet the pained
response, 'thus I am doomed to be a poor man for the remainder
of my existence for I must share my crust with him as long as
he lives'.[36] It turned out his father would receive half-pay, and
Moore then wrote to his mother berating her for her low spirits
when so many were suffering so much more: 'If you knew the
hundreds of poor clerks that have been laid low in the progress

of this retrenchment that is going on, and who have no means in the world of supporting their families, you would bless our lot, instead of yielding to such sinful despondency about it.'[37] Moore therefore supplies a straitened society with images of fanciful copiousness. Passages in *Lalla Rookh* tantalize with the erotic ease of the 'florid, fanciful music which pleased his time'[38] or indeed of modern television fantasies. *Lalla Rookh* was a Regency anticipation of televisual opulence:

> Meanwhile, through vast illumunated halls,
> Silent and bright, where nothing but the falls
> Of fragrant waters, gushing with cool sound
> From many a jasper fount is heard
> Young Azim roams bewildered – nor can guess
> What means this maze of light and loneliness.
> Here the way leads o'er tesselated floors
> Or mats of Cairo, through long corridors
> Where, ranged in cassolets and silver urns
> Sweet wood of aloe or of sandal burns;
> And spicy rods, such as illumine at night
> The bowers of Tibet, send forth odorous light
> [. . .]
> And here, at once, the glittering saloon
> Bursts on his sight, boundless and bright as noon
> Where, in the midst, reflecting back the rays
> In broken rainbows, a fresh fountain plays
> High as th'enamell'd cupola, which towers
> All rich with Arabesques of gold and flowers.

Such writing has a strange mesmeric absurdity, a kind of accumulative ease, the oriental equivalent of what Robert Welch had identified as the 'static non-progressive grace'[39] of *The Irish Melodies* which kept in suspended animation the real suffering of a people. Poverty is unthinkable in the copious proliferation of Moore's fancy in *Lalla Rookh*. English life may be economically straitened, Ireland and the Orient the prey of a fanatacism which only a rational imperialism can restrain, but the satisfactions of the ornamental are endlessly and easily available in the realms of wish-fulfilment. But through *Lalla Rookh*, as metaphors of a deadened silence in the *Melodies* had reminded of a pain Moore could not begin to address directly, so in the mellifluous oriental and Irish muddle of his wildly successful romance a compulsive note of necrophilia is struck. Obviously included as necessary to the genre (the macabre model of Beckford's *Vathek* was clearly in Moore's mind),[40] one also senses an unconscious recognition in these strange passages that not all the perfumes of the Orient could sweeten the stench of a nation decaying in defeat.

NOTES

1. It was Professor Dowden who in 1879 refused to serve on the Moore com-memoration committee in Dublin since he thought Moore was not 'in a high sense of the word "great"' nor worthy of 'national homage'. See *The Letters of Edward Dowden and His Correspondents* (London, New York 1916), p. 133.
2. I am grateful to Professor David Webb, FTCD, for this information.
3. *The Letters of Thomas Moore*, Vol. 1, ed. Wilfred S. Dowden (Oxford 1964), p. 20. Henceforth, *Letters*.
4. W. F. Trench, *Tom Moore: A Lecture* (Dublin 1934), Preface.
5. *Ibid.*, p. 1.
6. *Ibid.*, p. 3.
7. Stopford A. Brooke, 'Thomas Moore' in *A Treasury of Irish Poetry*, ed. Stopford A. Brooke and T. W. Rolleston (London 1900), p. 35.
8. *Ibid.*, p. 38.
9. *The Letters of W. B. Yeats*, ed. Allan Wade (London 1954), p. 447.
10. Patrick Kavanagh, *Collected Poems* (London 1963), p. 84.
11. Tom Paulin, *Ireland and the English Crisis* (Newcastle -upon-Tyne 1985), pp. 40-41.
12. See *Letters of W. B. Yeats*, p. 877.
13. Anthony Cronin, *Heritage Now* (Dingle 1982), p. 36.
14. Terence de Vere White, *Tom Moore* (London 1977), p. 77.
15. Seamus Heaney, Introduction to *A Centenary Selection of Moore's Melodies*, ed. David Hammond (Skerries, Co. Dublin 1979).
16. George Saintsbury, 'Lesser Poets, 1790-1837' in *The Cambridge History of English Literature*, Vol. XII, eds Sir A. W. Wood and A. R. Waller (Cambridge 1932), p. 102.
17. *Ibid.*, p. 103.
18. *Ibid.*, p. 104.
19. *Ibid.*, p. 106.
20. See Derek Beales, *From Castlereagh to Gladstone, 1815-1885* (London 1969).
21. *Letters*, Vol. II, p. 821. The word 'Lalla' in Hindi means 'a collector of dues'. It was an appropriate title. I am grateful to Dr Ganesh Devi for this informa-tion.
22. For a summary of these see John O. Hayden, *The Romantic Reviewers 1802-1824* (London 1969), pp. 220-24.
23. For a detailed study of the European as well as British success of *Lalla Rookh*, see Thérèse Tessier, *La Poesie Lyrique de Thomas Moore* (Paris 1976), pp. 323-35.
24. Trench, *op. cit.*, p. 13.
25. Seamus Deane, *Celtic Revivals* (London 1986), p. 14.
26. Edward W. Said, *Orientalism* (London and Henley 1978), p. 118. In view of

the coyly salacious quality of Moore's oriental imaginings in *Lalla Rookh,* it is interesting to note that Said identifies a good deal of Victorian pornographic fiction as employing oriental settings.

27. *Byron: Poetical Works,* ed. Frederick Page, a new edition corrected by John Jump (London 1970), p. 277.

28. Cited in *The Poems of Gray, Collins and Goldsmith,* ed. Roger Lonsdale (London 1978), p. 366.

29. John Wilson, *Blackwood's Edinburgh Magazine,* Vol. 1, No. 111 (June 1817), p. 279.

30. Francis Jeffrey, *The Edinburgh Review,* No. LVII (Nov. 1817), p. 1.

31. *Ibid.,* pp. 1-2.

32. John Wilson in *Blackwood's* responded to this sense of universal order in the poem, admiring 'the utter hopelessness of ultimate success' with which Moore endows his revolutionaries in *Lalla Rookh.* Wilson wrote of 'The Fire-Worshippers': 'The feelings, therefore which he acts upon are universal, and free from ali party taint – a vice which, we cannot help thinking, invested several of Mr Moore's shorter poems. . .' *Blackwood's Edinburgh Magazine,* Vol. II, No. V (1817), p. 509.

33. *Letters,* p. 359. We know he had completed a fair amount of *Lalla Rookh* when he wrote this letter, for it is dated 10 April 1815, and on 15 April 1815 he wrote to Longman that he had 'copied out fairly about 4000 lines of my work' (*Letters,* p. 360). Moore was punctiliously honest with his publisher.

34. Cited in Stephen Gwynn, *Irish Literature and Drama in the English Language: A Short History* (London 1936), p. 41. Of this Gwynn wittily remarked that Ireland found itself 'about as much at home as is the ordinary European in oriental costume at a fancy dress ball'. Quoted by L. A. G. Strong, *The Minstrel Boy: A Portrait of Thomas Moore* (London 1937), p. 169.

35. See Beales, *op. cit.,* pp. 36-9.

36. *Letters,* Vol. 1, p. 408.

37. *Letters,* Vol. 1, p. 411.

38. Brooke and Rolleston, *op. cit.,* p. 38.

39. Robert Welch, *Irish Poetry from Moore to Yeats* (Gerrards Cross 1980), p. 26.

40. Moore had offered to review *Vathek* for *The Edinburgh Review* in 1816 (see *Letters,* Vol. 1, p. 394) but although Francis Jeffrey accepted this offer the review never appeared. For the orientalism of *Vathek* and the tradition in which Moore was working, see Byron Porter Smith, *Islam in English Literature* (Beirut 1939).

3

EDWARD DOWDEN: IRISH VICTORIAN

In June 1879 Edward Dowden, the distinguished Professor of English Literature at Trinity College, Dublin, wrote to his brother telling him of a week of dissipation. The high-spot of this was, it seems, a soporific evening in the company of the poet Aubrey de Vere in the home of the antiquary and poet, Samuel Ferguson. There they played a new game: 'that of poets trying to put one another to sleep with sonnets'. Dowden reports his victory in this dispiriting competition: 'I think I stayed awake longest'.[1] At that stage in his career Dowden could scarcely have believed (his book on Shakespeare behind him, a projected study of Goethe in hand) that he would be remembered, if remembered at all, as one of the most representatively tedious of the Irish Victorians. For in the autobiography of the poet W. B. Yeats, under the title 'Reveries Over Childhood and Youth', the unfortunate Dowden is made to bear the responsibility for Victorian Unionist Ireland which, in Yeats's sense of things, put entire generations to sleep with its cultural and political inadequacies, its tiresome evasions, its reactionary torpor. In Yeats's account, Dowden, a man of some undoubted gifts, had betrayed them in typically Unionist fashion to provincial security. His most famous work had unforgivably turned Shakespeare into a British Benthamite and his 'ironical calm' was merely 'a professional pose'.[2]

When Yeats was waiting for the publication of the memoirs in which the portrait of Dowden appears, he felt some qualms. He was after all treating with a good deal less than respect one of his father's oldest friends, one who despite many temperamental differences had remained loyal and practically helpful to the constitutionally impractical portrait-painter. And Dowden, too, had been encouraging to W. B. Yeats himself at a time when it matters most to a young poet, when he published his first book. Yeats's letters indeed on that occasion reveal how much Dowden's commendation of *The Wandering of Oisin* meant to him, as he gratefully reported the professor's *imprimatur* to all and sundry. But the structure of 'Reveries', as Ian Fletcher has pointed out, required the arrangement of characters into revelatory juxtaposition in which Dowden inevitably came off the worse in a comparison with 'O'Leary's noble head'. As Fletcher has it, 'Dowden's ironic calm and O'Leary's moral genius, passionate, Roman, Hebraic, confront one another'.[3] So the poet, who knew he was picturing Dowden as 'a little unreal, set up for contrast behind the real image of O'Leary', nervously, even apologetically wrote to his father in late 1915:

I think you will very much dislike my chapter on Dowden, it is the only chapter which is a little harsh. . . . I couldn't leave Dowden out, for, in a subconscious way, the book is a history of the revolt, which perhaps unconsciously you taught me, against certain Victorian ideals. Dowden is the image of those ideals and has to stand for the whole structure in Dublin, Lord Chancellors and all the rest. They were ungracious realities and he was a gracious one and I do not think I have robbed him of the saving adjective.[4]

Part of the ungracious reality of that Dublin which Dowden (despite his personal qualities) represented for Yeats was of course the university in which the critic and scholar had made his career. And for Yeats (though the poet had hoped to succeed Dowden in his chair), Trinity College, Dublin, had long been, as it had for most Irish nationalists in late nineteenth and early twentieth-century Ireland, the chief symbol of the Anglicizing forces at work in the country which it was the duty of a patriotic Irishman to resist. Trinity, too, with its predominantly Unionist politics and historic Protestantism, was regarded as an instrument of British control in Ireland, as much a part of imperial influence as Dublin Castle and the Vice-Regal Lodge. As a young man Yeats had published bitter polemics against the college and its professoriate, damning the latter as a collection of mediocrities who in general appeared 'at no time to have thought of the affairs of their country till they have first feared for their emoluments'.[5] Cut off from the national enthusiasm in the country, the college had 'shut itself off from every kind of ardour, from every kind of fiery and exultant life',[6] only excelling in such subjects as mathematics or metaphysics. It was probably inevitable, therefore, that Dowden in the youthful poet's mind should have become identified with everything the poet found reprehensible in the institution the professor served, and that his portrait of him in 'Reveries' should have been so lacking in the graciousness he admitted was Dowden's saving characteristic.

Yet in choosing Dowden as the representative Irish Victorian among the classicists, historians, philosophers and mathematicians, among the Fellows and professors of Trinity College, Yeats in fact appears a good deal more perspicacious than perhaps he knew. For in many respects Dowden was the Trinity don of the period in whom the currents of the Victorian age ran most freely. Indeed, as two recent historians of the college have suggested, there was a tendency in the second half of the nineteenth century for the faculty of that institution to adopt an attitude which they identify as 'a spirit of self confidence'[7] and which others might associate the more with outright arrogance. Its effect, when it 'degenerated into provincial complacency',[8] was that it 'enabled even the most acute and scholarly minds in Trinity to ignore the controversies which were raging in England and allowed the new ideas to seep in so slowly as to cause no shock'.[9] The dons concerned themselves principally with classics, physics and mathematics in an intellectual climate where 'the numbers of intellectuals who were concerned with biology, geology, philosophy, literary criticism or the fine arts were very small'.[10]

The prevailing intellectual tone in the college, indeed, may account for the number of writers and artists who have recorded their disapproval of, or disappointment with, the Victorian college when it was at the height of its wealth and international reputation. John Butler Yeats himself (who entered Trinity in 1857) had found 'the Trinity College intellects noisy and monotonous, without ideas or any curiosity of ideas, and without any sense of mystery, everything sacrificed to mental efficiency'.[11] For him the college was 'intellectually a little Prussia'.[12] Such fictional accounts as exist of undergraduate life in the period (and the absence of Irish equivalents of the many contemporary Oxford and Cambridge novels is surely significant) tend to highlight not the Germanic efficiency of the intellectual life to be discovered there but rather the bacchanalian excesses of the studentry. Charles Lever's Trinity is famous for its portrayal of unregulated undergraduate boisterousness and alcoholic exploit. But it is in the one nineteenth-century novel that deals directly and at length with Trinity student life (T. Mason Jones's novel of 1867, *Old Trinity*) that Trinity's deficiencies are most clearly adumbrated. 'Stand at the college gates, from two o'clock 'till six,' counsels one of the novel's characters,

and watch the crowd of idle men that go streaming by. I have been in all the capitals of Europe, and in no other city have I seen so many thousands of idle young men as you find in this city of Dublin. [. . .]

They are doing nothing or worse than nothing. They are waiting for commissions in the army; expecting government appointments; loafing about billiard rooms and taverns, cooling their heels in waiting rooms at the Castle. Their ambition soars no higher than shirt collars and kid gloves.[13]

The hero of *Old Trinity* is a sensitive and well-read young man who finds Trinity a profound disappointment. What he had expected is nowhere to be encountered. The college chapel affords no spiritual guidance to a young man undergoing a Victorian crisis of faith: 'I heard there the poorest preaching and the most execrable reading I ever listened to. The preaching had not even the poor merit of variety. It all consisted of one standing dish – Bishop Butler.'[14] The classroom offers no improvement: 'Instead of being high priests of learning, as my imagination had pictured them, I found the Fellows, with one exception, clever matter-of-fact men of the world.'[15]

Jones was writing of the early 1850s. One wonders whether the single don to escape his condemnation was John Kells Ingram, author of that ballad of the Ninety-Eight, 'The Memory of the Dead', or perhaps it was John Anster, the translator of Goethe. Both of these men gave lectures on English literature in the college as they were to continue to do even after the appointment of the first professor of English in 1867, the year in which Jones published his bleak assessment of Trinity's intellectual life.

Edward Dowden came of a Cork family. His father, John Wheeler Dowden, was an Anglican whereas his mother had been raised as a Presbyterian.[16] The family business was the linen trade and Edward's uncle, Richard, had served as mayor of the city in 1845. A supporter of Daniel O'Connell, he had published a book on Irish flowers in 1852 and in Edward's youth in Cork he was City Librarian, presiding over a library of about 24,000 volumes, which interestingly enough was about the same number of books Edward Dowden held in his own personal library when he died in 1913. Dowden, the second son, was born in 1843. The home was devoutly Christian and marked by evangelical puritan taboos against the theatre and secular enter-tainments, especially those which might desecrate the Sabbath. Indeed the young Dowden had some difficulty in convincing himself that the theatre was not 'worldly' and therefore suspect when he came as a student to Trinity at the age of sixteen. He read Mental and Moral Science with distinction and although his mind was more historical and literary than philosophical, the encounter with abstract ideas and with the history of thought gave to his subsequent writing a sense of the significance of ideas and metaphysical pre-suppositions in the literary works which commanded his critical attention.

His first ambitions were poetic. A Trinity chair was very much a second best and was only contemplated because his early marriage in 1866 to Mary Clerke, a woman ten years' his senior had laid responsibility on his shoulders, making him a hostage to the most obvious of the enemies of promise, respectable domestic-ity. It was his ready acquiescence in this that irritated his friend John Butler Yeats, who whatever his weaknesses never betrayed his talents to domestic security.

Dublin did not attract Dowden as a young man. In May 1867 he wrote to his brother: 'I don't consider a Professorship in Trin-ity College the slightest honour; and in fine, we both find Dub-lin, as I always did, an unsatisfactory place. I should be glad to be in Yeats's company going to London, and I suppose in the end London will engulf me',[17] and in July 1867 he further informed John Dowden: 'If I don't get the English Lit. I don't see that it would be well to stay in this miserable Vice-Regal world of Dublin.'[18] In noting Dowden's iconoclasm about a Trin-ity professorship, it must be remembered that such a post in the nineteenth century commanded neither the respect nor the emoluments of the altogether more desirable and powerful Fellowship which was the object of most scholarly ambition in Irish academe. Dowden's chair at its inception enjoyed a salary of £100 per annum. In 1869 this was increased to £140, in 1871 to £300 and in 1885 it was set at £500, at which sum it remained for the rest of Dowden's career.[19] By way of contrast we may cite Dowden's famous contemporary, John Pentland Mahaffy, who from the early 1870s was in receipt of a Fellow's salary of about £700, and who in later years was very comfortably placed with salaries which rose from £800 to £900 and, when he became senior college officer and Senior Fellow, £1500.[20] But Dowden found even his modest middle-class competence enough to keep him in the Dublin which as a young man he had found so dispiriting. So he settled down in the suburbs with his new wife and set about the business of his professorship, but not without continuing qualms. In September 1869 the poet John Todhunter wrote to tell him that John Butler Yeats thought that he was 'sinking into the sleep of death and that nothing but instant emigration from Ireland can save you'.[21] Dowden's response combined prudence with an exact appreciation of his powers and his likely fate in a metropolis:

It is impossible from me to go at present on a visit to London, and I regret it very much. For a permanent place of residence I believe neither Dublin nor London would do me good. Dublin has the evils of city life without its compensations. London would be a whirl of ideas, and the best flows out of me, not in the obsession of many ideas, but in the calm brooding possession of a few. I wish I could live in the deepest solitude with a few friends and no acquaintances! But if I were to give up my Professorship I should be obliged to work for my bread, and to go to London and become a hack for the magazines, which consummation I fully intend to avert.[22]

And so he did, foregoing the bohemianism which attracted that part of a nature which was not in bondage to security. Dublin offered it no opportunities. 'I am afraid', he wrote to Elizabeth Dickinson West, the young woman he had met in 1867 and with whom he corresponded throughout his long and less-than-satisfactory marriage, in an epistolary, intellectual love affair, 'there is no such thing as bohemianism proper in this little city, no truantship of losels, to the loss of us God-fearing housechildren, and one can't cultivate truantship at my age.'[23]

So the young man who had aspired to poetry settled for the life of university don and a reputation as a highly productive man of letters, publishing widely in the English reviews and achieving his significant contemporary reputation with his study of Shakespeare, *Shakespere: His Mind and Art* (1875). (Dowden adopted the spelling of the bard's name insisted upon by Furnival.) In his writings and in his letters, as well as in the volume of poems he published in 1876, we encounter a Victorian sensibility of a highly characteristic kind, and a mind involved in the intellectual issues of Victorian Britain as a whole in a way which was not so very common in nineteenth-century Ireland, even among Dowden's Unionist colleagues in Trinity College. His mind was open, too, to European influences so that the critic John Eglinton's claim that 'For many years Dowden's mind was probably the first point touched by anything new in the world of ideas outside Ireland' does not seem entirely fanciful. Indeed Eglinton suggests that Dowden was 'first to speak of Nietzsche, Ibsen, Bergson'.[24]

Dowden was a typical Victorian in the nature of his personal religious crisis and in the ways he attempted to resolve it. A youthful earnest piety which never really deserted him gave way to a sceptical rationalism about revealed religion. In his letters we come on a reckoning with that biblical criticism through which German scholarship was unsettling many Victorian minds. He reads Newman – the *Apologia* of course but also *The Grammar of Assent*. Is not impressed; but even less is he impressed by Keble or Faber ('The wantonness of piety').[25] Matthew Arnold in his *Literature and Dogma* (1873) is more to his taste as he finds much in it, on the interprepation of the Bible and other subjects, which agrees with what he 'had made out'[26] for himself. In the absence of faith in a revealed religion there is such solemn reflection in many of his letters on the possibility of transcendence, in the manner whereby the Victorian age established doubt as a kind of extra Christian virtue. He ponders Transcendentalism, Deism (which 'with a tendency to develop itself on the side of Pantheism, has a great attraction'[27] for him), and he ponders the claims of Auguste Comte and Herbert Spencer. In Christianity, 'apart from the historical uncertainty of the whole story of Jesus Christ',[28] he senses a lack of all that the pagan world had represented in the figure of the Venus de Milo (a miniature of which, he confesses to his epistolary confidante, Miss West, he keeps in his own study). In a European or indeed English context none of this is really very remarkable (though it is valuable to have in these letters the ruminations of a second-rate sensitive mind responding to the issues of faith and doubt), but it should be remembered that in the Ireland of the 1870s, when Dowden was most attentive to matters religious, very little attention was being paid to the kind of questions which were so disturbing the faithful in England and Europe. For many of the majority confession, *The Syllabus Errorum* (1864) had settled matters, and even where the Protestant mind might have been expected to be taking full account of developments in historical biblical criticism, there tended to be disinterest, as inter-Church polemics absorbed most energies. So George Salmon, perhaps Trinity's most distinguished nineteenth-century theologian (though the competition was not intense), is remembered for his *The Infallibility of the Church* (1889), a polemic against ultra-montanism, and is recorded in the college history as a strenuous opponent of the Tübingen School of Higher Criticism. And John Kells Ingram, who had adopted the creed of Comptean positivism, thought it wise to hide the light of that particular faith under the barrel of discreet silence in a college where orthodoxy was espoused so complacently, if unconvincingly, by such as the redoubtable Reverend Mahaffy.

In his published writings Dowden made it quite clear that the question of belief was highly problematic, both for the age and for the critic himself. The work in which these facts are assumed is not his famous study of Shakespeare nor indeed the 'official' life of Shelley which drew Matthew Arnold's feline contempt, but his first collection of critical essays, published under the title *Studies in Literature: 1789-1877* in 1878.

The essays in this assured volume are arranged in historical order to suggest the developing crisis endured by the literary and philosophical imagination since the late eighteenth century: an era of revolution has been followed by a period in which two modes of thought, the transcendental and the positivist, have sought to comprehend the meaning of human existence. Largely descriptive, these essays do nevertheless amount to a cultural history of nineteenth century thought (conducted it must be admitted with a certain bland air of personal self-confidence which tends to suggest a factitious capacity on the critic's part to cope with any intellectual challenge, however disturbing). In this conspectus, although religious writings are given respectful attention, it is perfectly evident that a relatavistic agnosticism is the author's personal outlook in relation to the claims of revealed religion. Indeed what concerns him much more intimately, and in this he is the quintessential Victorian, is not how religion can withstand the assaults of scepticism, but how humane culture, the life of the imagination, can cope with the increasing power, authority and philosophic certitudes of modern science. In his letters it is evident that he attends to the various Victorian debates about Darwinian evolutionism but without the kind of anguish which so many of his contemporaries endured in their encounters with that most influential of Victorian texts, *The Origin of Species*. Rather, he acknowledged that 'There is such a thing as the passion of scientific discovery – of which the nobility consists in its freedom from vulgar utilitarian motives and I, by a leap of faith and not logic, declare there must be a warrant for and beauty in every disinterested intellectual eagerness in high minds.'[29] Accordingly, in *Studies in Literature*, the essay on 'The Transcendental Movement' is followed by an essay entitled 'The Scientific Movement in Literature' which prepares the way for a celebratory assessment of the George Eliot in whose writings the religious, artistic and scientific spirits meet in a rich, humanistic synthesis.

In 'The Scientific Movement in Literature' Dowden accepts that science has changed Man's relationship with the universe and that literature must be expected to take account of and reflect this change. A new sense of the vastness of the universe, of the antiquity of the species and of the planet, of the relativity of knowledge and of historical era and a belief in evolutionary rather than revolutionary progress, are things which Dowden accepts as the legacy of the now-dominant scientific world view. And art must accept the new set of pre-suppositions about reality:

If then our views of external nature, of man, his past history, his possible future – if our conceptions of God and his relation to the universe are being profoundly modified by science, it may be taken for certainty that it must in time put itself in harmony with the altered conceptions of the intellect.[30]

Dowden is able to contemplate this profound shift in human consciousness with a kind of magisterial calm, since he is pleased to accept a role for individual and collective life in a grand imperial vision of universal processes. And he admires George Eliot particularly because of her reverence for all of mankind's past, together with her dignified, ethical optimism about the future which depends upon her commitment to dutiful self-surrender to the 'life of our whole race, descending from the past, progressing into the future, surrounding us all at this moment on every side'.[31] Dowden seems genuinely stirred by this vision with its imperialism of the mind, its assumptiom of universal Law at work in the world. He asks, as if there could be only one reply:

If man be made the measure of the universe, the universe becomes a parish in which all of the occupants are interested in each petty scandal. Who would not choose to be a citizen of a nobly ordered commonwealth rather than to be lord of a petty clan?[32]

With views like these it is not in the least surprising that the young Yeats, averse to Victorian science which he thought had robbed him of his faith in the mysterious, and ready to embrace Irish nationalism as a kind of surrogate enthusiasm, should have found the professor who advised him to read George Eliot a representatively disagreeable and intimidatory presence. So he remembered in 'Reveries' the dislike he felt on reading Eliot, encountering there a scientific spirit of a kind which Dowden had admired but which he loathed:

She seemed to have a distrust or distaste for all in life that gives one a springing foot. Then too she knew so well how to enforce her distaste by the authority of her mid-Victorian science or by some habit of mind of its breeding, that I, who had not escaped the fascination of what I loathed, doubted while the book lay open whatsoever my instinct knew of splendour. She disturbed and alarmed me. . . .[33]

The complacent democracy of Dowden's thought must also have irritated the poet. For Dowden combined his exalted calm about human progress in a universe obeying comprehensible scientific Law, with a faith in a general historical growth in democracy. Indeed democracy was one of the inestimable gifts that it might be supposed were the fruits of British Empire. Dowden, though, more interestingly associated the spirit of democracy with the New World where the poetry of Walt Whitman (with whom he corresponded and whose work he championed) reflected the advanced spirit of the age. Indeed his essay on Whitman, 'The Poetry of Democracy', allows the poet a prophetic role at the end of *Studies in Literature* which had begun with the literature of the French Revolution. Whitman's energe-

tic optimism, bred of a spontaneously warm faith in com-
radeship and an ebullient democracy of feeling, makes him the
ethical genius of a materialistic civilization, one who may
spiritualize the earth: 'But the great Mother – the Earth – is one
in character with her children of the democracy, who, at last,
as the poet holds, have learnt to live and work in her great
style.'[34] The Yeats who only momentarily flirted with William
Morris socialism and who was exploring an altogether more
esoteric, less terrestial form of spirituality, must surely have
found such enthusiam uncongenial and not a little vulgar. The
consistent moral strain in Dowden's criticism cannot have
appealed much either.

Dowden as a critic is principally concerned to discover the
author in his texts and to reflect on his relationship with 'the
good forces of nature and humanity that play in and through
him'.[35] There was in fact something almost bluff in his Victorian
commitment to what he called 'Life' ('We must read. . . for *life*;
we must read in order to live'[36]) and in his condemnation of mere
aetheticism: 'Those who feel sanely and nobly in matters of literature and art keep themselves in vital relation with the great
facts and laws of life and nature, and refuse to immure themselves in any monastery of art, or so-called culture.'[37] The
antagonist in Dowden's mind here is of course the aesthetic
Walter Pater, of whom he wrote in 1873: 'Pater is a Rossetti
among critics, each essay is most exquisite, but the whole book
[*Studies in the History of the Renaissance*] leaves on me a feeling of
hot-house culture, and his style is over-superintended and
mannered.'[38]

As a biographical and psychological critic, Dowden has his
strengths. He was especially able to write appeciatively and
instructively of the philosophical and ethical assumptions which
preoccupy the writers upon whose works he expatiates. But
often his desire to read a spiritual history in an *oeuvre*, a biography in a *corpus*, renders his writing tiresomely speculative
and flaccid (making his famous book on Shakespeare more of a
period piece for the modern reader than a useful introduction
to the subject). For he permits himself spacious passages of
hypotheses about lives and states of mind, only infrequently
attending to style and structure of individual texts. The manner
too often suggests that characteristic Victorian figure, the popular lecturer, who combined sensibility with secular uplift for a

middle-class audience anxious for spiritual sustenance of an easily digestible kind in the absence of secure religious faith. And Dowden, in the polite circles of the university, Alexandra College and the Protestant Dublin middle-class, did achieve something of the status of literary sage, interpreting the great for lesser mortals, assimilating them to an acceptably ethical sense of an orderly world. Dowden himself knew that there were risks in the kind of life he had allowed himself to adopt. At the start of his career he confessed to Miss West: 'My fear about myself – as a critic – is that in trying to get *inside*, my method is coarse and unfeeling. The flush and changing colour on the cheek tells of life as much as counting the beats of the big muscle, but I seem to overlook this fact.'[39] But it was what he felt most able to perform and the young man who had hoped to be a poet settled for the life of man of letters and such eminence as his professorship, his critical reputation and acquaintance with the great gave him.

As one of the early professors of English Literature in the British Isles he did play his part in the establishment of English as an academic discipline in the universities. And as one of his successors, H. O. White, has noted, his influence was marked. At his death thirty of his students occupied chairs of English literature in various countries. But as with his criticism he had his doubts about professing English literature in the academy. Writing to Miss West in 1874 he reported;

There is quite an extraordinary zeal, and not without knowledge, at present among some undergraduates about English literature, and some unusually good men among them. I am unhappy about this, because I see it runs the risk of becoming a mere piece of scholarship and refined culture, severed from the deeper interests of life, and I fear the guilt may in part be mine. I meant them to be literary in order to be something more and better than literary, and I shall have to try to give this little College zeal a turn lifewards and away from books, if possible.[40]

And he had serious misgivings about examining in the subject (finding the marking of examinations a weariness of spirit, as who does not): 'think of having to torture Adonis into questions, and then to find that one's own questions are indeed poetry compared with the answers a foolish conscience obliges me to read.'[41]

Dowden, however, was a slave of Victorian duty, committed to ideas of education rooted in a vision of a liberal clerisy whose humane culture would be a leaven in social life. What he hoped for in his labours was 'a school of honest and skilled craftsmen in literature. . . a body of trained scholars' who would be part of 'the intellectual aristocracy of a democratic age. . .'[42] And in his forty-six years in Trinity College he established English as a central part of the Arts curriculum[43] despite the contempt of such as the odious Mahaffy, who told W. B. Yeats when the poet sought his opinion on his chances of succeeding Dowden, 'He has been teaching here for thirty years and hasn't done a pennyworth of good to anybody. Literature is not a subject for tuition.'[44] And there were the quiet satisfactions of a life of reading. For if anything really lasting comes from Dowden's large critical output (though his essays on Whitman, George Eliot and two later essays on Pater and Ibsen[45] are individually stimulating accounts of these differing writers), it is a sense that a life of learning and reading is in no way an ignoble one and that literature provides plentiful resources for the human spirit as it seeks meaningful existence.

Mahaffy, in damning Dowden to Yeats, did at least grant his dead colleague his reputation as a scholar. But it was as a poet he had first hoped to enter the literary lists. He did of course publish one collection of poems in 1876 and a posthumous volume (*Poems by Edward Dowden* appeared in 1914) which added poems of later years, but these are almost all marred by a worthiness of tone and rhythmic banality which suggest the week-end versifier whose literary sensibility rarely quickens into poetry. One poem, 'In the Cathedral Close', which has acquired some life in the anthologies, does skilfully indicate however the poet's appreciation of music (Dowden was a frequent attender at concerts) in a manner which anticipates Betjeman, and there is a suggestion that Dowden had a larger theme if he had chosen to explore it more fully and with more courage – that notion of a buried life that Matthew Arnold as poet made his own. Throughout his verse is not only the theme of lost vision, that familiar nineteenth-century trope, but of emotion buried by duty and too much commerce with a busy world. Underneath flows 'the unregarded river of our life'. So the poet in 'Among the Rocks' by the sea-shore confesses to the mute stones:

> Down upon you I sink, and leave myself,
> My vain, frail self, and I find repose on you,
> Prime Force, whether amassed through myriad years
> From dear accretions of dead ancestry,
> Or ever welling from the source of things
> In undulations vast and unperceived,
> Down upon you I sink and lose myself.[46]

But there is little real sense in the poetry that Dowden was prepared to penetrate the depths of his own being as an artist. W. B. Yeats in 'Reveries' was to record his disappointment with Dowden's verses when he learned through the practice of his own art 'that certain images about the love of woman were the properties of a school', having earlier believed that the professor had 'loved, unhappily and illicitly'.[47] Dowden, of course, had so loved, but within the strained bonds of Victorian and Protestant Dublin's proprieties about marriage and separation. But one would not guess the fact from his poetry or his writings (though perhaps his attempt to exonerate Shelley from every mis-demeanor in his marital and erotic entanglements, which drew from Arnold the famous riposte 'What a set', may, in part, have their origin in his own insecure and difficult position at the apex of an eternal triangle). What his life and his work suggest is a man who, less than fully experienced in self-analysis, believes himself to be serene (and in his letters he frequently expresses a satisfaction in the life he has known) and who accordingly pre-sents to the world a mask of achieved serenity, whatever the cost. That Dowden was less than serene and that his role as the most Victorian of Irishmen was not something which could be adopted without the strains showing, becomes clear when we consider his attitudes to his native country and the ways in which those attitudes expressed themselves in action.

Dowden, although his intellectual life was predominantly focussed on England, by no means felt himself to be English. Indeed he had the typical Anglo-Irishman's sense of superiority in relation to the ordinary English citizen. On a visit to the neighbouring island in 1873 he wrote from Harrowgate to Miss West of his distaste for its people and the kind of civilization they were creating:

Each time I come to England it seems newer and more foreign. I think on the whole I am glad to be Anglo-Irish rather than English. The British breed has certainly the robust frame and the energy, out of which in the end, all good will come: but, so far, I think they have evolved out of this fine material as much barbarity as most peoples. Life is something quite dreadful in a city like Manchester.[. . .] This hotel, which is a good one, is resorted to chiefly by the married business people of Leeds, Bradford and Huddersfield, and the rich impenetrable vulgarity of these Britishers is without parallel, I fancy, among us.[48]

But such feelings did not incline him to entertain any sympathy for Irish nationalism. Throughout his career there seemed something verging on the neurotic in his commitment to a universal and therefore somehow sanitized and serene version of literary culture over against the offensive demands of the local, with all the risks they involved of parochialism and misjudgment. One senses a curious revulsion from something in Ireland for which a bland style and a cosmopolitan range are the necessary drapes. He wishes to be intimate with the elect of all ages, immune from the contamination of the vulgar and the enthusiastic. He seems to wish to keep his distance from all easy enthusiasm which, like childhood faith, can so readily prove insubstantial. So he wrote as a young man to his brother in a passage both revelatory of his own disturbed relationship with his native place and ironical when one considers in whose pages he has been set in amber as Victorian eminence:

We are heirs of all the ages, and lucky fellows to have come so soon after Gothe [sic]. . . Frightful thought though! – there may be another Gothe just half a century ahead of us (your grandson perhaps), ay or a Shakespere, since nature is inexhaustible. I can't, however, believe that Ireland will produce such a thing, or anything but more long-haired assess (or at most a Duns Scotus or two); the idiotic noises the true Irishman makes from generation to generation are certainly not human, but are part of the irony on humanity of the Aristophanic Spirit who presides over the World-Drama – a chorus of asses.[49]

A licensed jest? Perhaps. But there is something almost pathological in the instinctive racism of the drollery. It sets in unnerving context Dowden's advice to Aubrey de Vere to avoid Irish mythical or early historical subject in his poetry since they confine 'the full enjoyment of the poem to a little circle'.[50] That he can't have been too pleased when the same de Vere told him that his own verses possessed what he regarded as 'an Irish characteristic of poetic genius'[51] is clear in the fact that he later had serious qualms about appearing in an anthology of Irish poetry. He commented then: 'What I have written has really no right to appear in a specially Irish Anthology, and if anything is worth living in it, it comes out of the general mother, Earth; so I would be content to be one of the general crowd of small singers rather than one of the local group.'[52]

The local group when Dowden wrote these words in 1898 was of course that led by the son of his old friend, J. B. Yeats, with whom he had been in public conflict for some years. For the Dowden who had strenuously thrown himself into opposing the Home Rule Bill of 1886 saw little but political risk and artistic provincialism in the Irish Literary Revival. It was not that he could not recognize the artistic potential in the Celtic past that the Revival was popularizing. In 1882 he admitted to de Vere that the story of Deirdre which he knew principally from Ferguson's prose and verse was 'one of the greatest tragic stories of the world' and he recognized with some prescience that it was 'like some of the subjects of Greek tragedy' capable of being 'handled again and again by different poets'. He also reckoned the Táin 'a subject of great grandeur'.[53] But the aims and aspirations of the Revival writers drew his opposition in public debate in 1895 (the disappointed poet in him, the man who had made universal culture his creed, seemed almost affronted by Revival fervour), and in the same year he still thought it necessary to preface his *New Studies in Literature* by reprinting a warning on the dangers of 'the separatist tendency. . . in literature',[54] despite the fact that Yeats had insisted on its anachronism. He advised his readers and the new movement: 'If the Irish literary movement were to consist in flapping a green banner in the eyes of the beholders, and upthrusting a pasteboard "sunburst" high in the air' that he 'for one should prefer to stand quietly apart from such a movement'.[55] He ignored the fact that Yeats and his movement were at work on the de-Davisization of Irish poetry and wrote with an ill-considered contempt of something he clearly had not really chosen to understand, deserving Yeats's censure that he was 'no authority at all when he speaks of Irish verse or Irish legend, but a partisan ready to seize upon any argument which promises a momentary victory'.[56]

So in Dowden's response we come upon what Seamus Deane has described in a memorable phrase (unfairly used, I believe, to characterize a famous passage by Yeats himself) as 'the pathology of literary Unionism'.[57] We encounter a wilful blindness, an irrationality in one who clearly prided himself on the universal composure of his understanding. For Ireland could not be allowed in fact what he admitted was possible in theory – 'an Irish literary movement which should command our deepest interest and sympathy'.[58] And he could not bring himself even to consider whether what he had described as occurring in another colonial world had any parallel in his own country. To set his noble words on the origins of American literature beside his later ungracious words about the beginnings of the Irish Renaissance ('I confess that I am not ambitious of intensifying my intellectual or spiritual brogue'[59]) is to understand the kinds of deformations of sensibility that colonial experience effected on one of Victorian Ireland's most attentive minds. For of those origins he had written:

The New World, with its new presentations to the senses, its new ideas and passions, its new social tendencies and habits, must surely, one thinks, have given birth to literary and artistic forms corresponding to itself in strange novelty, unlike in a remarkable degree those sprung from our old world, and old-world hearts. . . it is as much to be expected that poems and pictures requiring new names should be found there as that new living things of any other kind, the hickory and the hemlock, the mocking bird and the katydid should be found. [. . .]
    The fact is that, while the physical conditions, fostering certain forms of life and repressing others, operated without let or hindrance, and disclosed themselves in their proper results with the simplicity and success of nature, the permanent moral powers were met by others of transitory or local, but for the time being, superior authority, which put a hedge around the literature and art of America, enclosing a little paradise of European culture, refinement, and aristocratic delicatesse from the howling wilderness of Yankee democracy, and insulating it from the vital touch and breath of the land, the winds of free, untrodden places, and the splendour and vastness of rivers and seas, the strength and tumult of the people.[60]

Dowden saw this insulation of the American mind from American reality coming to an end in the poetry of his beloved Whitman. Whatever the critic today makes of Yeats's problematic relationship with Irish reality, it is surely revelatory that the Victorian critic who wrote these words could not even consider whether a similar process was at work in his own country in the writings of a poet who sought to invest *his* verses with 'the vital touch and breath of the land' of Ireland. And so we were robbed of the critical writings Dowden might have given us on the works of a generation of Irish writers who were changing the literary map of Europe, that map which had so absorbed his attention in the past.

NOTES

1. *Letters of Edward Dowden and His Correspondents* (London 1914), p. 137. Henceforth *Letters*.
2. W. B. Yeats, *Autobiographies* (London 1955), p. 95.
3. Ian Fletcher, *W. B. Yeats and His Contempories* (Brighton 1987), p. 133.
4. Allan Wade (ed.), *The Letters of W. B. Yeats* (London 1954), pp. 602, 605.
5. W. B. Yeats, 'The poetry of Sir Samuel Ferguson' in John P. Frayne, *Uncollected Prose by W. B. Yeats* (New York 1970), p. 104.
6. *Ibid.*, p. 233.
7. R. B. McDowell and D. Webb, *Trinity College, Dublin, 1582-1952: an academic history* (Cambridge 1982), p. 240.
8. *Ibid.*
9. *Ibid.*
10. *Ibid.*
11. Quoted by William M. Murphy, *Prodigal Father: The Life of John Butler Yeats* (Ithaca and London 1978), p. 33.
12. *Ibid.*
13. T. Mason Jones, *Old Trinity: A Story of Real Life*, Vol. I, with an introduction by Robert Lee Wolff (New York and London 1897), pp. 161-2.
14. Jones, *op. cit.*, Vol. II, p. 71.
15. *Ibid.*
16. See H. O. White, *Edward Dowden* (Dublin 1943), for a biographical sketch by one of Dowden's successors.
17. *Letters*, p. 38.
18. *Ibid.*, pp. 38-9.
19. These figures have been abstracted from the College Calendars.
20. See W. B. Stanford and R. B. McDowell, *Mahaffy: A biography of an Anglo-Irishman* (London 1975), p. 28.
21. Murphy, *op. cit.*, p. 67.
22. *Letters*, p. 45.
23. *Fragments from Old Letters: E. D. to E. D. W.*, First Series (London 1914), p. 119. Henceforth *Fragments I*.
24. *Letters*, p. xv.
25. *Fragments I*, p. 46.
26. *Ibid.*, p. 67.
27. *Ibid.*, p. 116.
28. *Ibid.*, p. 166.

29. *Ibid.*, p. 113.
30. Edward Dowden, *Studies in Literature, 1789-1877* (London 1878), p. 86. Henceforth *Studies*.
31. *Ibid.*, p. 253.
32. *Ibid.*, p. 95.
33. W. B. Yeats, *op. cit.*, p. 88.
34. *Studies,* p. 515.
35. Edward Dowden, 'The Interpretation of Literature' in *Transcripts and Studies*, second edition (London 1896), p. 252.
36. *Ibid.*
37. *Ibid.*, p. 257.
38. *Fragments I*, p. 68.
39. *Fragments from Old Letters: E. D. to E. D. W.*, Second Series (London 1914), p. 1. Henceforth *Fragments II*.
40. *Fragments II*, p. 89.
41. *Letters*, p. 131.
42. Edward Dowden, 'Introduction' to *New Studies in Literature* (London 1895), pp. 20-21. Henceforth *New Studies*.
43. Edward Dowden was the first professor of English Literature in Ireland. Chairs of English had already been established in London, Manchester, Glasgow and Edinburgh (for the history of English in the universities see D. J. Palmer, *The Rise of English Studies* (London 1965)). From the start Dowden lectured on the whole course on English literature in a two-year cycle of lectures. But although such contemporary authors as Tennyson, Matthew Arnold and Ruskin were included in the examination syllabus, the formal course throughout Dowden's career remained fairly restricted. No novels were set for examination study and it was not until the academic year 1905-6 that drama other than that by Shakespeare appeared on the reading list in the College Calendar. In that year students were required to include Sheridan's *The School For Scandal* in their examination reading. Marlowe was included in 1912-13. No American authors were set for examinations and the course was rarely changed, so that although Dowden represented recent literature when he was appointed, by the end of his occupancy of the chair the course, which in its early years seemed adventurous in its recognition of the major Romantic poets, with Tennyson as their successor, had a distinctly antique air. It is a point worth noting, however, that the year after the admission of women to the university in 1904, Tennyson's 'The Princess' appeared as an examination text.
44. Allan Wade, *op. cit.*, p. 557. See also Philip Edwards, 'Yeats and the Trinity Chair' in *Hermathena*, No. CI (Autumn 1965), pp. 5-12.
45. See Edward Dowden, *Essays Modern and Elizabethan* (London 1910), p. 65.
46. Edward Dowden, *Poems* (London 1914), p. 65.
47. W. B. Yeats, *op. cit.*, p. 86. In a lecture given in July 1988, Philip Edwards suggested that Dowden feared the feminine in his own nature, reading his book on Shakespeare (which extols the dramatist's pragmatism) and his political Unionism as compensatory modes of thought and activity. Miss West certainly seems to have been the stronger partner in the relationship.
48. *Fragments II*, pp. 28-38.
49. *Letters*, p. 24.

50. *Ibid.*, p. 68.
51. *Ibid.*, p. 103.
52. *Ibid.*, p. 285.
53. *Ibid.*, pp. 184-5.
54. *New Studies*, p. ix.
55. *Ibid.*, p. 18.
56. Frayne, *op. cit.*, p. 353.
57. Seamus Deane, *Heroic Styles: the tradition of an idea* (Derry 1984), p. 10.
58. *Transcripts*, p. 18.
59. *Ibid.*, p. 19.
60. *Studies*, pp. 468-9.

4

THE CHURCH OF IRELAND AND
THE CLIMAX OF THE AGES

In James Joyce's *A Portrait of the Artist as a Young Man* (1916) the young coldly arrogant Stephen Dedalus delivered a judgment on Protestantism that was clearly intended to be a magisterial last word on the subject. Discussing with his fellow undergraduate a disinclination to make his Easter duty, Stephen replied to Cranly's question 'You do not intend to become a protestant?'

I said that I had lost the faith. . . but not that I had lost self-respect. What kind of liberation would that be to forsake an absurdity which is logical and coherent and to embrace one which is illogical and incoherent?

Stephen's contemptuous dismissal of Protestant Christendom was, it has generally been assumed, a direct expression of Joyce's own view, and indeed the only unambiguously Protestant body of thought that Joyce admits to Stephen's protracted cerebrations as worthy object of his sustained attention in *Ulysses* is that of the Bishop of Cloyne. Beyond that it seems Protestantism had little to offer intellectually to a sensibility formed by Roman Catholicism but in humanistic rebellion against it.

In twentieth-century Irish literature in English the central religious conflicts have seemed to be those defined by Joyce – between authority and freedom, between the absolute demands of an all-powerful traditional Church and the assertion of human potential. Few Irish writers have chosen to explore the field of Christian belief and practice in terms other than those established by Joyce, Stephen Dedalus's resolute *non serviam* having apparently defined the dialectics of the religious issue. Accordingly, the most frequent explicitly religious theme in twentieth-

49

century Irish writing is the struggle of the individual against the constraining nets of an all-encompassing religious authority and its demands. George Moore's *The Lake* (1905), for example, explores the psyche of a priest whose sense of a stable reality is challenged by the sexual courage of a woman parishioner; Austin Clarke's collection of poems, *Night and Morning* (1938), recounts the struggle of a humanistic conscience with the fears induced by religion; Patrick Kavanagh's long unfinished poem, *Why Sorrow* (1942), ponders the dilemma of a priest who cannot respect the Jansenistic extremism of much of the Irish Church; while in Patrick Power's moving account of priesthood, *The Hungry Grass* (1969), the solitary sacrifice of celibacy demanded by the Church is set against the human instinct for family and fatherhood.

The problems and issues which have preoccupied Protestant Christendom since the nineteenth century and which have found reiterative expression in English literature have scarcely been touched on by Irish writers. The conflict of science and religion has rarely been matter for Irish writing other than in certain occult poems of Yeats who adopted his reactive strategies to escape the problems occasioned by it. Otherwise many Irish writers have tended to explore religious themes as if Darwin had not challenged the Christian conception of man, historical research the status of holy texts, and psychology and sociology the nature of human responsibility. Nor has the perception that humanistic and individual values can be subject to secular totalitarianisms much troubled the Irish writer. So, all these themes which have been matter for Christian reflection elsewhere and for treatment in fiction, drama and poetry, have not found expression in Irish writing in English. Instead, the characteristic Irish religious theme in literature remained, even in the 1960s and '70s, the conflict of the individual with ecclesiastical authority and tradition. Thomas Kilroy's novel *The Big Chapel* (1971), in its study of the nineteenth-century Church, of the struggle between local religious practice and the ultra-montanist tendencies of the period, was just such a work; while one of the most experimental plays of the decade was Thomas Murphy's *The Sanctuary Lamp* (Abbey Theatre, 1975), which achieved a note of genuine humanist iconoclasm by the simple ploy of setting its tale of betrayal and individual suffering in a Roman Catholic church.

If, then, for many Irish writers the fundamental religious issue has been that so precisely dramatised by Joyce in *A Portrait*, it might have been expected that writers who chose to explore the social world of Irish Anglicanism would have discerned there religious dialectics more akin to those that have disturbed Protestantism elsewhere since the mid-nineteenth century in a Church less dominated by conceptions of absolute authority and long open to developments in modern liberal theology and contemporary thought. The fact is that very few writiers have ever chosen to write of Irish Protestant ecclesiastical life, and there are no works of modern literature that could be said to emerge directly from the complex of concerns, ideas and feelings that have preoccupied Irish Anglicanism in the period. Despite the riches that have been available even in local events (the period surrounding Disestablishment, for example, would surely have provided novelists with rich grist to their mills), there has been no Irish Trollope. Even George Birmingham, who comes closest to treating of Irish Anglicanism in a way that reminds of Trollope, was more concerned with the problem of how to be Anglican and an Irish nationalist than he was intent on examining and portraying the full range of the conflicts, ideas and feelings within the Anglican community in Ireland in the early twentieth century. And there has been no poet whose sense of life has been continuously informed by Christian feeling and thought as mediated through Anglican worship and practice in the manner of an R. S. Thomas or indeed a Geoffrey Hill. Accordingly, the Church of Ireland has been directly present in Irish literature throughout most of the modern period only in brief images and allusions, as a social presence that can be variously represented in fiction, drama or poetry without the need for any sustained examination. The result has been, therefore, that the literary treatment of Irish Anglican life has largely consisted of a series of clichés and programmatic responses. These have been of three primary varieties.

First, the Church of Ireland has been represented as expressing the hard, bitter face of privilege, as a Church that can only with difficulty hope to atone for its association with a hated Ascendancy and its reputation for exploitation of the Irish people. The grotesque, monstrous figure of the Reverend Phineas Lucre in Carleton's novel *Valentine M'Clutchy* (1845), for example, was a terrible propagandist indictment of a Church whose clergy did not always reckon their ministry to be principally amongst the meek and downtrodden. He is, Carleton informs us acidly, 'one of the first fruits of that which is called modern sanctity or saintship, being about two thirds of the Tory and High Churchman, and one of the Evangelical'. With two rich livings (one of his livings was worth £1800 per annum) and a private income of £1400 a year, he is 'a portly gentleman, having a proud consequential air stamped upon his broad brow and purple features'. Here is Carleton's damning estimate of the man, couched in terms of a heavy but well-deserved irony:

Without piety to God, or charity to man, he possessed, however, fervent attachment to his church, and unconquerable devotion to his party. If he neglected the widow and orphan whom he could serve, he did not neglect the great and honourable, who could serve himself. He was inaccessible to the poor, 'tis true; but, on the other hand, what man exhibited such polished courtesy, and urbanity of manner to the rich and exalted. Inferiors claimed that he was haughty and insolent; yet it was well-known, in the teeth of all this, that no man ever gave more signal proofs of humility and obedience to those who held patronage over him. It mattered little, therefore, that he had not virtues for the sick, or poverty-stricken, in private life, when he possessed so many excellent ones for those in whose eyes it was worth while to be virtuous as a public man.

Such an image of a Church and a corrupt social order, inextricably linked, had a powerful longevity in Irish literature. So, for Patrick Kavanagh in his poem *The Great Hunger* (1942), 'tall hard as a Protestant spire' is an appropriate metaphor to suggest the rigorous hold a mother can lay upon her bachelor son, and such spires can provoke even the customarily urbane Seán Ó Faoláin to the following reflection in his book *The Irish* (1947):

The barrier. . . which originally existed between Normans and Gaels, and which was in the end worn away, was erected again by the Anglo-Irish. [. . .]
   The barrier which was to prove the most formidable of all was the difference in religion. . . The outward symbol of that barrier is the Catholic church relegated to a remote or back street (cheaper ground, also less likely to attract attention) and the Protestant church plumb in the middle of a town square, or on the hill: and one will note how often the Catholic church is without a spire – that little arrogance forbidden by law. Thus in my native city of Cork the great trident of the spires of the Protestant Cathedral dominates the city, all the older Catholic

churches are hidden away, and none has a spire. These things remind us that one of the most cultivated and creative societies in western Europe during the eighteenth century was also politically barbarous.

But in direct contrast with such imaginative presentation of the Church of Ireland as the Church of an alien Ascendancy, Irish writers have also chosen to supply portraits of individual Protestant clergy which suggest that not all of them were in any sense complicit with that political barbarism which O Faoláin so frankly identified. The motif of the humble, truly saintly priest, a figure as old in English literature as Chaucer's poor parson surrounded on the road to Canterbury by examples of rampant ecclesiastical corruption, is a literary convention Irish writers have felt able to exploit in the treatment of the Church of Ireland. Even in Carleton's *Valentine M'Clutchy*, the essentially vicious Phineas Lucre is made to seem the more horrible in comparison with his curate, Mr Clement. Subsisting on a stipend of £60 per annum (though Lucre should pay him £75) he is intimate with the sufferings of the poor and has little time or inclination to engage in the sectarian polemics of his rector:

The severe duties of so large a parish, the calls of the sick, the poor, and the dying, together with the varied phases of human misery that pressed upon their notice as they toiled through the obscure and neglected paths of life, all. . . constituted a sufficiently ample code of duty.

In Irish writing Mr Clement has his literary descendants, as Chaucer's parson had his descendants in English literature in Fielding's Parson Adams, for example, and even in Trollope's Mr Harding. The innocent, unworldly priest who lives a life of genuine spirituality recurs in George Birmingham's novel of the land war, *The Bad Times* (1908), where the humble and earnest Rev. Eugene Hegarty, at the novel's climax, forgives the murderers of a wife, who is innocent victim of an attempt on another's life. And as evidence that such a portrait is not merely the wish-fulfilment of the Anglican Canon Hannay (George Birmingham was the *nom de plume* of the Church of Ireland cleric who achieved considerable fame and success as a popular novelist)[1] we may recall the gentle John Crosthwaite in the Catholic Canon Sheehan's novel of 1912, *Miriam Lucas:*

He was universally beloved. He trod on no man's corns by excessive learning; he flattered everyone's vanity by his exceeding humility. He was one of those delightful beings who, with much knowledge, retained all the simplicity and unconsciousness of a child, never seeing a blunder, never blushing at a solecism, always humble, suave, deprecatory; and everyone loved him, because he appealed to their pity and never challenged their pride. The farmers' sons in his neighbourhood, Catholics all, would leave their own harvest work unfinished to cut or thresh his corn; and, stranger still, they worked from dawn to dark for him with no greater stimulant than tea or coffee, whilst porter was the inevitable accompaniment and reward of their own generosity elsewhere.

A similarly genuine spiritual worth is the object of Seán O'Casey's celebration in his play *Red Roses for Me* (1942), where the Anglo-Catholic priest, The Rev. E. Clinton, rector of St Burnupus (based, in fact, on a figure who had exercised a considerable influence on the young O'Casey, Dr Edward Morgan Griffin of St Barnabas'),[2] outfaces Orange bigotry to allow the hero of the play his liturgical and symbolic due. But perhaps it is in Louis MacNeice's poetic reflection on the life of his father, The Rev. John Frederick MacNeice, that the literary trope of the sincerely Christian priest had its fullest expression in Irish literature's treatment of the Church of Ireland.[3] MacNeice's beautiful epitaph for this father in 'The Kingdom' is a moving exploitation of the motif, made intense with personal feeling:

> All is well, said the voice from the tiny pulpit,
> All is well with the child. And the voice cracked
> For the preacher was very old and the coffin down in the aisle
> Held the body of one who had been his friend and colleague
> For forty years and was dead in daffodil time
> Before it had come to Easter. All is well with
> One who believed and practised and whose life
> Presumed the Resurrection. What that means
> He may have felt he knew: this much is certain –
> The meaning filled his actions, made him courteous
> And lyrical and strong and kind and truthful,
> A generous puritan. Above whose dust
> About this time each year the spendthrift plants
> Will toss their trumpets heralding a life
> That shows itself in time but remains timeless
> As is the heart of music.

In contemporary literature the most resonant image of the Church of Ireland is of a Church in irresistible decay, evoking a poignant poetry through its association with the *ancien regime* and in its declining membership. Such feeling it was which provoked John Betjeman to these lines in 'Ireland with Emily' as he pondered a ruined Irish abbey:

> There in pinnacled protection,
>   One extinguished family waits
> A Church of Ireland resurrection
>   By the broken, rusty gates.
> Sheepswool, straw and droppings cover,
> Graves of spinster, rake and lover,
> Whose fantastic mausoleum
> Sings its own seablown Te Deum,
>   In and out the slipping slates.

And such a sense of melancholy and pathos in these lines, redolent of Protestant hymns and liturgy, is subtly employed by Samuel Beckett in his dramatic presentation of terminal states of being. In *Krapp's Last Tape* (1958), for example, the deterioration of Krapp's mental faculties and his atrophied emotional life are hauntingly linked to his memories of the evening hymn, 'Now the day is over'. *All That Fall* (1957), Beckett's radio play set in South County Dublin, the title alluding to a biblical text, presents the thoughts of an elderly woman, Mrs Rooney, as she journeys to meet a train. Her comic and pathetic reflections, contained within the musical frame of Schubert's 'Death and the Maiden', are interrupted by various encounters, one of which is with Miss Fitt (the name is an obvious pun), a lady in her thirties who worships at the same Protestant church as does Mrs Rooney. Beckett's verbal portrait of Miss Fitt is unnervingly suggestive of her social and emotional vulnerability, of her hectic fragility as a neurotic middle-class member of a declining religious minority:

Oh but in church, Mrs Rooney, in church I am alone with my Maker. Are not you? (Pause) Why even the sexton himself, you know, when he takes up the collection, knows it is useless to pause before me. I simply do not see the plate, or bag, whatever it is they use, how could I? (Pause) Why even when all is over I go out into the sweet fresh air, why even then for the first furlong or so I stumble in a kind of daze as you might say, oblivious to my co-religionists. And they are very kind I must admit – the vast majority – very kind and understanding.

That the phrase 'the vast majority' has ironic implications when applied to many Church of Ireland congregations (though not surely to those of Beckett's Foxrock boyhood) is perhaps part of the black humour of Beckett's characterization here. And indeed the image of the tiny congregation is one that has often appealed to writers for its poignancy and nostalgic possibilities. In 1966 the late Jack White made a clever play about just such a congregation in *The Last Eleven*. As early as 1906 (in *Hyacinth*) George Birmingham had noticed the numerical difficulties faced by Irish Anglicanism. Here he describes a congregation in a country town:

. . . the church was never full, even under the most favourable circumstances, more than half full. The four front seats were reserved for a Mr Stack, on whose property the town of Ballymoy stood. But this gentleman preferred to live in Surrey, and even when he came over to Ireland for the shooting rarely honoured the church with his presence. A stone tablet, bearing the name of this magnate's father, a Cork pawnbroker, who had purchased the property for a small sum under the Encumbered Estates Court Act, adorned the wall beside the pulipt. The management of the property was in the hands of a Dublin firm, so the parish was deprived of the privilege of a resident land agent. The doctor recently appointed to the district was a Roman Catholic of plebean antecendants, which reduced the resident gentry of Ballymoy to the Quinns, a bank manager, and the Rector, Canon Beecher. A few farmers, Mr Stack's gamekeeper, and the landlady of the Imperial Hotel, made up the rest of the congregation.

In 1975 Derek Mahon, in his poem 'Nostalgias', recognized the almost comic finality implicit in such a scene:

> The chair squeaks in a high wind,
> Rain falls from its branches,
> The kettle yearns for the
> Mountain, the soap for the sea.
> In a tiny stone church
> On the desolate headland
> A lost tribe is singing 'Abide with me'.

And perhaps it is an indication of the limited role the Church of Ireland plays in the modern Republic of Ireland that in 1985 Eoghan Harris's play *Souper Sullivan* could be performed in the Abbey Theatre without protest. For in that play of the Famine, a Protestant priest and his convert are the heroes, as if to give the lie to Carleton's furious cartoon in *Valentine M'Clutchy*.

If, then, modern Irish writing in English has not to any great extent treated directly of themes rooted in the Church of Ireland's life, and has tended to present that Church only in terms of rather conventional, even sometimes hackneyed images, there is nevertheless a very significant if indirect sense in which the experience of the Church of Ireland and the Irish literary tradition can be said to have been fruitfully associated at one time. For many of the writers whose work from the 1880s onwards came to be identified with that cultural and imaginative awakening known as the Irish Literary Revival were, as has often been noted, of Protestant, Church of Ireland background. Simply to name them is to remind one of how great was Protestant Ireland's contribution to the literature of the period: Standish O'Grady, Lady Gregory, Douglas Hyde, W. B. Yeats, John Synge, Sean O'Casey.

Until very recent times no really convincing reasons were adduced by literary and cultural historians to account for the curious fact that Protestant Ireland gave to the Literary Revival so remarkable a pantheon of creative writers. It was often simply taken for granted that the mythological and historical traditions of Ireland were so compelling an inheritance that minds encountering them could not but fall under their spell. The contribution of men and women of Anglo-Irish backgrounds was most usually conceived of in terms of a national duty at last recognized by individuals from within the colonial world upon their discovery of Gaelic antiquity. More recently, however, explanations to account for Protestant Ireland's production of a generation of literary activists in a national mode has concentrated on the history of the Anglo-Irish as a colonial class faced by a nascent Catholic nationalism in the late nineteenth and early twentieth centuries. In this understanding of things, certain sensitive individuals, conscious of the insecurity of Anglo-Ireland's social and political position, and possessed to greater or lesser extents by racial guilt, sought to contribute to the national cause, doing so in a way that would allow for the establishment of an Irish cultural identity that did not derive solely from the Catholic nationalist majority.[4] In this thesis, Anglo-Ireland's social and political condition was emphasized, not its religious aspect. Anglo-Ireland's Protestantism was only one attribute of a colonial class or caste whose entire political, social, cultural and religious inheritance was to become increasingly suspect as modern Ireland forged an identity largely Catholic in complexion and Gaelic in aspiration. Out of the anxieties and the stimulus of the insecurity bred of these circumstances flowed, the thesis suggested, the rich stream of Anglo-Irish Revival literature.

In the last decade scholarship has begun to complicate this picture in a very interesting way, tentatively shifting the centre of gravity so that features of nineteenth-century Irish cultural life can be seen as reflecting developments in the British Isles as a whole as well as those in the specifically Irish context. The concept of Victorian Ireland has begun to gain currency.[5] And a consequence of reflecting on nineteenth-century Irish cultural history as a manifestation of Victorianism will be, I believe, to introduce the topic of nineteenth-century Irish Protestantism as a social, cultural and theological phenomenon to the study of the origins of the Literary Revival. For Irish Protestantism was a principal channel that allowed the Victorian frame of mind access to the country. To state the matter in simple terms: pondering the Revival as an expression of Irish Victorianism will lead back to a study of Irish Protestantism not only as one more lamentable attribute of a colonial class which largely sets its face against the emergent nation but as a much more interesting element in a complex of ideas and modes of feeling and action which compromise the Irish Victorian world in which that Revival came to life.

In a lecture delivered in 1979, Vivian Mercier inaugurated such a study.[6] Outlining features of Irish Anglican thought in the nineteenth century which paralleled the ideological impulses of the Literary Revival (each for example, asserted its commitment to a genuinely Celtic, pre-conquest, national authenticity), he identified the evangelical movement as a peculiarly powerful influence on Victorian Irish Anglicanism, as it also was on English religious life in the same period. In such a context it becomes possible to consider the emergence of numbers of writers of Protestant backround in Ireland not only as the inevitable product of the dynamics of late colonialism but as an Irish example of a development in the British Isles as a whole. For the religious pilgrimage, whereby sensitive young men and women found in literary and cultural activity a surrogate religosity for the abandoned emotional certainties of an evangelical childhood, is a commonplace of nineteenth-century and early twentieth-century English literary history, as its most explicit (and, indeed, grotesque) in Edmund Gosse's *Father and Son* (1907) and exemplified in Ireland by the career of Edward Dowden. And the chiliastic note so frequently struck in late-Victorian literature can be accounted for in such as John Ruskin, for example, not only as a pessimistic response to a troubled and troubling age but as a transference of evangelical preoccupation, rendered theologically unsustainable by scepticism, to social and aesthetic dimensions. Analogously, it may be possible to associate the apocalyptic obsessions of Yeats's poetic with the calamitarian mood of late-Victorian Britain in which eschatological modes of thought, so characteristic of the evangelical temper of Victorian religious feeling, were available to mythologize a generally perceived social crisis. Accordingly, when Yeats wrote as follows of his youth, he was exhibiting the degree to which nineteenth-century Ireland was a Victorian Ireland. His religious conflicts were typical of the age:

I am very religious, and deprived by Huxley and Tyndall, whom I detested, of the simple-minded religion of my childhood, I had made a new religion, almost an infallible Church of poetic tradition, of a fardel of stones, and of personages, and of emotions, inseparable from their first expression, passed on from generation to generation by poets and painters with some help from philosophers and theologians.

An early poem expressive of this aesthetic and mythic religiosity, 'The Valley of the Black Pig' (in *The Wind Among the Reeds*), was cast in terms of apocalypse, and shows how, almost from the first, Yeats's imagination had been drawn to one of Victorianism's dominant obsessions, even though in his immediate family background evangelical religion (in which that widespread obsession probably had its deepest roots) had scarcely made itself felt. Apocalypse was to become a primary symbol for the poet and was to retain its power for Yeats's imagination throughout his career.

Yeats's remarkable meditation of 1909, *The Death of Synge*, sounds an explicitly eschatological note, intensely familiar from the evangelical homiletic tradition:

Celebrations

1. He was one of the unmoved souls in whom there is a perpetual 'Last Day', a perpetual trumpeting and a coming up for judgment.
2. He did not speak to men and women, asking judgment, as lesser

writers do, but knowing himself part of judgment he was silent.
3. We pity the living and not such dead as he. He has gone upward out of his ailing body into the heroical fountains. We are parched by time.

There is a haunting appropriateness in Yeats's choice of metaphors here, with their evangelical provenance disturbed by a hint of classical paganism in the image of the 'heroical fountains'; for John Synge had experienced as a youth just the kinds of religious and personal tensions that had characterized the early lives of so many of his English Victorian contemporaries. Indeed, the intellectual biography of the dramatist must provide persuasive evidence for those prepared to account for the Irish Literary Revival not only in the broad terms of the history of colonialism but more particularly in relation to developments within the Irish Anglican community.[7]

Synge's family, with its complement of clergy and medical missioners, had long been familiar with the fervent values of evangelicalism, and Synge himself was touched intimately by them in the person of his devout mother. The story of his intellectual break with his mother's creed is recounted intelligently in Edward Stephens's *Life of J. M. Synge* (1974), and the account unfolds a tale which undoubtedly had parallels in the lives of many literary Victorians. For an awakening speculative intellect posed for the growing boy a painful if commonplace dilemma: 'John saw that if he arrived at the logical conclusion of Darwin's argument, as it now appeared, he would be faced not only with religious difficulties but also with the outraged feelings of almost everyone he knew. . .'. Edward Stephens's editor, Andrew Carpenter, has suggested that Stephens probably exaggerated the degree to which Synge was affected by the tensions generated in him by his mother's creed. Stephens, Carpenter argues, interpreted Synge's career in the light of his own belated rejection of evangelical certainties. But Stephens, although he relates Synge's plays rather too directly to the biographical facts of the dramatist's life, does have the evidence of Synge's own assessment of his adolesence to sustain his view that Synge's youthful religious crisis was a severe one, likely to have affected adult experience and activity. Synge wrote of his intense feelings when the repository of faith was assaulted by his discovery of Darwin:

I flung the book aside and rushed out into the open air – it was summer and we were in the country – the sky seemed to have lost its blue and the grass its green. I lay down and writhed in an agony of doubt. . . . In a few weeks or days I had regained my composure, but this was the beginning.

Furthermore, Synge seemed perfectly conscious how his developing nationalism and involvement with the ideals of the Literary Revival could be seen as a surrogate for the religious enthusiasm which had been an ever-present reality of his childhood world.

Soon after [he wrote] I had relinquished the Kingdom of God I began to take a real interest in the Kingdom of Ireland. My patriotism went round from a vigorous and reasoning loyalty to a temperate nationalism, and everything Irish became sacred.

He recognized that 'Patriotism gratifies man's need for adoration and has, therefore, a peculiar power upon the imaginative sceptic' and in his own case that 'The Irish country rains, mists, pale insular skies, the old churches, manuscripts, jewels, everything in fact that was Irish had a charm neither human nor divine, rather perhaps as if I had fallen in love with a goddess.' A critical enterprise therefore exists to show in what degree, in W. J. Mc Cormack's words, 'Synge's mythology was a mask for tensions in his Protestant upbringing.'[8] Mc Cormack hints at a reading of his plays which notes how each of them concludes 'with images of death, of death necessitated and desired as the culmination of life'.[9] This would provide a tantalizing starting-point for a full study, for not only does such a perception remind of the Yeatsian epitaph's eschatalogical implications, but relates Synge's *œuvre* to the apocalyptic aspects of the religious tradition in which he was reared.[10] In such a reading evangelical eschatology is transferred to the dramatic world of an *œuvre* dominated by a sense of the absolute demands of death and by the symbolic presentation of a world under judgment. Rejecting the crude certainties of an evangelical Protestantism Synge did not, in his espousal of a new national and literary set of values, necessarily shake off the apocalyptic elements of his mother's world view. So, Synge can be seen as exhibiting to a marked degree the tendency of Irish Revival writing to reflect a Victorian cultural development whereby writers forsook childhood certainties but continued to express in symbolic form the same chiliastic anxieties that evangelical religion expressed in directly theological terms when it discerned in the disorders of the times 'signs' of an imminent climax of the ages.

This interesting complex of ideologies, social facts and of feelings was, as it happens, identified precisely as its effects were being felt in the literature of the Revival. In 1906 George Birmingham published his novel *Hyacinth*. In this astute if formally diffuse work Birmingham detected how a feeling for the Irish nation can function as a surrogate religion for a young man raised within the emotional certainties of an evangelical Christianty. Young Hyacinth, the novel's hero, is the son of a missionary with a Protestant organization (possibly the notorious Irish Church Missions) dedicated to the conversion of the Irish, who has lost his proselytising zeal but has maintained a primitive, almost mystical faith. Hyacinth is marked for Holy Orders and leaves his western home for Trinity College, Dublin, where he finds love for Ireland, unconsciously instilled by his association with the native folk among whom he has hitherto lived, affronted by the unabashed Unionism and imperialism of teachers and taught alike in the Divinity School as the Boer War rages. He becomes involved with a group of hyper-nationalists and forsakes his studies: he has found a new creed. But it is one that can feed his imagination with symbols not so different from those that absorb his father's mind. The faith of his father and his new enthusiasm are closely related, Birmingham implies. And in both the metaphor of Armageddon is centrally powerful, and perhaps that accounts for Hyacinth's attraction to nationalism – it is a secular religion serving as a replacement for the faith he has lost. Hyacinth's father, just before he dies, recounts a strange vision to his son in which he prophesies a great final battle: 'And the battlefield is Ireland, our dear Ireland. All these centuries since the great saints died He has kept Ireland to be his battlefield.'

That night Hyacinth has his own vision, which blends evangelical fervour, a literary nationalism and apocalyptic imaginings in a way that casts a strong if slightly too heated light on the issues which have now begun to attract scholarly attention in Ireland:

For a long time after he had gone to bed Hyacinth lay awake haunted by his father's prophecy of an Armageddon. There was that in his nature which responded eagerly to such a call to battle. In the presence of enthusiasm like his father's. . ., Hyacinth caught fire. His mind flamed with the idea of an Independent Ireland resplendent with her ancient glories. He embraced no less eagerly the thought of his father's battle and his own part in it. Groping for points of contact between the two enthusiasms, he caught at the conception of the Roman Church as the Antichrist and her power in Ireland as the point around which the fight must rage. Then with a sudden flash he saw, not Rome, but the British Empire, as the embodiment of the power of darkness.

So, the history of the Church of Ireland may come to be considered as bearing intimately on the Irish Literary Revival as scholars draw out the implications of the 'contact between two enthusiasms'. And in that event, developments in a Church that since the eighteenth century of Swift and Berkeley has made little apparent impact upon Irish literature may well come to be seen as crucial to a full cultural, social and intellectual portrait of the Irish Victorian age.

NOTES

1. For a study of Hannay's nationalism and involvement with the Gaelic League see R. B. D. French, 'J. O. Hannay and the Gaelic League', *Hermathena*, No. CII (Spring 1966), pp. 26-52.
2. See Alan Simpson, 'O'Casey and the East Wall Area of Dublin', *The Irish University Review*, Vol. 10, No. 1 (Spring 1980), pp. 41-51, and Garry O'Connor, *Sean O'Casey: A Life* (London 1988).
3. For MacNeice's poetic treatment of his father see my 'MacNeice: Father and Son' in *Time Was Away: The World of Louis MacNeice*, eds T. Brown and A. Reid (Dublin 1974), pp. 21-34.
4. F. S. L. Lyons's book, *Culture and Anarchy in Ireland, 1890-1945* (Oxford 1979), was a notable contribution to the debate on the origins of the Revival cast largely in these terms. See also F. S. L. Lyons. 'The Battle of Two Civilizations' in *Ireland Since the Famine* (London 1973), pp. 224-46.
5. See W. J. Mc Cormack, *Sheridan Le Fanu and Victorian Ireland* (Oxford 1980). See also F. S. L. Lyons, 'Yeats and Victorian Ireland' in *Yeats, Sligo and Ireland*, ed. A. Norman Jeffares (Gerrards Cross 1980), pp. 115-38.
6. See Vivian Mercier, 'Victorian Evangelicalism and the Anglo-Irish Literary Revival' in *Literature and the Changing Ireland* (Gerrards Cross 1982), pp. 59-101.
7. It is, of course, arguable that the Irish Protestant Churches were so influenced by the evangelical revival of the nineteenth century because the colonial predicament of the Irish Protestant middle-class intensified the sense

of insecurity that the middle-classes felt generally in the British Isles as new social conditions and a quickening pace of intellectual change disturbed bourgeois complacency and religious certainty. The Calvinist ideas within much of the evangelical movement – of special election, imminent Armageddon and necessary social separation from the lost – have a peculiar force in a colonial setting, where the nascent national majority practises a suspect version of Christianity. In this sense evangelicalism in Ireland cannot be fully understood without consideration of the colonial facts of nineteenth-century Ireland. But that evangelicalism was also a local expression of a phenomenon which had profoundly affected the United Kingdom as a whole.

8. Mc Cormack, *op. cit.*, p. 6.

9. *Ibid.*, p. 265.

10. It seems clear that Synge's mother was deeply evangelical. In the dramatist's memory of his religious experience in childhood he remembers precisely those things which one might associate with that fervent version of Christiantiy – a sense of a personal conviction of sin, fear of hell and an encouragement to seek personal salvation. Synge reflects that his upbringing was not especially Calvinistic, and Ann Saddlemyer tells us that his mother's favourite religious injunction was, 'Come you out and be you separate'. These facts strongly suggest that, although the family attended at the Church of Ireland St Patrick's Cathedral, in Dublin, her faith was significantly influenced by the attitudes of the Brethren. This was a sect which had been founded by John Nelson Darby in Wicklow and Dublin in the 1830s. An outgrowth of this movement became the fairly widespread religious sect known as the Plymouth Brethren. Darby, whose faith was strongly emotional and not markedly Calvinistic, in fact broke with the movement and was leader of a remnant who believed in the separation of the Christian from the world to await the Second Coming which, scripture suggested, could not be long delayed; an extreme doctrine which he preached in terms of Mrs Synge's favourite injunction. The Darbyites remained quite strong in Wicklow during Synge's childhood. They were keen students of biblical prophecy, earnest to read the signs of imminent apocalypse. This tradition had been established by Darby himself (he died abroad aged eighty-two in 1882) when between 1832 and 1838 many meetings had been held to study the prophetic scriptures in Lady Powerscourt's home in the company of eminent Anglican clergymen.

5

CANON SHEEHAN AND THE CATHOLIC INTELLECTUAL

In December 1903 Canon Sheehan, the popular Irish novelist, addressed the students of his *alma mater* in the *Aula Maxima* of St Patrick's College, Maynooth. His lecture, stirringly entitled 'The Dawn of the Century', challenged his audience in a way to which they were not, by all accounts, accustomed:

One safe principle may be laid down – that the Irish priest must be in advance of his people, educationally, by at least fifty years. The priests have the lead, and they must keep it. But the right of leadership, now so often questioned, must be supported by tangible and repeated proofs; and these proofs must concern not only your spiritual authority, but your intellectual superiority. The young priest who has lectured on 'Hamlet' in the Town Hall on Thursday night is listened to with deeper respect on Sunday morning. The priest who conducts a long and laborious experiment before a literary and scientific society in any of our cities is, henceforward, an acknowledged and unquestioned guide in his village. And the priest who, quietly and without temper, overthrows one of those carping critics at a dinner-party, may confirm, without the possibility of its being disturbed again, the faith of many who are present, and whose beliefs, perhaps, are rudely shaken by the impertinence of the shallow criticism to which they had just been listening.[1]

The educational deficiencies of Maynooth, whatever its success as the clerical powerhouse of the increasingly dynamic Catholicism of later nineteenth-century Ireland, were a recurrent complaint of Victorian social commentators. In 1840 those prolific scribblers Mr and Mrs S. C. Hall had written disparagingly in their three-volume tour of the country of the narrow, illiberal education offered there to a socially undistinguished studentry, lamenting its location in a cultural backwater: 'the college should be, undoubtedly, removed from the miserable

village where it at present stands to the immediate neighbourhood of some city; where, while the students are subjected to
wholesome and sufficient restraint, they may be permitted occasional intercourse with mankind'.[2] A Royal Commission of 1854-
5 tended to confirm the Halls' jaundiced opinions, and subsequent literary and autobiographical reminiscence of Maynooth
life suggests that few improvements were effected in the following decades. Patrick Augustine Sheehan himself entered
Maynooth in 1869. His memories were less than enthusiastic.

I think it was on the 25th August, 1869, I passed through the Sphinx-
guarded gates of Maynooth College, and stood near what was then the
Senior Chapel, and saw, with a certain melancholy feeling, the old keep
of the Geraldine castle lighted up by the rays of the sinking sun. I
remember well that the impression made upon me by Maynooth
College then, and afterwards, when I saw its long stone corridors, its
immense bare stony halls, the huge massive tablets, etc., was one of
rude, Cyclopean strength, without one single aspect or feature of refinement. So too with its studies. Relentless logic, with its formidable
chevaux-de-frise of syllogisms, propositions, scholia; metaphysics, sub-
lime, but hardened into slabs of theories, congealed in medieval
Latin. . . . The Graces were nowhere. Even in the English Literature
or Belles Lettres class, as it was called, the course seemed to be limited
to hard grinding Grammar and nothing more.[3]

Upon ordination Sheehan quickly realized how little his
Maynooth career had prepared him for what he increasingly felt
was required in modern pastoral life, intellectual as well as
spiritual leadership of the kind he commended in his lecture of
1903. Accordingly, almost all of his published work affords us
a fascinating opportunity to observe the complex relations between a committed Catholic intellectual and Irish society in the
period when modern Irish nationalism was forming itself into
the force which would shape a new Ireland in the first two
decades of the twentieth century. For throughout his career as
essayist, novelist and priest, Sheehan remained vigorously
engaged in the project of establishing an intellectual Catholic
presence in a country he believed was in dire need of such.
Indeed the almost obsessional way in which the topic recurs in
his writings suggests how desperate in his opinion was the lack
of that leaven.

In Sheehan's writings the Irish Catholic of intellectual and
cultural aspiration is confronted at the outset by a terrible aware-

ness – that is of the comparative impoverishment of the country in almost every sphere of humanistic achievement. An early veneration at the shrine of Carlyle had given him an appreciation of all things German and amongst his first literary and cultural exploits had been a series of essays on the German university system, beside which Ireland's halls of higher learning seemed pitiably inadequate. In modern Germany, it seemed to him, as had not been the case since the days of the Greek Academy, an 'aristocracy of talent' held sway in a climate where 'chief prominence is given to religious science'.[4] And of the country he could claim 'infidelity is making no headway amongst any class in Germany'.[5] In his novel *Luke Delmege* (1901) we are introduced to a priest, one of the many interesting minor characters in the work, who has spent two years studying in Germany. His experience there compares sadly with the hero's period of cultural deprivation at Maynooth and the generally depressed quality of life in Ireland. Of this character Sheehan informs us: 'And when by degrees he began to realize that this country, which but a few years back had been cursed by a foreign tongue, had now, by a supreme effort, created its own language, and a literature unsurpassed for richness and sweetness, he saturated himself with the poetry and philosophy of the country, which gave a new colour and embellishment to life.' But it is in Sheehan's last novel, *The Graves at Kilmorna* (1915), that the romance of the European, and of Germany in particular, receives its fullest expression. Sheehan had himself holidayed in Germany in 1904 and in *The Graves at Kilmorna*, written in 1911, he has an ageing Fenian, depressed and discouraged by developments in Ireland, discover there a world more headily attractive than any he had hitherto encountered. But the experience is no unalloyed pleasure:

As they advanced, and new worlds of wonder opened up to this view, and he saw what education and civilization had wrought; and how human life and its surroundings were lifted up and on to a high plane of refinement and culture; how literature and the arts sweetened toil. . . he became moody and silent and abstracted. He was thinking of the motherland; and how far she was in the rear of all modern civilization. . . . He would not admit for a moment that Nature had done less for Ireland than for the favoured countries of Europe; but oh! when it came to human effort and human genius, what a deplorable contrast.

Sheehan had in fact good reason to praise the quality of German civilization, for in that country his own work was much esteemed. In particular his fine semi-autobiographical account of the intellectual pilgrimage of a priest in *Luke Delmege* was admired by German readers. In that work one character had indeed conceived an ambition to engraft 'German ideas and German habits and manners in the peasantry at home', which improbable enterprise must have commended him to a German audience. But a more compelling aspect of *Luke Delmege* is its exploration of a sensitive and intelligent Irishman's encounter with the riches of Victorian English culture. Sheehan's enamourment of German life and letters was a matter of books and the romanticism of the distant – he presents Germany in his novels in terms of fictional tourism. His relationships with England was the fruit of his two years' service on the English mission. As a consequence his study of Luke Delmege's complex and varying responses to England amounts to one of the most subtle, psychologically developed portraits in all his fiction.

Luke Delmege has graduated with his academic honours from Maynooth and is plunged into priesthood in a land he cannot easily comprehend. His initial response is in terms of an Irish nationalist stereotype whereby England is apprehended in all its vast materialism in contrast to the spirituality of Ireland:

Everywhere it was the same. Whilst all around the splendid materialism of England asserted and showed itself; whilst shops were packed full of every kind of luxury and necessary, and the victuallers and pork-butchers vied with the fruit-sellers in exhibiting every form of human food; whilst public baths were springing up in all directions, and everything ministering to human wants was exhibited in superabundance, whilst a perfect system of police and detective supervision guarded human life and safety, each solitary individual walked alone.

The English state seems to Luke 'a huge piece of perfect and polished mechanism – cold, clean, shining, smooth, and regular; but with no more of a soul than a steam engine'. Slowly, however, he finds himself penetrating the cold surfaces of English personality: 'he got used to it, and his nerves were gradually toned down into the silky smoothness that reigned everywhere around him. And he began to see great deeps of affection and love far down beneath the icy surface, and every day he was made aware of genuine kindness, gentle, undemonstrative, unobtrusive, until he grew to love those grave, pleasant people, and they loved him in return'. Furthermore, he is transferred to a curacy where he has the opportunity to preach to an educated, urbane congregation and begins to make a mark as a Catholic apologist. A liberal, cultivated social circle introduce him to the range of contemporary English intellectual life:

The beautiful, smooth mechanism was affecting Luke unconsciously. He no longer heard the whir and jar of machinery, or saw the mighty monster flinging out its refuse of slime and filth in the alleys and courts of southwest London; but the same smooth regularity, the same quiet, invincible energy was manifest here in the sleepy Cathedral town. Here was the beautiful tapestry, pushed out from the horrid jaws of the great mill; beautiful, perfect, with all fair colours of cultured men and stately women, and woven through with gold and crimson threads of art and science and literature. And Luke felt the glamour wrapping him around with an atmosphere of song and light and he felt it a duty to fit himself to his environment.

England has seduced an Irish intellect and sensibility. A visit back to his home village confirms his national disenchantment: 'As they drove along, the aspect of the landscape seems intolerably melancholy and dull. The grey fields, that had not yet sprung into green, the thatched cottages, the ruined walls, the broken hedges, the ragged bushes all seemed to Luke, fresh from the prim civilization of Aylesburgh, unspeakably old and wretched. Ruin and delapidation were everywhere.'

Sheehan of course is not satisfied to show us in his fiction only the effects on the culturally starved of the rich diet of English and European civilization. He is perhaps even more absorbed as an artist with the problems confronting the Irish Catholic intellectual who wishes to influence his country through the broader cultural perspectives provided by English and European experience. The latter half of *Luke Delmege* therefore has Luke back in Ireland engaged in a vain attempt to teach his Irish charges the ways of English punctuality, self-improvement and personal independence. The result is catastrophic for Luke. But in a more muted, less schematic fashion Canon Sheehan's best-known and most popular work, *My New Curate* (1900), is preoccupied with precisely this theme. The degree to which this work revolves about this major concern of Sheehan's own intellectual life may surprise the reader who comes to this book in the knowledge of its Irish reputation as a benevolent, humorous, engaging series of scenes from Irish clerical life. In fact the work, for all its occasional drollery of tone and urbanity of manner, is a study in failure. The genial humour of the book derives from its central character, the quizzical, good-tempered, elderly classicist Father Dan (he is one of Sheehan's most attractive and credible creations). His new curate is the impetuous, culturally ambitious, energetic social improver, Father Lethenby. Father Lethenby's enterprises, however, come to grief. His efforts to establish a factory and a fishing industry prove disastrously ineffective and almost bring him to financial and personal ruin. But the novel makes clear too that Father Dan, now the repository of the calm wisdom of the aged, had once nurtured similar ambitions until the years taught him sense:

I remember what magnificent ideas I had. I would build factories, I would pave the streets, I would establish a fishing-station and make Kilronan the favourite bathing resort on the western coast, I would write books and be, all round, a model of push, energy, amd enterprise. And I did try. I might as well have tried to remove yonder mountain with a pitchfork, or stop the roll of the Atlantic with a rope of sand. Nothing on earth can cure the inertia of Ireland. It weighs down like the sweeping clouds on the damp, heavy earth and there's no lifting it, nor disburthening of the souls of men of this intolerable weight. . . It was a land of the lotus. The people were narcotized.

We know from Sheehan's biographer[6] that he himself had experienced something of the same frustration when he returned from the English mission to a curacy in Mallow. Accordingly, it is hard not to read in Sheehan's fiction a kind of intellectual and spiritual autobiography in which he sought to come to terms with difficulty, frustration and even failure. In each of his novels in which he explores the dilemma of the priest as intellectual, *My New Curate, Luke Delmege* and *The Blindness of Dr Gray* (1909), he makes his heroes learn the hard lesson of the inadequacies of intellect unless it is warmed by the fires of faith and feeling. Luke Delmege is brought to acknowledge that the spirituality of the Irish will never be satisfied by any philosophy rooted in the materialism of English ideas of progress. Father Lethenby comes to understand the role of suffering in the truly beneficent life and Dr Gray must learn that the letter of an abstract and perfect law is what kills the spirit, where love gives life. The fact that these profound Christian apprehensions are mediated by Sheehan in his novels through scenes and events reminiscent of the most tendentious and propagandist of Victorian evangelical fiction is probably the principal aspect of his work that has sent his once bright literary reputation into eclipse. Too much, far too much, is made of fallen women, sacrificial sisters, miraculously heroic acts of piety. As spiritual resolutions to sensitively explored psychological dilemmas, these Victorian motifs seem inadequate and aesthetically unsatisfying. In relation to Sheehan's own biography it is hard not to entertain the suspicion that these pietistic dénouements represent some kind of wish-fulfilment. Be that as it may, what is even more telling is the fact that at no point in any of these three intriguing if flawed novels does Sheehan give more than a hint of how the spiritually humbled Catholic intellectual should relate to his society, the error of his earlier ways reckoned with and cast aside. Father Lethenby's financial and personal survival is what is at stake at the end of *My New Curate*, Dr Gray in *The Blindness of Dr Gray* is close to death when his spiritual re-birth takes place, and most significantly *Luke Delmege* begins with the death of its hero. In this latter work it is as if Sheehan has taken Luke to the point of transformation but then cannot conceive of what to do with him. So he opens the work with Luke's death as a lonely, slightly eccentric figure who has apparently found no significant social role in the Irish priesthood, despite the spiritual chastening, we learn by the novel's end, he has experienced.

Indeed, sounding as a bass-note through much of Canon Sheehan's fiction, deeper even than the prevailing *pietas*, is a sense of the intense solitude of priestly life, particularly as experienced by those of intellectual and cultural distinction. A passage such as the following, where Luke Delmege is set against the Irish landscape, is typical and furthermore gives some sense of the power which Sheehan can release in his work, suggests the very real strengths of this extraordinary uneven, but under-estimated novelist:

The very solitude, which had oppressed him with such lonely and melancholy feelings, began to assume a strange and singular charm. There was a mysterious light over everything that gave an aspect of dreamland and enchantment, or of old, far-off times, even to the long, lonely fields, or the dark, sullen bogland. He could not well define it.

There was some association haunting everything, inexpressibly sweet, but so vague, so elusive, he could not define what it was. The fields in the twilight had a curious colour or cloudland hanging over them, that reminded him of something sweet and beautiful and far away; but this memory or imagination could never seize and hold. And when, on one of those grey days, which are so lovely in Ireland, as the light falls sombre and neutral on all things, a plover would shriek across the moorland, or a curlew would rise up and beat his lonely way, complaining and afraid, across the ashen sky, Luke would feel that he had seen it all before in some waking dream of childhood; but all associations had vanished.

Throughout his career Sheehan had indicated in his fiction that nationalism as a social and cultural movement of high idealism could provide an intellectually aware priesthood with the means whereby it might achieve the leadership of the people in a worthwhile, ennobling cause. Novels like *Lisheen* (1907) and *Miriam Lucas* (1912) had made clear his views on the social evils of landlordism and unbridled capitalism (the motif of absentee landlordism plays a part, too, in *Luke Delmege)*, while *Glenanaar* (1905) with its vivid story of O'Connell and the Doneraile conspiracy had firmly nailed Sheehan's colours to the mast of Irish national aspiration. But the subtle-minded, vigorous imagination of the novelist could not observe the developments of late nineteenth-century Irish nationalism without serious reservations. His novel *The Graves at Kilmorna* (1915), therefore, written when Sheehan knew of his own terminal illness, is a work of remarkable interest as an analysis of the varying strands of modern Irish nationalism about which Sheehan clearly felt less than happy. Late in his life, the force that once might have allowed the Catholic intellectual to participate in Irish society as an enthusiastic leader is viewed with anxious concern.

The Graves at Kilmorna recounts a tale of the Fenian rising and tells the life-story of one of the activists, Myles Cogan, who survives into a period of unheroic disillusionment. In this respect the novel is curiously anticipatory of a later work of revolutionary frustration by that other Cork writer, the Seán O Faoláin of *Bird Alone* (1936).

Sheehan was a student in St Colman's College in Fermoy, Co Cork, when the incidents of 1867 took place which form the basis of his later novel. He would probably have known of the antagonism of many in his Church towards the Fenian martyrs but was clearly impressed, as his own record tells us, by the brave death of Peter O'Neill-Crowley, leader of the East Cork Fenians in Kilcloony-wood, holding at bay an entire British regiment and a posse of police. He remembered, too, how the curate of Mitchelstown ran to give the dying hero the last sacraments and how as a boy he himself had watched the huge funeral procession that bore O'Neill-Crowley to his patriot grave: ' the dark masses of men swaying over the bridge, the yellow coffin conspicuous in their midst'.

Fenianism in *The Graves at Kilmorna* is associated with high idealism, spirituality, an inclusive national vision derived from Thomas Davis, John Mitchel and the Young Irelanders. It opposes the acquisitive, degenerate corruption of conventional political and economic life. The Fenians are drawn from the most honourable, the most educated (the martyr Halpin is a schoolteacher), the most religiously scrupulous of the populace. Its soldiers are dominated by a vision of Ireland's heroic past, her physical beauty and her cruel subjugation. They combine pride, honour, duty with chivalric intensity. What Sheehan seems to be doing in this work of 1911 (it was published posthumously) is proposing a theory in which the corrupt materialism of an Ireland adapting itself to the modern world of commerce, power politics and pragmatism, will always stimulate a minority to acts of what they believe to be redemptive violence. In so doing he is interpreting the Fenian Rising less in its own terms than in terms of what he feared might occur in twentieth-century Ireland. This is quite clear when we consider the following extraordinary percipient conversation in the novel. Myles Cogan is consulting with his leader, James Halpin, on the prospects for the Rising. He is told the outcome can only be disaster in military terms, but,

'The country has become plethoric and therefore indifferent to everything but bread and cheese. It needs bloodletting a little. The country is sinking into the sleep of death; and nothing can awake it but the crack of the rifle. . . . You and I will be shot. Our bodies will be stretched out on the Irish heather; our blood will have soaked back into our mother's breasts. . . and the political degradation of the people which we shall have preached with our gaping wounds will shame the nation into at least a paroxysm of patriotism once again.'

'That means', said Myles Cogan after a long pause, 'that we, Fenians, are not soldiers, but preachers.'

Such an interpretation of the Fenians' purposes is, of course, something of an historic anachronism but one charged with accurate premonition. The full sense of Fenian martyrdom only came after the execution of the Manchester Martyrs but it was such a reading of the past and the future which was to spur a new generation to rebellion a few years after Canon Sheehan's death. The revolutionary sermon was to be preached once more.

The personal consequences of a sacrificial role are explored in the second half of Sheehan's novel where we see Myles, released from prison in England, attempting to come to terms with the Ireland he has so despised in the past. He cannot do so. He makes efforts to promote social improvement in his home town but holds himself apart from the new political nationalism of the Land League and Parnellism. He becomes isolated, politically uninvolved and remote from reality: 'He seemed to be drifting further and further from public life. He read the morning paper, watched with languid interest the course of that wretched gamble, called politics, then went back to his poets and philosophers, and grew absorbed in the serenity of their ideas and their lives.' On a holiday in Germany he is highly attracted by the anti-democratic, elitist fantasizing of a German aristocrat whom he encounters. The Thuringean counsels a form of authoritarian nostalgia:

Democracy has but one logical end – socialism. Socialism is cosmopolitanism – no distinction of nationalities any longer; but one common race. That means anti-militarism, the abolition of all stimulus and rivalry. And who is going to work or fight, my friends, for that abstraction, called Humanity? Not I. But, thank God, we have the Past to live in. They cannot take that from us.

Myles's nostalgia is for the revolutionary absolutism of the Fenians which draws him, towards the end of his life, to an extremism of religious renunciation, to a fiercely puritan vision of Irish Christiantiy. His contempt for the new materialism of the country, together with a sense of ideals frustrated, revolutionary hope disappointed, has bred in him a kind of life-denying zeal – he seems finally satisfied when his Cistercian spiritual confessor assures him of the nation's ascetic destiny:

The nation will go on; grow fat like Jeshurun, and kick. And then it will grow supremely disgusted with itself; it will take its wealth, and build a monastery on every hilltop in Ireland. The island will become another Thebaid – and that will be its final destiny!

Sheehan seems to be saying in the novel that he fears the narrow, zealous ascetic and self-destructive nationalism that must be the outcome when the noble idealism of a minority encounters the prudent, cautious, self-interested national feeling of an increasingly materialistic, even socialist majority.[7] That there might be another way is suggested in the book by the figure of Father James, a wise older priest, who tries to save Myles from himself. In him is embodied Sheehan's own sense, which *was* his despite admiration for the nobility of the Fenians' chivalric gesture, that a more fruitful nationalism must be rooted in intellectual renewal. 'It is not', he advises Myles, 'by the pike and the gun, but with the voice and the pen that Ireland's salvation can be worked out.' Education must inform the majority's nationalism so that the fatal dialectic between nobility and pragmatism can be transcended in a new national order.[8] The tragic conclusion to the book suggests that Sheehan feared events had gone too far in his own day to permit of any such new departure. Myles in the end is prevailed upon to speak on behalf of a parliamentary candidate who has Father James's support and who seems to represent something of the cultivated generosity of mind that a true Irish nationalism should represent. Speaking before an audience who find his evident contempt for them wholly inflaming, he is struck down by a stone and dies. Sheehan seemed incapable of showing how his intellectual clerical heroes might relate in any creative way with their own society. Similarly, he seems at the end of this dark and prescient work to prophesy, in the death of its hero at the hand of his own people, a period when the role of the Catholic intellectual in Ireland, and of a clergy culturally as well as spiritually endowed, would be overshadowed by the kind of cruel dialectic of revolutionary violence and reaction which destroyed Myles Cogan. Canon Sheehan had spent much of his life in the encouragement of a cultural leavening of Irish life. That the twentieth century was, he sensed, to make many of his labours irrelevant perhaps accounts for the sombre words with which this strange but compelling book concludes, as Father James gives the oration over the graves at Kilmorna which contain both Halpin and Myles Cogan:

There lie two Irish martyrs – one, pierced by an English bullet on the field of battle; the other, after spending the best ten years of life in English dungeons, done to death by his own countrymen. There they lie; and with them is buried the Ireland of our dreams, our hopes, our ambitions, our love. There is no more to be said. Let us go hence!

NOTES

1. Canon Sheehan, 'The Dawn of the Century' in *Literary Life* (Dublin n.d.), pp. 145-6.
2. Cited in John A. Murphy, 'Priests and People in Modern Irish History', *Christus Rex*, Vol. XXIII, No. 4 (1969), p. 251. I am indebted to this detailed study.
3. Sheehan, 'The Irish Priesthood and Politics' in *Literary Life*, pp. 112-13.
4. Quoted by Sheehan, *Irish Ecclesiastical Record* (August 1886), p. 690.
5. Sheehan, *Irish Ecclesiastical Record* (July 1886), p. 629.
6. See Herman J. Heuser, D. D., *Canon Sheehan of Doneraile* (London 1917), pp. 73-86.
7. In a letter of 1911 Sheehan told a friend, 'I have a new novel completed; it deals with Socialism in Ireland and many other matters.' Heuser, *op. cit.*, p. 258.
8. I was aided in my interpretation of this novel by the helpful reading Austen Corcoran supplied in his unpublished doctoral thesis, 'Violence and the Form of the Irish Novel' (University College, Dublin, 1981).

6

YEATS, JOYCE AND THE IRISH
CRITICAL DEBATE

The nascent nationalism of the early twentieth century in Ireland generated the movement known as Irish Ireland – a movement earnest to celebrate the authentic life of a nation long subjected to alien suppression. It saw as one of its enemies the Anglo-Irish Ascendancy which had been, so Irish Ireland reckoned, the chief agent of Anglicization in the country, that Anglicization which had eclipsed the Gaelic world. The literature it identified with that caste, Anglo-Irish literature, was received with the profoundest suspicion. For critics like D. P. Moran, Eoin MacNeill and Daniel Corkery, the question of Anglo-Irish literature posed an issue which in fact generated a critical discourse more sustained and coherent than anything produced by a person or group sympathetic to the achievement that literature represented.[1] And the ways in which Irish Ireland reflected on Anglo-Irish literature have proved remarkably long-lived in the country, contemporary critical debate often being conducted in terms that Irish Ireland would have found congenial. So powerful indeed has been the influence of the Revival that seventy years after Irish Ireland's first assaults upon Anglo-Irish literature the question of that literature's relationship with Irish life remains contentious and vexed, around which the nearest thing to a contemporary body of Irish criticism revolves.

The central thrust of Irish Ireland's critique of Anglo-Irish literature was that it lacked national authenticity, was not truly indigenous. A second, subsidiary element in Irish Ireland's polemical assault upon Anglo-Irish literature was that it was inauthentic because it failed to appreciate the deeply European nature of Ireland's local life. In *The Hidden Ireland* (1924) Corkery evokes the indigenous life of peasant Ireland as one that has escaped the universalizing forces of the Enlightenment, retaining in its customs and beliefs a link with the mediaeval world of Catholic Europe. Furthermore, in his celebration of the Gaelic big houses of the eighteenth century it is their European awareness and that of their poets which he particularly esteems: 'To these, Paris was nearer than Dublin, and Vienna than London'[2] and 'contact with Europe, then, was one of the notes that distinguished the culture of the Catholic Gaels from that of the Planters'.[3]

Irish Ireland's critique was a powerful and pugnacious polemic vitiated by a major weakness most evident in the work of its principal advocate, Corkery himself. It lacked an exemplary contemporary figure to set against the exotic, inauthentic and non-European literature of the Revival, to confirm the analysis by an evident national authenticity and continental imaginative range. In the 1920s a number of literary commentators in Ireland began to identify James Joyce in such terms, finding that his career and work more closely approximated to Irish Ireland's cultural map than the John Synge whom Corkery himself tried to incorporate into his own analysis as an exemplary and explanatory figure. An early and amusing instance of this cultural strategy was provided by Joyce's friend, the writer and subsequent Registrar of Ireland's Supreme Court, C. P. Curran. Reflecting in AE's *Irish Statesman* on that most profound of Irish polarities, the North and South side of the Hibernian metropolis, he asserted, 'the North side is the Gael's, the South the Pale's'. And it is in the Gaelic North side that the city's most vibrant cultural energies are located:

I suggest geographically that the Northern frontier of the South side stretches from the Brewery to Trinity College. I do not deny that breweries and colleges produce literature of a sort, nor do I fail to recognise the existence of many admirable suburban and austral poets. But they seem to me to lack some toughness of fibre, the intensity, the austerity, the virile, sometimes astringent quality that makes good North side literature. Aungier Street could write sweet verses about Bendemeer's stream, and Merrion Square poets may write about salley gardens and more obscurely about cats and the moon. What is all their praise to them who tread in the footsteps of the Nameless One dreeing his weird between the river and the famous back-parlour in North Charles Street where he consorted worthily with his peers, Petrie,

O'Donovan, O'Curry, O'Langan, and the rest who made the lower end of the North Circular Road the bright focus of Irish literature. . . . Nor does the way-worn, travel-stained Ulysses himself ever stray for long from this consecrated ground.[4]

Here, in jocose fashion, Curran proposes Joyce, in a manner that was to become conventional in Irish cultural debate, as an adversary to his great contemporary, Yeats. Joyce, in the person of his hero Bloom, is associated with the virile energies of the Gael, with Mangan and the exploits of Gaelic scholarship; Yeats with effete Celticism, the exotic otherworldliness of the occult and the Moore of *Lalla Rookh*.

Also in the 1920s, Joyce's achievement began to be identified as a European phenomenon by Irish critics keen to discover in an indisputably indigenous writer evidence of Ireland's continental patrimony which set it apart from the neighbouring island and from the cultural hegemony of the Anglo-Saxon world. In 1929 the poet Thomas MacGreevy (who had already contributed to *Our Exagmination Round His Factification for Incamination of Work in Progress* in Paris) took Seán O Faoláin sternly to task for his unfavourable response to *Anna Livia Plurabelle*. MacGreevy berated O Faoláin for adding his voice to 'the prim and priggish university intelligences of England and America':

These two countries, which reek with puritanical hypocrisy, have both banned Mr Joyce's most important work, and it seems to me a pitiable thing to see a young Irish critic of some education helping, however disinterestedly or unconsciously, to find aesthetic justification for their moral cowardice.[5]

An understanding of the European significance and Catholic nature of Joyce's achievement, MacGreevy asserts, allows his work to be properly apprehended. The clear inference is that the Anglo-Saxon world is incapable of such a reading which Ireland and Europe can provide:

The conception of *Ulysses* as a modern equivalent of the *Inferno* of Dante did not strike a great many of the people who thought it infernal. They all screamed 'pornography' and attributed evil motives to the author, though no single one of the eternal moral values is altered in the book.[6]

So situated in the context of European intellectual and religious tradition, *Work in Progress* can readily be understood, in MacGreevy's view:

The new work regarded as a Purgatorio falls into place at once. A Catholic imaginative writer like Mr Joyce may well seize on aspects of the purgatorial ideas that were not treated by Dante, and may invent a technique suggested by some more modern writers than Dante, such as Vico, the 18th century Neapolitan philosopher, to express them. And this is to some extent what has happened.[7]

In the 1930s Irish Ireland's polemic against Yeats and Revival literature became strident, even at times grotesque. A Mr James Devane (author of *Isle of Destiny*, 1936, and described by his editor as a 'dermatologist, who since his return from India has invaded Irish letters and vied with his Jesuit brother in enriching the controversial pages of Irish journalism') took Yeats to task in *Ireland To-day*. 'Why', he asked, 'does Yeats. . . who has done so much for our national culture. . . these later days, speak of the Irish yeoman in the traditional Anglo-Irish accents of contempt.'[8] Yeats has often been attacked for a sentimental idealization of the Irish peasant; rarely has he been thought inadequately appreciative of the Irish yeoman, whoever he might be. Devane is representative, however, in his sense that Yeats's cosmopolitan eclecticism is somehow alien to the Irish majority – his 'choice and eclectic diet may suit the tender palate of a poet, but it will scarcely agree with the rough digestion of a crofter, a Connemara fisherman, a country shopkeeper, a country doctor, a lawyer, a policeman, soldier'.[9] In the 1930s, however, there was little sense of Joyce as a radical alternative to the Yeatsian model of an artistic relationship with society. At one level that is hardly surprising. To many, in a decade of aggressive nativism, Joyce's European literary aspirations must have seemed an affront. Official Ireland in 1932 had issued a *Hand Book* in which the litterateur Robert Lynd in an article on 'Anglo-Irish Literature' had restricted himself to the cautious observation, 'Critics differ in their estimates of the genius of Mr George Moore and Mr James Joyce, but they are at least two writers who have had an enormous influence on the English novel of our time.'[10] And this in a survey which took for granted the brilliant dominance of the Irish literary firmament by the Yeatsian star. To many, such caution, however, would have seemed only good sense in such a context, given the moral opprobrium Joyce had drawn upon himself. Indeed, L. A. G. Strong reported seventeen years later how when '. . . invited to lecture to the Royal Dublin Society', and when he had proposed to speak on Joyce, he was 'informed in tones of dignified reproach that such a subject would not be acceptable to the members'.[11] Strong concluded in his study of Joyce, published in 1949:

Such views may not seem worth mentioning, when Joyce's status is so generally admitted, but his case remains to be argued in his native land, and an Irish writer must sometimes argue it – even though an attempt to rebut the false case which Irishmen have hatched up against Joyce be foredoomed before it is made.

At another level it is surprising that Joyce's developing international reputation in the 1930s did not challenge younger Irish writers to assess his achievement as a counterweight to Yeats's august and intimidating magnificence. In fact *Ireland To-day*, the one periodical in the 1930s which sought to reflect on Irish social and cultural, as well as literary, matters contained no reference to Joyce whatsoever, apart from a few cursory reviews of *Work in Progress* and of republished works.

It was the short-story writers Seán O Faoláin and Frank O'Connor who in the 1940s reformulated the Yeats/Joyce polarity which had achieved embryonic form in the 1920s. They did not deny Yeats's grandeur, nor even the European dimension of his imaginative synthesis, but considered their own work a realistic exploration of aspects of Irish life more in the tradition of Joyce than Yeats. O'Connor makes the matter plain:

When O'Faolain and I began to write it was with some idea of replacing the subjective, idealistic, romantic literature of Yeats, Lady Gregory and Synge by one modelled on the Russian novelists.[13]

In so doing, O'Connor almost unconsciously associates the enterprise with the writings of Joyce: 'it is time that the literature of Catholic Ireland (and one needn't go beyond Joyce to prove it) is dominated by its material in a way in which the work of Synge and Yeats rarely was',[14] setting the key for what O Faoláin was to declare twenty years later:

There is no longer any question of dishing up local colour (The Noble Peasant is as dead as the Noble Savage. Poems about fairies and leprechauns, about misted lakes, old symbols of national longing, are over and done with). We need to explore Irish life with an objectivity never hitherto applied to it – and in this Joyce rather than Yeats is our inspiration.[15]

For O'Connor and O Faoláin, Joyce is a more appropriate inspiration for an Irish writer because a post-revolutionary phase in Irish history demands a realism, in O Faoláin's words, 'knitted with common life'.[16] Yeats is not deemed to lack national authenticity, as Irish Ireland had insisted he did. He is merely a magnificent anachronism.*

The O'Connor/O Faoláin critique of Yeats and Joyce took the poet's greatness for granted but assumed that his imaginative idealism could not greatly affect writers in a more prosaic age. In recent decades Irish critical thought has sought to reassess Yeats in ways that owe more to Irish Ireland's original assault upon the poet. Such reassessments do not of course indulge in the crude nationalism of the earlier movement in denying Yeats his national authenticity. They do nevertheless challenge his imaginative procedures, fearing indeed that these may have a baneful influence on contemporary Ireland. For Yeats, in these critics' view, was guilty of a highly damaging imaginative evasion. And Joyce in their writings is comparatively adduced as the truly enabling presence.

It was the poet Thomas Kinsella who first put this argument in a powerful lecture in 1966.[17] His brooding reflection on 'The Irish Writer' brings him up immediately against his sense of the Irish tradition as gapped, discontinuous, terrifyingly disabling. The loss of the language is felt as a crippling wound. Corkery's analysis of the effects of this catastrophe is fully endorsed – the effect is one of fundamental deprivation, the modern Irish world almost completely unrealized in the country's literature. Yeats, in Kinsella's view of things, accepted the isolation such a state of things necessarily created, making a brilliant if fundamentally dubious virtue of it. Yeats created his own tradition in isolation and 'it is still a coherent entity, at a graceful elegiac height above the filthy modern tide'.[18] The consequence of this act is that Yeats 'refused to come to terms with the real shaping vitality of Ireland'.[19] And a further consequence is that Yeats, so masterful and energetic a presence in the Irish world, who might have brought healing to the Irish tradition, in fact irritated the wound:

Yeats bestrides the categories. He had a greatness capable, perhaps, of integrating a modern Anglo-Irish culture, and which chose to make

* For a fuller treatment of O Faoláin's critique of Yeats and the Revival, see pp. 93-5 below.

this impossible by separating out a special Anglo-Irish culture from the main unwashed body.[20]

There is a harshness about this argument, bred of pained regret and a sense of national requirement which reminds of Corkery. For it seems unduly judgmental to assume that Yeats deliberately chose to make an integrated culture impossible (there is an uneasy vagueness, too, in the notion of a 'greatness' chosing). At this point in Kinsella's thesis Corkery indeed is once more directly invoked. In *Synge and Anglo-Irish Literature* (1931) that critic had identified three forces which give 'Irish national being its Irishness' and which must be expressed in any truly national literature: (1) the Religious Consciousness of the People, (2) Irish Nationalism, (3) the Land. Kinsella observes that Joyce's Stephen Dedalus is conscious of two of these forces, and although he rejects them he does not evade them. Joyce, by extension from Stephen, is introduced to the argument as the exemplary alternative to Yeats:

His stomach, unlike Yeats's, is not turned by what he sees shaping the new Ireland: the shamrock lumpen proletariat, the eloquent and con- niving and mean-spirited tribe of Dan. Daniel O'Connell or de Valera or Paudeen do not deter him from his work; they are his subjects. He is the first major Irish voice to speak for Irish reality since the death of the Irish language.[21]

So Irish Ireland's main polemical thrust is reaffirmed (Yeats, although a major voice, does not truly speak for 'Irish reality') and the force of that earlier cultural analysis is augmented by the incorporation of Joyce into the dialectics:

So, the Irish writer, if he cares who he is and where he come from, finds that Joyce and Yeats are the two main objects in view; and I think that he finds that Joyce is the true father. I will risk putting it diagram- matically and say that Yeats stands for the Irish tradition as broken; Joyce stands for it as continuous or healed – or healing – from its mutilation.[22]

A further strain of Irish Ireland's cultural critique is reaffirmed in Kinsella's lecture, though in modulated key. For Irish Ireland, indigenous Irish life was essentially European, which set it apart from the provincialism of Anglo-Saxon culture. Kinsella allows Joyce a similarly synthetic cultural comprehensiveness beside which Yeats must appear curiously parochial in his basic archaism. Joyce's is an urban, and therefore modern, imagination:

The filthy modern tide does not only run in Ireland, of course, and Joyce's art of continuity is done with a difference: he simultaneously revives the Irish tradition and admits the modern world. It is symptomatic that for Corkery's third force, the Land, Joyce substitutes the City. He makes up all the arrears at once.[23]

Subsequent Irish critics have echoed Kinsella's stern view, censuring Yeats for his Anglo-Irish élitism and finding in Joyce an exemplary and inspirational democrat of the imagination. A number of critics associated with the Dublin-edited periodical, *The Crane Bag* (which began publishing in 1977), and with the Derry-inspired and published Field Day Pamphlets (which began publication in 1983), have indeed mounted what has almost seemed a kind of cultural crusade in these adversarial terms. Declan Kiberd, in a lecture in the series, 'Ireland: Dependence and Independence', had this to say of Yeats in the rhetoric of the debating chamber:

Having dazzled himself with this Ireland of stolen children and fairy forts, of serene towers and violent highways, of big houses and cosy cottages, Yeats then employed his immense rhetorical powers to enrapture everybody else. The result is that Irish people no longer live in a country of their own making, but in a kind of tourist's film set.[24]

It seems hard to blame Yeats for the vulgarization of his symbolic imagination, but the forensic trajectory of this kind of writing needs a villain beside whose misdeeds the radically innovative quality of James Joyce can appear all the more compelling. Joyce is reckoned a socialist and his socialism is a product of his European sensibility (the European is now socialist, not Catholic, as it was for Corkery and MacGreevy):

There was, however, a second form of Irish revival, an alternative to the one led by Yeats and de Valera. It was pioneered by men like Connolly and James Joyce, men who began with the courageous admission that there is no such thing as an Irish identity, ready-made and fixed, to be carried as a passport into eternity.[25]

Similarly Richard Kearney, in his Field Day Pamphlet 'Myth and Motherland', proposes Yeats and Joyce as representatives in literary terms of a tendency in Irish life to reflect a tension between mythic and anti-mythic forms of discourse. Less polemically assured than Kiberd, Kearney nevertheless sponsors the Joycean alternative to Yeatsian myth-making. Joyce in Kearney's view indicates how Irish identity can be reformulated not in nationalistic fashion but in European and indeed universal modes, which can liberate from myth conceived of in absolute terms, and from provincial stereotyping.

Finnegans Wake teaches us that Dublin is 'Doublin' – itself and not itself. It teaches us that our sense of tradition is not some pre-ordained continuity which makes us all the same. Myth is revealed as history and history as myth. Joyce thus shows that our narrative of cultural self-identity is itself a fiction – an 'epical forged cheque' – and that each one of us has the freedom to re-invent our past.[26]

Yeats, it seems, passed the Irish nation a dud local cheque – Joyce can draw on the inexhaustible credit of the European and world banks.

This is why Joyce presents Anna Livia Plurabelle as a model of *unity in plurality*, a 'bringer of plurabilities' who is 'every person, place and thing in the chaosmos of alle. . . moving and changing every part of the time'.[27]

It has, of course, been Seamus Deane who has developed the most sustained and exactingly brilliant critique of Yeats in recent years in Ireland. Since 1974, when he delivered a lecture in Canada on 'The Literary Myths of the Revival', he has subjected Yeats's historiography to an icily angered analysis. In that lecture (recently republished in revised form) he is manifestly incensed that Yeats should have bestowed a retrospective dignity by a piece of historical sleight-of-hand on a discredited social caste, the Anglo-Irish. So great is this offence that Deane finds it difficult in the lecture to arrive at any unambiguous estimate of Yeats's artistic achievement, though his indignation is blended with admiration at the poet's 'almost inexhaustible resourcefulness'.[28] That imaginative resourcefulness expressed itself on the stage, and Deane in an essay of 1978 did extend Yeats the recognition (even if at the expense of Sean O'Casey) that in his experimental theatre, 'despite its esoteric ambitions, its aristocratic gestures and its select audience',[29] he does discover 'the tragic possibilities of political action and the contemplative alternative to it'.[30] The year before Deane had indeed sought to reckon with Yeats as a colonial poet whose *œuvre* nevertheless challenges both Ireland and the contemporary world in useful ways. 'To describe Yeats's politics and, to a large extent, his achievement as colonial is not at all to diminish it',[31] Deane avers, identifying in Yeats's form of traditionalism a radical rebuke to the spiritual impoverishment of modern capitalism. But even here the critic can only allow the poet a negative virtue. By the time he wrote his Field Day Pamphlet, 'Heroic Styles; the tradition of an idea' (1984), qualification was overtaken by condemnation. Yeats is subsumed in a general sentence passed with magisterial distaste on the cultural manoeuvrings of a fading class – the Anglo-Irish Ascendancy:

Irish culture became the new property of those who were losing their grip on Irish land. The effect of these re-writings was to transform the blame for the drastic condition of the country from the Ascendancy to the Catholic middle classes or to their English counterparts. It was in essence a strategic retreat from political to cultural supremacy. From Lecky to Yeats and forward to F. S. L. Lyons we witness the conversion of Irish history into a tragic theatre in which the great Anglo-Irish protagonists – Swift, Burke, Parnell – are destroyed in their heroic attempts to unite culture of intellect with the emotion of the multitude, or in political terms, constitutional politics with the forces of revolution.[32]

The judge's distaste for the prisoners in the dock is here all too evident; Yeats does not escape indictment. He is indeed seen to exhibit 'the pathology of literary unionism'[33] and must, it seems, pay the price before the bar of history.

The main thrust of Irish Ireland's critique of Yeats and of the Literary Revival as a whole was augmented, as I have argued, by the recruitment of Joyce to the dialectical polemics as an exemplary democrat. Surprisingly in Deane's criticism, which must remind of Corkery in its ideological rigour, and the extent of its influence – Joyce too must abide our question. In his essay of 1982, 'Joyce and Nationalism', Yeats and Joyce are, familiarly, present as contrasting figures (though they are also seen to share a conviction that 'the supreme action was writing').[34] But it is not clear that the critic unreservedly approves the way, he discerns, that 'Ireland as an entity, cultural or political, was incorporated in all its mutations within Joyce's work as a model of the world and, more importantly, as a model of the fictive'.[35] In 'Heroic Styles' this sense of judgment reserved is overtaken by one of a critical summing up in which Joyce as well as Yeats must endure an austere scrutiny in a criticism which is genuinely dialectical rather than simplistically dualistic:

The pluralism of his styles and languages, the absorbing nature of his controlling myths and systems, finally gives a certain harmony to varied experience. But it could be argued, it is the harmony of indifference, one in which everything is a version of something else, where sameness rules over diversity, where contradiction is finally and disquietingly written out. In achieving this in literature, Joyce anticipated the capacity of modern society to integrate almost all antagonistic elements by transforming them into fashions, fads – styles, in short. Yet it is true that in this regard, Joyce is, if you like, our most astonishing 'modernist' author and Yeats is his 'anachronistic' counterpart. The great twins of the Revival play out in posterity the roles assigned to them and to their readers by their inherited history.[36]

What this says is that Irish Ireland may have been right about Yeats and the Revival in some crude senses, but that the Irish reality it so took for granted as an unqualified good, which the artist must celebrate, is deeply flawed. And it is flawed not only because it is a reality that includes the horror of incipient civil war ('contradiction') but one which allows the superficial styles of modern capitalism to delude the unwary into an egregious complacency. Certain readings of Joyce, Deane implies, encourage such evasive complacency as Yeats, read as he intended he should be, might encourage patrician and futile individual heroics. What makes this essay by Deane so important and necessary, it seems to me, is that it could provide a *terminus ad quem* to a debate Irish Ireland inaugurated at the beginning of the century, and clears the way for new readings of both Yeats *and* Joyce which would not see them in the starkly adversarial poses in which they have traditionally been presented. It might allow a less reductive estimate of Yeats's achievement if the case against him could be taken as resting (it has rarely been so starkly and persuasively stated) and permit a more searching Irish analysis of Joyce to proceed if it were recognized that his celebration of a fictively open, polysemic European consciousness, in Ireland's and Europe's contemporary circumstances, might itself lack full enabling significance.[37]

There is some evidence in Deane's own criticism indeed that, the case having been stated against the poet, it is now in order to reflect on other aspects of Yeats's career, not in some sentimental attempt to exonerate, but in order to come to terms with his undeniable power. The publication of John Kelly's first volume of *The Collected Letters of W. B. Yeats, 1865-95* seems to have provided the liberating occasion, not only for Deane but for his fellow Field Day director, Tom Paulin. Writing in *The London Review of Books* Paulin, with disarming frankness, admitted that he could not have imagined until he read the letters that the old man had so much blood in him:

I readied myself to take a sling-shot at the great Cuchulain – the impulse dissolved in helpless love, chortles, delight. The old boy, I realized, has managed here his last and finest trick, for he appears in these pages not as the superb glittering imago, but as pupil and pupa, an earnest, eager, driven young man who is unsure of himself, short of money, screwed by his publishers and in a desperate rush.

Seamus Deane in *The Times Literary Supplement* was more measured but clearly had been impressed by the way the young Yeats assiduously worked to create an audience for his poetry, and in a recent essay[38] he has developed his perceptions on Yeats's relationship with possible audiences into a comprehensive statement on the tragic nature of the poet's art and not simply of his essentially colonial cultural mission. This essay, while reckoning as fully as before with the deeply problematic quality of the Yeatsian poetic and cultural enterprise, does also suggest, against the critic's own inclination perhaps, the incontrovertible energy of the poet's creative achievement, and the ways in which his heroic failures stimulate neither emulation of a style not acts of heroic desperation, but a recognition of the tragic ambiguities of historic experience when comprehended in the terms of a Yeatsian dialectic:

Yeats's audience belongs to no immediate time. It lives in the future or in a past which will be the future. Between these two modes of time, past and future which is the more past, intervenes the cataclysm or crisis.[38]

And the poet of crisis is finally less an intimidatory precursor to be denied, than a warning to be heeded, a human voice to be listened to in admiration as well as exasperation, as we turn to our own problematic historic experience with its ambiguous demands and duties. One awaits Deane's further reflections on both Yeats and Joyce with keen anticipation.

NOTES

1. For studies of Irish Ireland see F. S. L. Lyons, *Ireland Since the Famine* (Glasgow 1973), pp. 224-46 and *Culture and Anarchy in Ireland, 1890-1939* (Oxford 1979), pp. 57-83. See also my *Ireland: A Social and Cultural History, 1922-79* (Glasgow 1981 and '85), pp. 45-78.

2. Daniel Corkery, *The Hidden Ireland* (Dublin 1967), p. 62.

3. *Ibid.*, p. 64.

4. C. P. Curran, 'On the North Side', *The Irish Statesman* (10 July 1926), p. 484.

5. Thomas MacGreevy. 'Anna Livia Plurabelle', *The Irish Statesman* (16 February 1929), pp. 475-6.

6. *Ibid.*, p. 476.

7. *Ibid.*

8. James Devane, 'Is An Irish Culture Possible?', *Ireland To-day*, Vol. 1, No. 5, (October 1936), p. 29.

9. *Ibid.*, pp. 30-1.

10. Robert Lynd, 'Anglo-Irish Literature', *Saorstat Eireann Official Handbook*, (Dublin 1932), p. 280.

11. L. A. G. Strong, *The Sacred River: An Approach to James Joyce* (London 1949), p. 13.

12. *Ibid.*

13. Frank O'Connor, 'The Future of Irish Literature', *Horizon*, Vol. V, No. 25 (January 1942), p. 58.

14. *Ibid.*, p. 59.

15. Seán O Faoláin, 'Fifty Years of Irish Writing', *Studies* (Spring 1962), pp. 100-01.

16. Seán O Faoláin, 'Yeats and the Younger Generation', *Horizon*, Vol. V, No. 25 (January 1942), p. 50.

17. Though the argument was present in an inchoate form in Kavanagh's critical comments on Yeats and on Joyce, whose *Ulysses* was one of his sacred books. See Alan Warner, *Clay is the Word, Patrick Kavanagh 1904-1967* (Dublin 1973), pp. 82-5.

18. Thomas Kinsella, 'The Irish Writer', *Davis, Mangan, Ferguson? Tradition and the Irish Writer* (Dublin 1970), p. 62.

19. *Ibid.*

20. *Ibid.*, p. 64.

21. *Ibid.*, p. 64-5.

22. *Ibid.*, p. 65.

23. *Ibid.*

24. Declan Kiberd, 'Inventing Irelands', *The Crane Bag*, Vol. 8, No. 1 (1984) (*Ireland: Dependence and Independence*), pp. 11-12.

25. *Ibid.*, p. 13.

26. Richard Kearney, *Myth and Motherland* (Derry 1984), p. 18.

27. *Ibid.*

28. Seamus Deane, *Celtic Revivals: Essays in Modern Irish Literature* (London and Boston 1985), p. 36. This volume usefully collects some of Deane's scattered

essays (with some alterations) on Irish writing which he has published since 1975.

29. *Ibid.*, p. 112.

30. *Ibid.*

31. *Ibid.*, p. 49.

32. Seamus Deane, *Heroic Styles: the tradition of an idea* (Derry 1986), pp. 7-8.

33. *Ibid.*, p. 10.

34. Deane, *Celtic Revivals*, p. 97.

35. *Ibid.*, p. 107.

36. Deane, *Heroic Styles*, pp. 16-17.

37. The degree to which this reading of twentieth-century Irish literary history has taken hold is exhibited in the fact that the two full-scale studies of post-Yeatsian poetry to appear to date have both assumed that the course of poetry since Yeats can best be understood as a kind of competition between Yeats and the rest in which Joyce is the truly progenitive precursor. See Robert F. Garratt, *Modern Irish Poetry: Tradition and Continuity from Yeats to Heaney* (Berkeley, Los Angeles and London 1986), and Dillon Johnston, *Irish Poetry After Joyce* (Mountrath and Indiana 1985).

38. Seamus Deane, 'Yeats: the Creation of an Audience' in *Tradition and Influence in Anglo-Irish Poetry*, eds T. Brown and N. Grene (London 1988).

7

AFTER THE REVIVAL: SEÁN O FAOLÁIN AND PATRICK KAVANAGH

'Is there in Ireland a real inadequacy?'
Seán O Faoláin

For the aspirant writer of the 1920s and 30s in Ireland the anxiety of influence pressed with a peculiarly intimate insistence. He was perhaps a rueful late guest at a literary feast celebrated as the Irish Literary Revival which, as Ernest Boyd announced in 1922, had done 'more than anything else to draw the attention of the outside world to the separate national existence of Ireland'. But conscious of the lateness of the hour, his insecurity was rendered the more discomforting since he was unsure that he had in fact received an invitation. George Russell (AE), minor poet and indefatigable editor of *The Irish Statesman*, might open the hospitable columns of that weekly to his youthful efforts, but Yeats, without whom the Revival could not have been conceived of, seemed a distant, unapproachable figure secure in his international reputation, crowned by a Noble Prize, lost in his own strange imaginative territory. And the summons to Coole, that signal of ultimate acceptance into the upper circle, seemed improbable indeed. Accordingly, one of the more entertaining aspects of literary life in 1920s Dublin was the spectacle of young men who had arrived too late challenging, in an outspokenness compact of insecurity and ambition, the national authenticity of the occasion at which they found themselves late and perhaps uninvited guests.

The idelogy of the Irish Ireland movement provided them with the weapons they needed for this youthful iconoclasm. That cultural and political movment, associated with the writings of

Douglas Hyde, Eoin MacNeill (the first Minister of Education in the Irish Free State), D. P. Moran (editor of *The Leader* newspaper and author of *The Philosophy of Irish Ireland*, 1905), and Daniel Corkery (Professor of English in University College, Cork), and expressed most vigorously in the activities of the Gaelic League, had preached since the turn of the century a doctrine of national distinctiveness where the only authentic national life was certainly Gaelic, and possibly Catholic as well. In the light of its exacting sense of national priorities, the Anglo-Irish Literary Revival was an exotic flowering of the colonial mind in which the true concerns of the Irish people did not find any adequate expression. In Daniel Corkery's very influential critical studies, *The Hidden Ireland* (1924) and *Synge and Anglo-Irish Literature* (1931), the reader may find the most eloquent, searching statements of this view, a view that was the staple of much cultural polemic in the first decades of Irish independence. Sentiments of the following kind (the author is the critic Stephen Brown, S.J., writing of Yeats and Synge) were the commonplaces of Irish Ireland commentary in the period:

. . . whatever their literary merits, the claim made for them that they interpreted the Gaelic thought-world, or that the qualities which they contributed to Anglo-Irish literature were authentic Gaelic qualities is quite another thing. One wonders, for instance, if there be anything in common between Mr Yeats and his shadowly, Celtic dreamland and the flesh and blood Gaels who wrote our Gaelic literature, from the unknown authors of the Tain, through Colmcille, the Medieval bards, Keating and the Munster poets, to Canon Peadar O Laoghaire.[1]

In the 1920s some of the younger writers (as we saw above) were willing to adopt such Irish Ireland conceptions, making them the catch-cries of an assault upon an older generation of writers. The first performance of Sean O'Casey's *The Plough and the Stars* in 1926 provided a ready-made opportunity for such literary warfare. Yeats, who had defended the play from the Republican charge that it demeaned the national struggle, found himself the object of attack by a group of young writers. One suspects that they were moved less by a veneration of the Gaelic past or the national struggle, or by genuine distaste for O'Casey's work, than by a desire to engage in polemic for its own sake, to the discomfort of Yeats and Russell. Liam O'Flaherty led the way with a letter to *The Irish Statesman* of February 20th

– 'The protest by Mr. Yeats, against the protest of the audience, was an insult to the people of this country'.[2] O'Flaherty was unwilling to state the quarrel in explicitly Irish Ireland terms but others felt no such compunction. Austin Clarke, in a further letter, clearly identified the play with an 'old Anglo-Irish school', stating that 'several writers of the new Irish school believe that Mr O'Casey's work is crude exploitation of our poorer people in an Anglo-Irish tradition that is now moribund'.[3] For F. R. Higgins it was 'quite evident that the main questions at issue are merely based upon a revival of that arrogance of the Gall, recently dormant, towards the Gael'.[4]

It would be satisfying to dismiss such literary ructions as simply the inevitable symptoms of the heightened anxiety states of weak writers in the presence of the indubitably strong. It would be simple furthermore to present the younger writers' suspicion that the Anglo-Irish Revival was in some fundamental sense unIrish (expressed as this was in the crude terminology of the Irish Ireland movement) as merely the effort of the intimidated young to create imaginative space for themselves at an already overcrowded table, presided over by a particularly domineering host. However, this would be to ignore the fact that the more intelligent of the younger writers who briefly employed Irish Ireland's categories in an opportunistic assault upon their elders soon moved on to a much more complicated understanding of the recent past, and that there were those who, without adopting the propagandist simplicities of Irish Ireland, nevertheless sensed a difference in their relationship with Irish reality to that of Yeats and his contemporaries. Accordingly, Austin Clarke, Frank O'Connor and particularly Seán O Faoláin shared a respectful critique of the Literary Revival which allowed for its genius but estimated that its legacy was of dubious value. Yeats, as the main force behind the Revival, had had different problems to solve than they, and while his example in its energy and uncompromising commitment to artistic values could prove inspiring, his career could not really help the younger writer who was faced with radically different tasks.

Writing an article entitled 'Yeats and the Younger Generation' in Cyril Connolly's *Horizon* in 1942, O Faoláin distinguished his own generation of writers from that of the Yeatsian past in the following terms:

They were faced with problems far more insistent: social, political and even religious problems. They had grown up in a period of revolution, were knitted with common life, and could not evade its appeal. As time went on these problems became savagely acute.[5]

O Faoláin, in a more systematic way than any of his peers, spent much time, over a period of thirty years, elaborating on this distinction. His analysis is highly persuasive, suggesting that when the young men in the 1920s expressed uncertainty as to the Irish authenticity of the Revival and of Yeats's work in particular, they were not only engaging in youthful iconoclasm but touching on some genuine conflict in Irish cultural life. The crux of O Faoláin's thesis is in that phrase 'knitted with common life'. Behind it lies a cultural and historical polemic that occupied O Faoláin over many years.

Seán O Faoláin was born John Whelan, the son of a constable in the Royal Irish Constabulary in Cork in 1900. As a young adult he had been caught up in the revolutionary enthusiasm that followed the 1916 Rising. He had shared in his generation's exhilarated discovery of the Irish language and the Gaelic past. The Civil War, following the Treaty of 1921, marked the beginning of his disillusionment with the charged romantic dream of that past which had fed the imagination of an insurrection and a revolutionary war. The Ireland that he discovered when he returned to civilian life following the defeat of de Valera's supporters in the Civil War was no Republic fit for heroes who had fought in the name of Cathleen Ni Houlihan, but a drab, dispiriting, ill-named Free State where the artist could scarcely make a home, assaulted as he was by the twin horrors of puritanical moralizing and patriotic philistinism. The 'common life' that O Faoláin began to know in the small-town Ireland (he spent a year as a teacher in a Christian Brothers' School in Ennis, Co. Clare, in the 1920s) was scarcely the imaginatively compelling estate that the Revival writers thought they had found in rural Ireland with its roots deep in the traditional Gaelic past, but a small-town provincialism that bore aggressively on the spirit. Ireland for O'Connor, for Austin Clarke and for O Faoláin, was not the land 'the poets imagined / Terrible and gay'[6] but a country where the novelist's realistic eye, the satirist's scalpel, seemed the only appropriate literary equipment to deal with its drab, unromantic actuality.

94

The writers of the Irish Literary Revival, in fact, for all their individual quarrels and disagreements with Irish nationalism and with its most vigorous representatives, the writers and thinkers of the Irish Ireland movement, had accepted the fundamental tenets of that faith. Ireland was an historic nation with its sources in pre-history. Gaelic civilization had been a glorious flowering of the Irish spirit, reborn in the Rising of 1916; and a modern imagination drinking at the well-springs of that world, even in translations of its literature, could enjoy a refreshment so revivifying that the splendours of that old spirituality might be born anew in a Europe grown weak and infertile in an old age of rationalism, science and economic utilitarianism. So Yeats, towards the end of his life, could affirm 'Gaelic is my national language, but it is not my mother tongue',[7] as earlier he had written, 'I might have found more of Ireland if I had written in Irish, but I have found a little, and I have found all myself.'[8] The Ireland he thought he had discovered in various translations from the national language, and in his imaginative sympathy with the Irish rural world, was that same Ireland the nationalists believed had survived the ravages of colonialism and which they thought had been partially restored in the founding of the new state. The young writers coming into their own in the early 1930s, inheritors of the post-civil-war disillusionment, could agree with the Yeats of the later poetry that the Irish Free State in no real sense re-established the values of the old Gaelic order, but they could not agree with him that the Literary Revival provided an adequate model of how such a re-establishment might be effected or indeed that such was possible or desirable.[9] Knitted with the common life of Ireland, the petit-bourgeois life of the towns, closer to the actual life of the small farms of rural Ireland than Yeats ever was, they knew the drab, unadventurous, unromantic, puritanically Catholic, English-speaking, economically prudent reality. They discerned in Ireland not the residual fire of a pagan and a Gaelic civilization ready to be fanned into new life, as the Revival writers had done, but a social enervation and an imaginative pusillanimity that seemed the antithesis of art. The young writer inspecting his social world with the artist's interest in material found little more, to quote Frank O'Connor, than

a vicious and ignorant middle-class, and for aristocracy the remnants of an English garrison, alien in religion and education. From such material he finds it almost impossible to create a picture of life which, to quote Dumas' definition of the theatre, will embody 'a portrait, a judgment and an ideal'.[10]

The writers accounted for this dismal state of affairs variously. Austin Clarke' volume of poems *Pilgrimage and Other Poems* (1929), evoking the Hiberno-Romanesque period in Irish history, implies that at certain moments in the old Gaelic order a happier balance between Christianity and paganism was struck than in the contemporary world. Much of his later satiric verse, in which he assails Church and State with an exacting distaste, can be seen as a necessary purge for his country, administered in the light of this ideal:*

> When the far south glittered
> Behind the grey beaded plains
> And cloudier ships were bitted
> Along the pale waves,
> The showery breeze—that plies
> A mile from Ara—stood
> And took our boat on sand:
> There by dim wells the women tied
> A wish on thorn, while rainfall
> Was quiet as the turning of books
> In the holy schools at dawn.[11]

Frank O'Connor chose to believe that the Literary Revival had been part of a momentary awakening of the Irish spirit in various restorative programmes that provided a framework within which an idealistic literature could find a place:

In those days there were at least half a dozen movements to which any young man of spirit could belong; all of them part of a general attack by the younger generation on the enemies within: the imitator of English ways – the provincialist; the 'gombeen man'—a very expressive Irishism for the *petit bourgeis*; and the Tammany politician who had riddled every institution with corruption. Irish literature fitted admirably into that idealistic framework; it was another force making for national dignity.[12]

The contemporary decline could be explained in terms of the break-up of the temporary Irish synthesis:

---

* For further treatment of Clarke's exploitation of the Hiberno-Romanesque, see pp. 130-1 below.

Irish society began to revert to type. All the forces that had made for national dignity, that had united Catholic and Protestant, aristocrats like Constance Markievicz, Labour revolutionists like Connolly and writers like AE, began to disintegrate rapidly, and Ireland became more than ever sectarian, utilitarian (the two nearly always go together), vulgar and provincial.[13]

For O Faoláin the matter was not quite so simple. After his brief intoxication with Irish Ireland he quickly became deeply sceptical about the possibility of reviving anything of real worth from the Gaelic past. He believed certainly that 'Gaelic, both the language and the literature, is like a well in whose dark silence one sees an image of that shadowy other-self which is our ancestral memory'[14] and in the need to communicate 'with those drops that are part of the whole stream that fed us,'[15] but he was persuaded that modern Ireland was an English-speaking nation formed by the struggles of the nineteenth century, shaped by the social experience of democratic nationalist politics. He believed that Gaelic Ireland, aristocratic, hierarchic, anti-democratic, died in the eighteenth century and that it was pointless to try and breathe life into a corpse. Modern Ireland had been, his thesis explained, invented by Daniel O'Connell in the nineteenth century. In his biography of the Great Liberator, *King of the Beggars* (1938), O Faoláin proposed this thesis with the greatest force (the thesis is the inspiration of many of his journal articles). What is clear in this masterful book is that O Faoláin does not regret the passing of the old order for all his distaste for contemporary Ireland. Indeed, the biography is essentially a polemic against those features of the modern Irish society he accepts as his own, that he found oppressive, since he believed they originated in a false understanding of Irish history which a true reading of O'Connell's life and work would correct. The romantic nationalism that had fed the revolutionary movement and the Literary Revival alike had fostered in O Faoláin's sense of things a view of Irish history that was idealistic to the point of fantasy. Despite all that had happened in the eighteenth and nineteenth centuries, that questionable creed asserted, Gaelic Ireland had remained intact and had been restored in acts of republican violence. The Rising of 1916 was a restorative culmination, not a beginning. O Faoláin thought such a view romantic claptrap, proposing by contrast a vision of Daniel O'Connell as King of the Beggars, a great utilitarian, English-speaking, anti-Gaelic, Irish leader who took a mob of disenfranchised helots whose civilization was in tatters and made of them a mass movement that bore fruit in the democratic achievements of the twentieth century. For O Faoláin the real Ireland, the only Ireland (the only Ireland because it was the real Ireland) was the Catholic, English-speaking, democratic, petit-bourgeois world he saw about him, troubled and oppressed by fanaticism and obscurantist doctrines of various kinds, bred of a romantic version of Irish history. Ireland was not the restored Gaelic nation, where defects could be accounted for in terms of inadequate restoration, but a new nation fashioned out of the scatterings of an old, where there still remained a great deal of nation-building to be done. For such a nation, the practical, almost Benthamite figure of O'Connell was a truer model that any idealistic image of Cuchulain or the Red Branch heroes.

The young writers' unromantic understanding of Irish society in the 1920s and 30s, at its most developed in the cultural and political polemic of Seán O Faoláin's *King of the Beggars*, certainly explains the alienation they felt from the idealism of the Revival. It also explains why a fundamental problem that they thought confronted them was the literary adequacy of Irish life. Realism of the kind represented in O Faoláin's celebration of O'Connell is, however one may wish to commend its accuracy, more suited to the polemicist, the political worker, the social activist, than to the writer. To recognize that the modern Irish nation is simply, a poor folk, but recently rescued from desperate actual and cultural impoverishment, at the very beginning of its life, might well inspire the active man but depress the contemplative poet, the novelist anxious for substantial grist to his mill. O'Connor sensed this when he feared that the social panorama in Ireland made it impossible to create a richly various picture of life, 'a portrait, a judgment and an ideal'. Again it was O Faoláin who addressed himself most fully to this problem.

In 1926 Seán O Faoláin set out for Harvard University where he was to study for three years. He left Ireland, as he tells in his autobiograpy *Vive Moi!* (1965), with 'a strong smell of moral decay'[16] in his nostrils, repelled by what he felt was 'the onset of . . . a new, native, acquisitive middle class intent only on cashing in on the change of governments.'[17] Towards the end of his years at Harvard his intuitive sense of the social deficiencies of the new Ireland became focussed upon Henry James's famous critique of life in Nathaniel Hawthorne's New England and the problems encountered there by that writer. He brooded upon James's formulation that 'it needs a complex social machinery to set a writer in motion,'[18] reflecting on its pertinence to the Irish situation, where the Anglo-Irish class had virtually disappeared and the new Ireland, outcome of O'Connell's great struggle, was at the beginning of its life. The society that he knew might provide 'complexity of manners and types'[19] and 'an accumulation of history and custom'[20] only in the folk sense. For the novelist with ambitions of a more urbane kind the outlook was apparently bleak. This is a theme O Faoláin explored again and again over the years. Returning to Ireland in 1929 with the determination to 'write about this sleeping country, those sleeping fields, those sleeping villages spread before my eyes under the summer moon,'[21] the fear dogged him, as it did for much of his career, that this might prove an impossible task. In 1949 he concluded, in a sourly depressed article entitled 'The Dilemma of Irish Letters':

The life now known, or knowable to any modern Irish writer is either the traditional, entirely simple life of the farm (simple intellectually speaking); or the groping, ambiguous, rather artless urban life of these same farmers' sons and daughters who have, this last twenty-five years, been taking over the cities and towns from the Anglo-Irish. . .[22]

There was little hope for the novelist:

In such an unshaped society there are many subjects for little pieces, that is for the short-story writer; the novelist or the dramatist loses himself in the general amorphism, unthinkingness, brainlessness, egalitarianism and general unsophistication.[23]

By 1949 such a passage in O Faoláin's *oeuvre* is no longer merely analytic; it is an admission of failure. For since his permanent return to Ireland in 1933 he had published three novels and had founded and edited a social and cultural review, *The Bell*, which had dedicated itself to discovering what variety of creative life truly existed in Ireland. The dismal fatigue of his 1949 article, with its admission that 'it all boils down to Hawthorne's "thin" society, stuff for the anthropologist rather than the man of letters. . . I think it obvious that realism as a technique for dealing with such material soon arrives at a dead end',[24] is O Faoláin's farewell to the realistic novel, an acceptance that the short story is his métier, despite earlier ambitions.

In his novels, O Faoláin had attempted to solve the problem of inadequate material, the problem posed for the novelist by what he sensed was the thinness of Irish life, through the simple expedient of the historical dimension. *A Nest of Simple Folk* (1934) opens in east Limerick in 1854 and ends in Cork in the revolutionary year of 1916. Given O Faoláin's understanding of Irish history, 1854 is a date deep in the past of the nation, almost at the edge of the known world. From this depth he traces three generations of a family as they move from country to city in an era of nationalist and republican politics. In such a work many of the novelist's generic problems are easily solved. Structure and the syntax of the action can be cast easily in terms of chronology. The unformed shapelessness of the society the novelist describes can be ignored as the work progresses steadily from period to period, event to event. Aesthetic satisfaction for the reader derives from the sense of historic depth, strata upon strata, slowly establishing itself through the book's action. O Faoláin believed that a novelist in a thinly composed society who is content as realist 'to describe without comment, the local life he knows intimately, will get one powerful book out of its surges and thrustings and gropings.'[25] *A Nest of Simple Folk* is that book.

But O Faoláin also realized that repetition of this formula would have been absurd. So, in his second novel, *Bird Alone* (1936), he attempted a complication. Like *A Nest of Simple Folk*, *Bird Alone* allows a sense of the historical development of Irish society to suggest thematic depth in the fiction. But, where in the earlier novel this had been the primary impression the work conveys, *Bird Alone* highlights the spiritual and emotional experience of a central character. The novel is narrated by an old man, Corney Crone, remembering his youth and young manhood in Cork during the years of Parnell's tragic career. Corney's father had been a respectable, pious, prudently conservative small builder whose values Corney, in admiration for his Fenian grandfather (diehard Parnellite and anticlerical stalwart), rejects with absolute conviction. The main action of the novel concerns Corney's sentimental, social and political education in a series of near-Gothic sexual and emotional encounters that bring him into direct conflict with his father's world, conflict which in the novel is associated with the grandfather's obdurate political integrity. Fenian anticlericalism and an almost perverse sexual ambition (Corney is exhilarated by the illicit nature of his love for a nun-like pious girl) cast the hero as social pariah as the novel ends. Much of the novel retains the tones and structural movment of family saga. But as the work reaches its climax O Faoláin, as if dissatisfied with the genre he had adopted, begins to darken the tone of the novel, complicates its emotional weather through the exploitation of Catholic conceptions of sin, guilt and redemption. Corney is transformed from a character in a historical novel to a figure who might more properly inhabit the fictional worlds of Mauriac or Graham Greene. The transformation is not a happy one, embarrassing in its emotional baring of the soul, in a book that has, I think, done little to prepare for baroque, sin-haunted confessionalism.

On the triangular candelabra a brown candle was extinguished, and the dark mass that watched the sacred play seemed to move and sigh. One other apostle had crept from the Master, the last slim candle of all on his peak of Gethsemane. From face to face I could cast my Judas-look, then, seeing in the crusted dust of an old woman's brow, in an old man's sad eyes that rose upwards and fell heart-brokenly, in the lips of a girl who kissed her cross with devotion, all that they felt, all by which they all lived, so pitying for their abandoned God, so loving of Him who for love of them suffered without a friend. . .
At that very moment, crushed around by them, inhaling their smell, mingling our breaths, I could feel all my solitariness, oozing away, and a craving in me, powerful as a lust, to yield up everything that divided me from them in order that I might be swallowed into their universal flesh.[26]

Bird Alone, therefore, in part depending on the significance of historic period for its emotional and thematic resonances, also tries to make aesthetic capital of Catholic feeling in a way that renders the final effect unsatisfactory. For the conclusion is disturbingly self-indulgent. We are left with a full flood of emotion that allows the work to end at a spiritual crescendo which, in fact, does little to confront, let alone resolve the conflicts of self and society, religion and politics, that the historical sections of the work have uncompromisingly raised in their examination of Parnellism in its period. One senses that O Faoláin, trying to transcend a simple realism in terms of Irish Catholic feeling, has found the primarily emotional categories of that faith inadequate

tools for intellectual comprehension. Feeling is therefore intensified and prolonged to embarrassing degrees in an effort to
compensate for that deficiency. To state it quite starkly, the content of Corney's emotional and religious experience at the work's
end gives no hint as to how a sensitive man like Corney could
relate to his society, a question which has been urgently posed
in the earlier sections of the novel, in terms other than religious
and romantic self-indulgence:

So, to rest, restlessly starting awake whenever a bout of sleep falls on
me. Some late reveller may see my light high up in the gable-end. . . .
  Only when the blessed morning comes and the day's work, and I
meet people and talk, am I content. I suppose there are many people
in the world like that, content enough while they forget; troubled only
in the silence of the night by thinking on those little accidents that have
prevented them, let us say, from taking part in the affairs of the city,
or from marrying a little wife and bringing up a family in the fear and
love of God.[27]

O Faoláin's final published realistic novel,[28] *Come Back to Erin*
(1940), supplied no further answer to this kind of question. Set
in the 1930s in a world that derived from the struggles of the
earlier periods, it takes its hero, a disillusioned Republican, outside the confines of a complacent petit-bourgeois Ireland to an
emotional and intellectual awakening in America, which, when
he returns to Ireland, can find no substantial expression within
the social possibilities of the country.

In fact O Faoláin found that he had brought the realistic novel
to an impasse in *Come Back to Erin*. He had sensed that historical
perspectives viewed chronologically might make up in at most
one or two novels for the paucity of a vivid contemporary social
scene, but the effort to explore Catholic feeling as a compensatory ingredient when the recipe palled, or as a resolving agent
when the problems exposed in such literary archaeology
demanded resolution, proved unsuccessful. As a writer of
fiction only the short story remained for him, where, as is
characteristic of almost all his efforts in the form, the brevity of
the action allows the emotional climaxes to seem less essentially
escapist than the climax of *Bird Alone*. The poignancies and
moments of pathos endured by so many of the alienated protagonists in O Faoláin's short stories therefore achieve the lyric
mood, which is acceptably managed because the realism of the

setting has not been oppressive, has not admitted historical and social problems to the degree where the author must attempt their intellectual resolution. As a result, O Faoláin's short stories are more successful works of art than his novels because they are less ambitious; they wisely settle for what the author believes is possible in a thinly composed society.

O'Faoláin's inability to advance as a novelist at the end of the 1940s may strike the reader as simply an indication of the writer's imaginative and technical inadequacies. Surely, it will be argued, greater writers have long made realistic fiction of unpromising material and O Faoláin's despairing analysis is simply a disguised form of artistic saving-face. A writer of essentially lyrical predilections took a wrong turning when he sought to write realistic fiction after the manner of Balzac and the Russians, and his failure does not require an elaborate explanation of the kind he himself attempted. Such an argument would, it must be admitted, carry a good deal of weight were it not that the career of another very different writer who began to publish in the 1930s suggests, as in certain crucial respects it parallels that of O Faoláin, that his analysis was something more than a mere *apologia pro vita sua*.

Like O Faoláin, Patrick Kavanagh (1904-67) believed he was knitted with common life as a writer in a way the Revival writers were not. Indeed, he was capable of denying the Revival's national authenticity with an almost Irish Ireland vehemence. Born the son of a shoemaker and small farmer in Co. Monaghan, he suspected that the Revival writers knew little of the actual conditions and realities of Irish rural life. His attitude to Yeats was constantly ambivalent (recognizing his genius despite himself), but to the Revival as a whole it was unambiguous. It did not spring from or reflect the essential life of the people. Synge bore his special condemnation:

His peasants are picturesque conventions; the language he invented for them did a disservice to letters in this country by drawing our attention away from the common speech whose delightfulness comes from its very ordinariness. One phrase of Joyce is worth all Synge as far as giving us the cadence of Irish speech. . .

Synge provided Irish Protestants who are worried about being 'Irish' with an artificial country.[29]

Late in life he was ready to dismiss the Revival 'which purported to be frightfully Irish and racy of the Celtic soil'[30] as 'a thorough-going English-bred lie'.[31]

The Irish reality that Kavanagh felt he knew more intimately than any Revival writer was that O Faoláin had evoked in his celebration of O'Connell, the English-speaking, Catholic world of the Irish small farmer. It was the world that William Carleton, the novelist, had rescued from obscurity in the nineteenth century, but whose actual life had been largely ignored in the Revival's romantic notions of the peasantry. The reality he knew was that of intellectual, emotional and actual poverty – 'My childhood experience was the usual barbaric life of the Irish country poor'[32] – and when he lifted his eyes from the watery fields and stony grey soil of Monaghan the spectacle of post-revolutionary Irish society seemed as uninspiring a contrast in its drab mediocrity as it ever did to O Faoláin when he left his native Cork. The poet, leaving rural Ireland to settle in Dublin in 1939, saw only a 'smug society that has climbed to power out of the bogs and cabins during the past century'[33] which 'has provided no place in its scheme for this awkward, troublesome creature – the artist. Mediocrity in the saddle assumes the role of moral arbiter, kicks the poet downstairs, and then putting on a dress-suit, goes off to a jazz dance'.[34] Like O Faoláin, Kavanagh sensed such a world demanded realism, not romanticism.

Kavanagh's early poems published in the 1930s (his first poem to reach a wide readership, 'The Intangible', was published by AE in *The Irish Statesman* in October 1929) were highly idealistic and romantic, some not dissimilar to the poems produced by minor poets associated with the Revival. But there was an innocence of expression, a direct statement of religious feeling and piety, that rescued some of these poems from the conventional, even in so conventionally titled a volume as *Ploughman and Other Poems* (1936). Yet concurrent with the development of Kavanagh's lyric art ran his interest in realistic prose. In 1938 his autobiographical work *The Green Fool* was published. Although Kavanagh was later to renounce the work as written 'under the evil aegis of the so-called Irish Literary Movement',[35] many passages in this work read as an authentic, fresh-minted record of the conditions of Irish rural society in the early decades of the century. Furthermore, for Kavanagh the writing of *The Green Fool* seems to have set in flow a stream of realistic writing that was to dominate his work in the early 1940s. For a period of two or three years it seemed uncertain indeed whether the essential Kavanagh was the lyric poet or a writer with an ambition rooted in respect for the achievements of realistic fiction. For the Ireland Kavanagh knew, the small farms of Monaghan and the newly rich middle class of Dublin, apparently lay open to the kind of realistic investigation a novelist attempts. And the discovery that obsesses him in three long poems, each grounded in realism, which he wrote in the early forties, 'The Great Hunger', 'Lough Derg', and 'Why Sorrow', as well as in his incomplete novel begun in 1950, *By Night Unstarred*, is the abject inadequacy of Irish life not simply as matter for the novelist's or poet's trade but as a condition of being. In each of these works a strain of outrage suggests that what appalls this angry, passionate man as he conducts his artistic investigations is whether there is any principle within the Irish world that can redeem it from nullity, can inspire it to that vivid, creative vitality and cultural and spiritual depth that Kavanagh, like O Faoláin, felt was so signally lacking in modern Ireland.

For Kavanagh the issue revolved around the role of Catholicism in Irish life. Instinctively religious, responsive to the liturgical and mythic dimensions of the Catholic faith, Kavanagh in these three powerful long poems (that have received scarcely any critical attention outside Ireland) confronts the inadequacy of Irish life in a savage realism that indicts a deficient Catholicism as a major source of Ireland's ills. A faith that should embrace life has fed on the most life-denying aspects of Irish experience, repressing instinct, joy, creativity. But in each of these darkly realistic works Kavanagh obsessively seeks to discover whether the grim waste of Irish Catholic life contains hints of more vital religious meanings. He hopes that his realism, probing the sources of contemporary distress uncompromisingly, will uncover intact the repository of a sustaining faith.

The most starkly oppressive of Kavanagh's realistic works is 'The Great Hunger' (1942) – in Ireland the Great Hunger is the disastrous potato famine of the 1840s. In this bleak work that horrendous period is associated with the emotional, sexual and cultural poverty of life on a small farm in Co. Monaghan in the twentieth century. Through fourteen sections, like fourteen personal stations of the cross, we follow Paddy Maguire, the central figure of the poem, as he ekes out a life of frustration and withering tedium. From the first we sense the religious blasphemy such a fate represents: it is a parody of incarnation:

> Clay is the word and clay is the flesh
> Where the potato-gatherers like merchanised scarecrows move
> Along the side-fall of the hill – Maguire and his men.
> If we watch them an hour is there anything we can prove
> Of life as it is broken-backed over the Book
> Of Death?[36]

At the last there is no revelation:

> The bedposts fall. No hope. No lust.
> Screams the apocalypse of clay
> In every corner of this land.
>
> (C.P., 104)

Maguire has been destroyed by a malign set of forces – economic insecurity and a widowed mother whose impossible demands for sexual loyalty reinforce the life-denying doctrines of the Church. Kavanagh's analysis of the Church's part in this tragedy is complex. He is not content simply to indict that institution. Rather he sees that a literal acceptance of the Church's doctrines is what can destroy a man, distracting him from natural fulfilment. Elsewhere religion can perhaps act as a necessary restraint on ungovernable passion, but in Ireland, when allied with the twin forces of necessity and family, it becomes a tyrant:

> 'Now go to Mass and pray and confess your sins
> And you'll have all the luck' his mother said.
> He listened to the lie that is a woman's screen
> Around a conscience when soft thighs are spread.
> And all the while she was setting up the lie
> She trusted in Nature that never deceives.
> But her son took it as the literal truth.
> Religion's walls expand to the push of nature. Morality yields
> To sense – but not in little tillage fields.
>
> (C.P., 89)

The whole of the poem is full of Kavanagh's own sense of the push of Nature, the disruptive energies of instinct and passion that might in a happier place make religion truly incarnational. One of the poem's most powerful effects is its sense of the movements of the seasons, of the blooming and withering of the natural cycle, of the almost sacramental beauty of flower and spring field. At moments even the clay-haunted Maguire can glimpse a richer mode of religious being in such natural life:

> Yet sometimes when the sun comes through a gap
> These men know God the Father in a tree:
> The Holy Spirit is the rising sap,
> And Christ will be the green leaves that will come
> At Easter from the sealed and guarded tomb.
>
> (*C.P.*, 84)

Plant, beast, bird, tree, wind, sun, rain, the very fish in the stream urge man to life, to belief in true Incarnation.

> The trout played in the pools encouragement
> To jump in love though death bait the hook.
>
> (*C.P.*, 92)

But Maguire, taking the bread of life, tied to mother and land,

> read the symbol too sharply and turned
> From the five simple doors of sense
> To the door whose combination lock has puzzled
> Philosopher and priest and common dunce.
>
> (*C.P.*, 88)

Maguire's tragedy is that of a misinterpretation which makes him a pauper in the midst of plenteous natural possibility. In the social world Kavanagh presents in 'The Great Hunger' such a miserable misinterpretation seems inescapable. It is this that makes the work, despite its energy and power, its vigorous impression of natural fertility, so bleakly harrowing, so dominated by its moods of anger and outrage. For nature cannot redeem Maguire from his deathly involvement with clay to

> that metaphysical land
> Where flesh was a thought more spiritual than music
> Among the stars – out of the reach of the peasant's hand.
>
> (*C.P.*, 89)

In 'Lough Derg' (first published in 1971) Kavanagh once again confronted the problems of the emotional and spiritual inadequacies of Irish life. Here, in even more direct fashion, the poet considers how Irish Catholicism bears on this melancholy estate. He does this by focussing on one of the more remarkable manifestations of piety in the country, the penitential pilgrimage of Irish men and women to endure the privations of a sojourn of three days and nights, fasting, on the holy island of St Patrick in Lough Derg in Co. Donegal. Kavanagh had visited the island in 1940 and in 1942 a second visit, shortly after the publication of 'The Great Hunger', bore fruit in a second long poem written before the year was out.

'Lough Derg', like 'The Great Hunger', has a distinctly documentary aspect. The poet seems intent on social analysis. Like the earlier poem, too, this stark work is partially structured as a narrative. Following a brilliant opening sequence of almost cinematic impressionism, the poet picks out three pilgrims from the crowd whose lives and religious motives he sets before us. One is an unfrocked Franciscan monk whose sin has been carnality, another a young girl who had murdered an illegitimate child, the third a small farmer with literary tastes, who is clearly representative of Kavanagh himself. For Robert Fitzsimons, the small farmer, 'a half-pilgrim who hated prayer' (*C.P.*,108), the question of the meaning of all this zeal weighs oppressively, as it does for the author. At one level the prayers of the people seem a ghastly acquisitive parody of true religious veneration:

> For this is Lough Derg, St Patrick's Purgatory.
> He came to this island-acre of limestone once
> To be shut of the smug too-faithful. The story
> Is different now.
> Solicitors praying for cushy jobs
> To be County Registrar or Coroner,
> Shopkeepers threatened with sharper rivals
> Than any hook-nosed foreigner
> Mother whose daughters are Final Medicals
> Too heavy-hipped for thinking,
> Wives whose husbands have angina pectoris,
> Wives whose husbands have taken to drinking.
>
> (*C.P.*,105)

Modern Ireland, which in wartime 'froze for want of Europe' (*C.P.*, 117), seems locked into a banal piety expressive of a peasant people's hold on land and property, where emotional savageries afflict the individual. But, as in 'The Great Hunger', that is not the whole of the story. Kavanagh allows Fitzsimons to sense an older, residual faith expressed in the rites of the people, a faith which perhaps predates Christianity and which in more humane times became wedded to Christian practice in a life-giving way. On one level Kavanagh himself can assert

Lough Derg is typical of what may be called the Irish mind. No contemplation, no adventure, the narrow, primitive piety of the small huxter with a large family.[37]

On another, he is impressed by

the freshness, the recency of Christianity. Lough Derg is no museum piece. The old stalk of Christianity ends in flowers that have both colour and scent – and thorns too.[38]

At Lough Derg

>   something that is Ireland's secret leads
> These petty mean people
> For here's the day of a poor soul freed
> To a marvellous beauty above its head.
> The Castleblaney grocer trapped in the moment's need
> Puts out a hand and writes what he cannot read,
> A wisdom astonished at every turn
> By some angel that writes in the oddest words.
> When he will walk again in Muckno street
> He'll hear from the kitchens of fair-day eating houses
> In the after-bargain carouses
> News from a country beyond the range of birds.

(C.P., 106)

Some almost eastern mystical principle perhaps guides the people to this holy place:

> These men and boys were not lead there
> By priests of Maynooth or stories of Italy or Spain
> For this is the penance of the poor
> Who knows what beauty hides in misery
> As beggars, fools and eastern fakirs know.

(C.P., 111)

In the poem Kavanagh fails to achieve certainty of any kind. At moments the poet is at one with the people, even sympathizing with their banal, poignant prayers; at others he is disgusted with the widespread expressions of spiritual acquisitiveness; occasionally he is conscious of deeper, more profound notes sounding through the babble of prayers and the ringing of bells. But we leave the poem remembering its realism, not its emotional or spiritual conclusions – a cinematic, documentary treatment of pilgrims representing various Irish social groups, and a bleak re-creation of a harsh place of rock, stone, water and cold air are its primary effects.

'Why Sorrow' may have been written before 'Lough Derg', although it was not published until 1946, and in Peter Kavanagh's edition of his brother's *Complete Poems* it appears according to its date of publication. Dealing with the spiritual problems of an Irish country priest, the poet takes him, as the poem itself breaks off *in medias res*, to Lough Derg.[39] The theme is certainly close to that of 'Lough Derg', though more sharply etched. Paganism and Christianity in this poem are frankly opposed. Much of the work is reminiscent of realistic fiction in an even more obvious way than 'The Great Hunger' and 'Lough Derg'. Father Mat, who is a priest forced against his inclinations (which are sensual and artistic) to preach a Jansenistic message in an emotionally starved countryside, is provided with a representative family history in Co. Clare, as in a work of realistic fiction.

> His father was a farmer in Corofin.
> He had six fields with soil like soap
> Where rushes grew and grasses like steel wires
> Blue in the sunshine. Down the shivering slope
> Water ran in sheets in winter.
> And out of this sour soil he squeezed
> The answer to his wife's wishes.
> In steely grass and green rushes
> Was woven the vestments of a priest.
>
> The eldest daughter rose to be
> A teacher in the school;
> Mat was the youngest. Father took
> His rosary and a stool,
> Knelt and prayed for something special,
> Something that was never mentioned,
> And the fire went out behind their heels
> And Mat grew up like July in the fields.
>
> (C.P., 169-70)

The social world from which Father Mat derives and to which he ministers seems to the tortured cleric quite antithetical to the wild pagan presence of Ireland herself:

> Ancient Ireland sweeping
> In again with all its unbaptised beauty.
>
> (C.P., 174)

The main thrust of the work is the conflict between the priest's sense of his duty to a frightened, impoverished parish which could be dreadfully harmed by any lapse in its spiritual director, and his own ungovernable desire for the pagan world of nature. 'The Great Hunger' and 'Lough Derg' tried to discern a relationship between Irish Catholicism and an older pagan feeling for natural fertility and the countryside, despite the rigors of contemporary belief and practice. In 'Why Sorrow' no such relationship is postulated. Rather the arid present seems the more desolate, with its severe psychological pressures on any who, like Father Mat, lift their eyes from the mud, because of the vital attractions of paganism. Kavanagh's realism has here discovered only anguish and masochistic submission.

For Kavanagh as for O Faoláin the Irish world, the people of O'Connell's Ireland, the Catholic majority of small-farmers, shopkeepers and priests, presents the artist with a diminished experience as his primary material. In his unfinished novel, undertaken in 1950 but posthumously published as *By Night Unstarred* (1977), Kavanagh admits as much. In this fragmentary but occasionally powerful work, we are introduced to the founder of a modern Irish dynasty, a small farmer in Co. Monaghan, one Peter Devine, born in 1867, who determines to amass a fortune and become a power in the land. Kavanagh early announces him as representative of his age and his society: 'So by the grace of God let him be revealed as a man, as a symbol of a new society, as a mirror for history.'[40] What Kavanagh's cruelly candid portrayal of this man does reveal is that in his society he is extraordinary only in the energy and singlemindedness of his ambition, not in the calculation and brutishness with which he pursues it. He inhabits a world where all social relations seem held in a balance of harsh economic fact, where only the exchange of goods and services, and the possession of land and power determine social and cultural life. The first half of the novel is therefore a horrifying portrait in savagely realistic terms of a man and a society governed only by envy, covetousness and naked greed. In the second part of the book we are brought forward to the early 1940s to meet the patriarchal Peter Devine once again, now the head of a dynasty that he has lived to see in important positions in Church and commerce in a new post-revolutionary Ireland. The self-congratulatory complacency of the family with its pretensions to social standing and culture, by comparison with the driving energy portrayed in the earlier sections of the book, seem at this point inadequate matter for the realistic novelist's searching, analytic powers. The truth is all too simple:

> Watching this artistic family with all the accoutrements of fashionable society upon them Patrick did not wonder that the glare and blare was designed to shut out their squalid past. The slime-stuck peasant unconscious of cities, of cultures, of everything but the power of money, had come to town. Money was everything – almost.[41]

In such a world realism has little to operate upon; it must give way to satire and polemic.

So, in the late forties and early fifties, Kavanagh, persuaded of the inadequacy of Irish experience as matter for realistic writing, as it was, more importantly, inadequate for imaginative living, turned to bitter, crude satires and violent denunciation. Irish society in these bitter poems and in the columns of *Kavanagh's Weekly*, which he edited and wrote with his brother in the spring and early summer of 1952, is excoriated for its mediocrity and provincialism, the Irish Free State and Republic comprehensively indicted:

> All the mouthpieces of public opinion are controlled by men whose only qualification is their inability to think.
> Being stupid and illiterate is the mark of respectability and responsibility. . .
> The country is dead or dying of its false materialism.[42]

O'Faoláin in 1940, when he sensed that he had exhausted the possibilities of realistic fiction in the Irish context, turned to documentary journalism and polemic in his periodical *The Bell*. It is striking that Kavanagh, too, reaching an impasse in imaginative work rooted in the realist tradition, turned to satire and polemic, sensing a need to start his own newspaper in order to have his say about the aesthetic and actual inadequacies of Irish life. For both of them journalism offered a partial release from similar frustrations.

It is in their subsequent achievements as writers that their careers diverge. That divergence, which was to take O Faoláin to a distinguished career as an urbane, broadly humanistic man of letters and professionally competent short story-teller, and to take Kavanagh to his late flowering as an original, if occasional, lyric poet, was grounded in their differing attitudes to the realistic work they had both attempted in their earlier years. Seán O Faoláin, one senses, chiefly experienced aesthetic disappointment when he discovered the inadequacy of Irish life for the kind of work he aspired to write as a young novelist. By contrast, Patrick Kavanagh was afflicted with moral and spiritual qualms when his realistic portraits of Irish society failed to uncover any convincingly creative principle in Irish life, particularly in the religious sensibility of the people. O Faoláin regretted the shapelessness of Irish life, the lack of a complex social machinery; Kavanagh, when he wrote realistically of Ireland's unformed, savagely simple life, was aghast to find there little more than harrowing bleakness and atrocity. Works rooted in that inadequate reality would inevitably bear the marks of a dominant despair, a terrifying simplicity. He became convinced, therefore, that writing about such a society in realistic or satiric terms was a spiritual wrong, an aesthetic crime. For the poet's mission, Kavanagh believed, is to 'excite the moment with hope'.[43] The task of a true art is to give expression to 'the quintessence of experience, so gay, so full of hope and faith, that lives at the heart of things'.[44] In a work like 'The Great Hunger' the poet had revealed 'some queer and terrible things',[45] but the whole had lacked 'the nobility and repose of poetry'.[46] And so Kavanagh turned away from society as a subject to the intimate histories of the self, expressed in a direct, improvisational style that achieves the lyric mood through a comic acceptance of the patterns life weaves in the midst of the everyday. The intellectual pretensions of realism and the desire for social analysis are abandoned by the mature Kavanagh:

What seems of public importance is never of any importance. Stupid poets and artists think that by taking subjects of public importance it will help their work to survive. There is nothing as dead and damned as an important thing. The things that really matter are casual, insignificant little things, things you would be ashamed to talk of publicly.[47]

In their place, in his later work, comes first the timeless world of the Irish countryside, treated as a personal, genially comic idyll in his semi-autobiographical novel *Tarry Flynn* (1948), and a pure lyric expression that unembarrassedly celebrates the adventures of self in the world and in time. 'Innocence' is a memorable example, bearing precisely on my theme:

> They laughed at one I loved –
> The triangular hill that hung
> Under the Big Forth. They said
> That I was bounded by the whitethorn hedges
> Of the little farm and did not know the world.
> But I knew that love's doorway to life
> Is the same doorway everywhere.
>
> Ashamed of what I loved
> I flung her from me and called her a ditch
> Although she was smiling at me with violets.
>
> But now I am back in her briary arms
> The dew of an Indian Summer morning lies
> On bleached potato-stalks –
> What age am I?
>
> I do not know what age I am,
> I am no mortal age;
> I know nothing of women,
> Nothing of cities,
> I cannot die
> Unless I walk outside these whitethorn hedges.
>
> (C.P., 241-2)

This is not an ironic, humane lyricism that issues from the poign-ancies of unresolved social tension, as in many of O Faoláin's later tales, but from the achieved self-confidence of a poet who is finally as ease with his material. That this material is the self in the ordinary Irish world represents Kavanagh's surest achievement. In moments of such charged lyric assurance he exhibits the possibility of an Irish art, that grounded in ordinary Irish reality excites 'the moment with hope'. Irish life transcends for an exemplary moment the problem of adequacy.

In the face of such gifts to insist that this transcendence is momentary and personal must seem the surliest form of ingratitude. Indeed, the liberating force of Kavanagh's later poetry on subsequent Irish poets, encouraging them to trust themselves and their own world, however diminished it might appear to them, is eloquent testimony to the cultural impact of Kavanagh's achievement in lyric art which cannot be gainsaid. But his career, like O Faoláin's, tantalizes in its sense of frustra-tion tearing at the heart of imaginative commitment. They each sensed their intimate involvement with an Irish reality that distinguished them from the writers of the Literary Revival. They aspired to major statement but found that ambition thwarted by what they felt were insurmountable deficiences, aesthetic and moral, in their material. For both writers the lyric and the lyric mood, even at its most ecstatic and intense as in Kavanagh's remarkable late work, was an acquiescence, a triumph of quietism. For both writers the lyric possibility offered a rhetoric of resignation.

NOTES

1. Stephen Brown, S.J. 'Gaelic and Anglo-Irish Literature – Contacts and Quality', *The Irish Statesman* (30 November 1929), p. 253.
2. Liam O'Flaherty, Letter to the Editor, *The Irish Statesman* (20 February 1926), p. 739.
3. Austin Clarke, Letter to the Editor, *The Irish Statesman* (20 February 1926), p. 740.
4. F. R. Higgins, Letter to the Editor, *The Irish Statesman* (6 March 1926), p. 797.
5. Seán O'Faoláin, 'Yeats and the Younger Generation, *Horizon,* Vol. 5, No. 25 (January 1942), 50.
6. W. B. Yeats, 'The Municipal Gallery Revisited', *Collected Poems* (London 1950), p. 368.
7. W. B. Yeats 'A General Introduction for my Work' in *Essays and Introductions* (London 1961), p. 520.
8. W. B. Yeats, 'Ireland and the Arts', *Essays and Introductions*, p. 208.
9. The fact that by the 1920s and 30s Yeats was incorporating the Anglo-Irish Ascendancy into his vision of an indomitable Irishry, made such agreement even less likely.
10. Frank O'Connor, 'The Future of Irish Literature', *Horizon*, Vol. 5, No. 25 (January 1942), p. 61.
11. Austin Clarke, *Collected Poems*, (Dublin, London, Oxford, New York 1974), p. 153.
12. 'The Future of Irish Literature', p. 56.
13. *Ibid.*
14. Seán O Faoláin, 'The Gaelic League', *The Bell*, Vol. 2 (1942), p. 80.
15. *Ibid.*
16. Seán O Faoláin, *Vive Moi!* (London 1965), p. 173.
17. *Ibid.*
18. *Ibid.*, p. 241.
19. *Ibid.*, p. 242.
20. *Ibid.*
21. *Ibid.*, p. 245.
22. Seán O Faoláin, 'The Dilemma of Irish Letters', *The Month*, Vol. 2, No. 6 (1949), p. 373.

23. *Ibid.* pp. 375-76.
24. *Ibid.*, p. 376.
25. *Ibid.*, pp. 376-7.
26. Seán O'Faoláin, *Bird Alone* (Dublin 1973), pp. 279-80.
27. *Ibid.*, p. 288.
28. Seán O'Faoláin's last novel *And Again?* (1979) is a comic fantasy in which the protagonist is permitted to live his life again, but backwards. Only superficially realistic, it is an exploration of the nature of psychological identity.
29. Patrick Kavanagh, 'Paris In Aran', *Kavanagh's Weekly*, Vol. No. 9 (7 June 1952), p. 7.
30. Patrick Kavanagh, *Self Portrait* (Dublin 1964), p. 9.
31. *Ibid.*
32. *Ibid.*
33. Patrick Kavanagh, *The Standard* (3 July 1942); reprinted in *The Journal of Irish Literature*, 6 (1977), p. 33.
34. *Ibid.*
35. Patrick Kavanagh, *Self Portrait*, p. 8.
36. Patrick Kavanagh, *The Complete Poems of Patrick Kavanagh*, collected, arranged and edited by Peter Kavanagh (New York 1972), pp. 79-80. Henceforth *C.P.*
37. Patrick Kavanagh, *Lapped Furrows*, ed. Peter Kavanagh (New York 1969), p. 58.
38. Patrick Kavanagh, *The Standard* (12 June 1942), in *The Journal of Irish Literature*, p. 33.
39. One critic has suggested: 'It is not unlikely that at this point Kavanagh was inspired to abandon 'Why Sorrow', at least for the time being, and devote a whole poem to Lough Derg. It doesn't seem probable that having exhaustively considered the Lough Derg material he would re-introduce it into 'Why Sorrow' a few years later'; Jude the Obscure, 'The H.U. Business Section', *The Honest Ulsterman*, No. 60 (July/October 1978), p. 75. This extended essay on Kavanagh's work was the first to alert readers to the importance of the realistic novel as an influence on the poet.
40. Patrick Kavanagh, *By Night Unstarred*, ed. Peter Kavanagh (The Curragh 1977), p. 26.
41. *Ibid.*, pp. 171-2.
42. Patrick Kavanagh, *Kavanagh's Weekly*, Vol 1, No. 1 (12 April 1952.)
43. *Ibid.*, p. 7.
44. Patrick Kavanagh, *The Standard* (25 October 1946), in *The Journal of Irish Literature*, p. 24.
45. Patrick Kavanagh, *Self Portrait*, p. 27.
46. *Ibid.*
47. *Ibid.*, pp. 20-21.

8

SOME YOUNG DOOM: BECKETT AND THE CHILD

The Beckett universe is a curiously childless one, even if at moments it admits the experience of childhood. Where consanguinity is admitted, as in Molloy's reflection on his mother or on the son he may have had, or in Moran's relationship with Jacques or where filial awareness plays a major part in a Beckett text, they are treated with mordant grotesque distaste as if for a Beckett persona any impairment of personal parthenogenesis and uniqueness of being is simply too much to be borne.[1] Where in Becket's work there is a sense of familial inheritance as in *Krapp's Last Tape* ('mother at rest at last'), *First Love, Footfalls, Rockaby*, it is usually an only child, like Molloy, who in old age is haunted by a parent. For Beckettt's families, such as they are, seem victims of inhibited fertility, impotence and sterility. Winnie and Willie cannot number among their happy days the birth of an heir, the tormented prisoners of *Play*'s eternal triangle are at least spared the complications of offspring within or without the bonds of matrimony. For the persona of A's story in *That Time*, childhood is remembered as a solitary condition in which he would hide among the rubble and nettles of a ruined building where 'no one came'. Hamm is the end of the line in *Endgame*.

When Beckett does allow his characters to contemplate a more fruitful domestic arrangement, they do so with a kind of wearied comic unenthusiastic gloom. Sapo, 'the eldest child of poor and sickly parents', is described by Malone in *Malone Dies* as the cause of futile parental endeavours.:

Nothing remains but to envisage a small house. But we are cramped as it is, said Mrs Saposcat. And it was an understood thing that this would be more and more so with every passing day until the day came when, the departure of the first-born compensating the arrival of the new born, a kind of equilibrium would be attained. Then little by little the house would empty. And at last they would be all alone with their memories. It would be time enough then to move. He would be pensioned off, she at her last gasp. They would take a cottage in the country, where, having no further need of manure, they could afford to buy it in cartloads. And their children, grateful for the sacrifices made on their behalf, would come to their assistance. It was in the atmosphere of unbridled dream that these conferences usually ended. It was as though the Saposcats drew the strength from the prospect of their impotence.

And Vivian Mercier has directed us to the one passage in Beckett's *oeuvre* where a text 'fully acknowledges the power of human fertility', noting that 'in that passage this uncontrollable and protean force pours out an almost inexhaustible supply of grotesques'.[2] The Lynch family in *Watt* hope that their combined ages can top the thousand. Birth and kinship are observed in this *tour de force* with a fascinated comic horror.

For Watt had not been four months with Mr Knott when Liz the wife of Sam lay down and expelled a child, her twentieth, with the greatest of ease as may well be imagined, and for some days after this agreeably surprised all those who knew her (and they were many) by the unusual healthiness of her appearance and by a flow of good spirit quite foreign to her nature, for for many years she had passed rightly for more dead than alive, and she suckled the infant with great enjoyment and satisfaction apparently, the flow of milk being remarkably abundant for a woman of her age and habit of body, which was exsanguinous, and then after five or six or perhaps even seven days of this kind of thing grew suddenly weak and to the great astonishment of her husband Sam, her sons Blind Bill and Maim Mat, her married daughters Kate and Anne and their husbands Sean and Simon, her niece Bridie and her nephew Tom, her sisters May and Lil, her brother-in-law Tom and Jack, her cousins Ann, Art and Con, her aunts-in-law May and Mag, her aunt Kate, her uncles-in-law Joe and Jim, her father-in-law Bill and her grandfather-in-law Tom, who were not expecting anything of the kind, grew weaker and weaker, until she died.

Minimal fertility, impotence and sterility are what characteristically absorb Beckett's personae as they reflect on the human condition and on the facts of reproduction. Imaginations so committed to terminal states of feeling and being as the object of obsessional attention find their other pole in bravura displays of comic repulsion from the details of the procreative act (the love affair between Moll and Macmann on the brink of the grave in *Malone Dies*, as Vivian Mercier has remarked, 'is calculated to undermine the reverence for life and awe before the reproductive processes of all but the most wholesome personalities')[3] and from the grotesque consequences of that act, the survival of the species.

It is such a context of Swiftian misanthropy, touched with nihilistic zest and frigid despair, that makes those moments in the Beckett canon when children appear without comment or interpretative sign so poignant and enigmatic. I am thinking particularly of the final moments of the two acts of *Waiting for Godot* when a message from Mr Godot arrives in the person of a timid boy (it is not the same child in the two acts, or so he says, though the *Dramatis Personae* only lists 'A Boy'). There is something peculiarly moving in the innocent simplicity of the messenger's demeanor in the face of Vladimir's insistent questioning. A childish acceptance of the world as it is challenges tonally the interrogative energy of the play's dialogue. In the theatre the mood is chilling, poignant and enigmatic simultaneously. Whose child is he? Who is his brother who minds the sheep, the goats? Why is one brother beaten by Mr Godot, the other not? What is the childish state of consciousness which is so acquiescent in its world, so untroubled by such questions.?

VLADIMIR: You're not unhappy? [*the* BOY *hesitates.*]
            Do you hear me?
BOY: Yes, sir.
VLADIMIR: Well?
BOY: I don't know, sir.

Similarly, in the final moments of *Endgame* Clov peers through his telescope and reports that without can be seen what may be 'a small boy'. Clov volunteers to go and check the matter. Hamm orders him to stay where he is.

CLOV: No? A potential procreator?
HAMM: If he exists he'll die there or he'll come here.
        And if he doesn't. . .
        [*Pause*]
CLOV: You don't believe me? You think I'm inventing?
        [*Pause*]
HAMM: It's the end, Clov, we've come to the end. I don't need you any more.

119

As the final moves of the endgame are played out, a tantalising image of continuance and rebirth (which Hamm and Clov fear) renders the clawed violence of the play's last moments all the more unbearable (a similar effect is created in Beckett's prose piece *The Calmative*), and we remember that Hamm has cursed his own father, 'Accursed progenitor', and has indulged in fantasies of testing a father's love for his son (a variant of Jahweh and Abraham, one supposes) and we remember too that Nagg, his own father, had asked:

Whom did you call when you were a tiny boy, and were frightened, in the dark? Your mother? No. Me. We let you cry. Then we moved you out of earshot, so that we might sleep in peace. . . I hope I'll live. . . to hear you calling me like when you were a tiny boy, and were frightened, in the dark and I was your only hope.

It is of course in Beckett's radio play *All That Fall* that a child plays the most crucial role. For it is the death of a little child who falls out of a carriage onto the line which delays the train that brings Mr Rooney from the city to his spouse waiting at the station.

They are a childless couple, Maddie and Dan Rooney, in a play dominated by references to sterility, childlessness and death. The play itself is framed by the strains of Schubert's 'Death and the Maiden', with its implications of a virginal demise. *En route* to the station by foot Mrs Rooney meets Mr Tyler, a retired bill-broker about whose daughter she solicitously enquires. 'Fair, fair', he replies, 'they removed everything, you know, the whole. . . er . . . bag of tricks. Now I am grandchildless.' Mrs Rooney gets a lift in Mr Slocum's automobile and the machine runs over an unfortunate hen, drawing from the terrified passenger a meditation on the bird's interrupted fertility:

What a death! One minute picking happy at the dung, on the road, in the sun, with now and then a dust bath, and then – bang! – all her troubles over. [*Pause*] All the laying and the hatching. [*Pause*] Just one great squawk and the. . . peace. [*Pause*] They would have slit her weasand in any case.

We know almost from the outset the reason for Mrs Rooney's preoccupation with sterility and death. The Rooneys' child, Minnie, has died young, or perhaps has never been born (Mrs Rooney is fascinated by a lecturer on psychology whom she once heard speak of a girl who 'had never been really born'): 'In her forties now she'd be, I don't know, fifty, girding up her lovely little loins, getting ready for the change. . . .'

But the death of the child in *All That Fall* is a mystery. Indeed the whole play has an air of the *policier* about it. It invites the hunt for clues. Dan Rooney is presented as a child-hating misanthrope: 'Did you,' he asks, 'ever wish to kill a child? [*Pause*] Nip some young doom in the bud. [*Pause*] Many a time at night, in winter, on the black road home, I nearly attacked the boy.' So suspicion must fall on him when we learn of the 'accident' that has delayed the train. Is he simply another of the Beckett personae whose loathing for the fact of human reproduction and family ties has led him to indulge a taste for child murder? Or has something even more horrible happened whereby the childphobic Dan has caused the death of a child, almost unconsciously? We know Dan is blind, much troubled with his health. He answers Mrs Rooney's enquiry for an explanation of the train's delay: 'We drew out on the tick of time. . . . on the tick of time. I had the compartment to myself as usual. At least I hope so, for I made no attempt to restrain myself.' How Dan may have frightened any occupant of his carriage, invisible to him, beggars the imagination. We know he probably suffers from prostate trouble for when the train does arrive (fifteen minutes late on a thirty minute run) he has immediately to be led to the 'men's, or Fir as they call is now'. Something nasty happened in the carriage and in some sense Dan is guilty of the child's death, even if we cannot go along with those critics who see him as a murderer, as a gratuitously anti-life nihilist, a performer of an *acte gratuit*.[4]

Dan is, as the play constantly reminds us, an Irish Protestant, a member of the Church of Ireland. Indeed the play is the most obviously localized and precisely situated of all Beckett's works. As a portrait of the Irish Protestant married male, Dan is a damning indictment. He fears emotion and the display of feeling: 'Kiss you? In public? On the platform? Before the boy? Have you taken leave of your senses?' He is hypochondriacal, mean, censorious ('Have you been drinking again?'), impatient, penny-pinching, callous (a psychologist to him is 'a lunatic specialist'). Throughout, he speaks with a kind of frigid contempt for his wife and, as one critic has suggested, 'ruled by fear of life and emotions, has always been obsessed by fantasies of killing the child (in himself)'.[5]

As a Protestant gentleman he values his privacy, his independence, his freedom from the 'horrors of home life' with its earthy involvements ('dusting, sweeping, airing, scrubbing, waxing, waning, washing, mangling, drying, moving, clipping, raking, rolling, scuffling, shovelling, grinding, tearing, pounding, banging, and slamming') and its adjacent fertility: 'And the brats, the happy little healthy little howling neighbours' brats'. His preference as life-hating solitary, reminiscent of those personae of Beckett's *Trilogy* whom Declan Kiberd[6] has celebrated as Protestant heroes, is for a state of death-in-life remote from the horrific challenges of home and children:

And I fell to thinking of my silent, backstreet, basement office, with its obliterated plate, rest-couch and velvet handings, and what it means to be buried there alive, if only from ten to five, with convenient to the one hand a bottle of light pale ale and to the other a long ice-cold fillet of hake. Nothing, I said, not even fully certified death, can ever take the place of that.

Like the personae of the *Trilogy*, Dan is determined to retain his independent self-hood, resenting his obvious dependence on his wife Maddy. His first word to his anxious spouse concerned about his delayed arrival is a cool 'Maddy'; and he immediately denies knowledge of his wife's birthday wishes despite the fact that he is wearing the tie she presented to him. He rejects, too, dependence upon any kind of supportive deity. When he learns the announced text for the next sabbath's sermon. 'The Lord upholdeth all that fall and raiseth up all those that he bowed down', the Rooneys 'join in wild laughter'. But as they move on in the wind and rain, Maddy, as if bereft of any divine consolation and aware of her husband's vulnerability, gasps 'Hold me tighter, Dan!'

In the *Trilogy*, as Kiberd has rightly pointed out, the Protestant puritan imagination is revealed in its austere integrity, its exacting confessionalism, its absolute commitment to individual conscience, until by the end of the work even Protestantism itself is subjected to an inexorable critique, conscience works on conscience until 'there is no consolation – merely the knowledge that Protestantism has ceased to be a potent myth and becomes a self-confessed fiction'.[7]

All That Fall shows us what that final state is like in its arid, self-destructive, life-denying cruelty. For there is a cruelty in the stripping away of communal, familial, religious support, in stripping away the layers of the self in what Hugh Kenner has brilliantly identified as the two spiritual traditions 'by which history has shaped the specifically Protestant character: the personal testimony and the *issueless* confrontation with conscience'[8] (emphasis mine). In the most obvious sense the confrontation with self in *All That Fall*'s Mr Rooney, resolutely retaining the fiction of independence, even when most dependent, blind, halting, leaning upon a spouse, is issueless, without issue, childless, destructive. In the person of Miss Fitt, too, whom Mrs Rooney meets *en route* to the station we see such self-delusion about self at its most ludicrous. She denies – this half-crazed, anorexic spinster, dieted with self – the communal aspects of her religious communion: 'In church, Mrs Rooney, I am alone with my Maker.' She is self-obsessed, to the point of self-destruction:

I suppose the truth is I am not there, Mrs Rooney, just not really there at all, I see, hear, smell, and so on, I go through the usual motions, but my heart is not in it, Mrs Rooney, my heart is in none of it. Left to myself, with no one to check me, I would soon be flown. . . home.

The childless Mrs Rooney has suffered in this world of Protestant virtues and self-absorption. The most warmly human, broadly humorous of all Beckettt's creations, for whom as one critic has noted 'life spills over its own boundaries'[9], Maddy Rooney has endured deep sexual frustration ('Love, that is all I asked, a little love, daily, twice daily, fifty years of twice daily love like a Paris horse-butcher's regular, what normal woman wants affection?') in this loveless environment of loveless selfhood: 'Oh I am just a hysterical old hag I know, destroyed with sorrow and pining and gentility and church-going and fat and rheumatism and childlessness.'

In part a creation drawing on the verbal panache and exuberance of the dramatist John Synge (whom Beckett greatly admired), it is difficult to believe indeed in Mrs Rooney as Protestant at all in this play. Her attitude to sexuality and procreation has an earthy uninhibited zest quite different from the prissy euphemisms of Mr Tyler, the frosty cruelty of Mr Rooney, the smarmy ingratiation of Mr Slocum, the high-pitched hysteria of Miss Fitt. Perhaps Beckett, imagining Mrs Rooney in terms of Synge's peasant heroines (and she employs Hiberno-English turns of phrase), unconsciously gave her attributes that set her apart from the obviously middle-class Dublin Protestants with whom she has to do. Or perhaps he has left us enough clues to suspect that she may in fact be an uncomfortable convert to her husband's Church and creed.

By her own account, she is a victim of gentility. Genteel she certainly is not.

Venus birds! Billing in the woods all the long summer long. (*Pause*) Oh cursed corset! If I could let it out, without indecent exposure. Mr Tyler! Mr Tyler! Come back and unlace me behind the hedge! [*She laughs wildly, ceases*]

Her attitude to the Irish language ('our own poor dear Gaelic') make her an unusual Irish Protestant of her generation,[10] as does her readily blasphemous tongue. ('Your arm! Any arm! A helping hand! For five seconds! Christ what a planet!') Beckett has Mrs Rooney 'left-handed on top of everything else', about to sing along with Newman's conversion hymn 'Lead Kindly Light', aware of her own linguistic peculiarity in an environment of circumspect colourless locutions and contemptuous of self-regarding Protestant virtue ('Pismires do it for one another. . . I have seen slugs do it'). The clues are there in this *policier* for a case to be built. But more crucially, and independently of Mrs Rooney's possible religious pilgrimage, the play repeatedly concerns itself with the theologically Protestant view of good works, an orientation Mrs Rooney does not share.

Protestanism at its most extreme insists that justification is by faith alone. Good works are expected of the individual believer if he is a true believer, but they must be the fruit of altruism. Throughout *All That Fall* the characters are required to perform corporeal acts of mercy and they reflect on the theological significance of these. Tommy, for example, against his will helps Mrs Rooney out of Mr Slocum's car, and comments, 'And that's all the thanks you get for a Christian act'. Miss Fitt is adamant when Mrs Rooney advises her (theologically heterodox as Mrs Rooney is in face of a Protestant purist):

MRS ROONEY: If you would help me up the face of this cliff, Miss Fitt, I have little doubt your Maker would requite you, if no one else.

MISS FITT: Now, now, Mrs Rooney, don't put your teeth in me.
Requite! I make these sacrifices for nothing – or not at all.

And when she accedes to Mrs Rooney's request for help it is
with a grudging, 'Well, I suppose it is the Protestant thing to
do.' That is, to do good deeds without hope of reward. And Mr
Rooney himself ponders the sources of human action when he
wonders what kept him from child-slaughter in the past, 'What
restrained me then? Not fear of man.' Fear of God, perhaps?
Right action can be in fear of punishment if not in hope of
reward.

By contrast with these calculating, self-regarding spiritual
accountants assessing their own theological worth according to
a creed which sets works at nought but demands them nevertheless, Mrs Rooney is a model of impulsive good heartedness who
has embarked on her wearisome journey to give her miserable
husband a surprise on his birthday.

So it is Protestantism which is indicted in *All That Fall*, with
its bleak, self-absorbed issueless creed. The life-denying forces
at work on the Protestant frame of mind are seen as those which
make Beckett's imaginative universe so childless a place in a play
about childlessness and a child's grisly death. These forces
account for the heroic individualism of his anguished self-
exoriating personae in many of his works but also, it may be
argued, for their misanthropic fear of consanguinity, reproduction, fertility, with their risks to self-hood's imagined integrity of being. Mrs Rooney could teach them all a lot.

NOTES

1. The only moment in Beckett's *oeuvre* where sonship and paternity are
viewed benignly is the end of Text 1 in *Texts for Nothing*. The narrator
remembers a tale told by his father. But this benign memory is undermined
by subsequent texts and even here the relationship only achieves its mellow
quality in a retrospection that implies a kind of parthogenesis: 'Yes, I was
my father and I was my son, I asked myself questions and answered as
best I could, I had it told to me evening after evening, the same old story
I knew by heart and couldn't believe, or we walked together, hand in hand,
silent, sunk in our worlds, each in his worlds, the hands forgotten in each
other. That's how I've held out till not. And this evening again it seems to
be working, I'm in my arms, I'm holding myself in my arms, without much
tenderness, but faithfully, faithfully. Sleep now, as under that ancient lamp,
all twined together, tired out with so much talking, so much listening, so

much toil and play.'
Everyman his own father and son. That at least is bearable.

2. Vivian Mercier, *The Irish Comic Tradition* (Oxford 1962, 1969), p. 74.
3. *Ibid.*, p. 76.
4. See Clas Zilliacus, *Beckett and Broadcasting* (Åbi 1976), pp. 35-7, for a summary of critics' responses to this conundrum.
5. Cited *ibid.*, p. 37.
6. Declan Kiberd, 'Samuel Beckett and the Protestant Ethic' in *The Genius of Irish Prose*, ed. Augustine Martin (Cork 1985), pp. 121-30.
7. *Ibid.*, p. 129.
8. Hugh Kenner, *A Reader's Guide to Samuel Beckett* (London 1976), p. 134.
9. Cited Zilliacus, *op. cit.*, p. 37.
10. It was Donald Davie who first pointed out that *All That Fall* 'is sited so firmly in a particular milieu, that some of the jokes need for their appreciation first-hand knowledge of the Republic of Ireland today'. Review of *All That Fall* in *Spectrum* (Winter 1958), 25-31. Reprinted in *Samuel Beckett: The Critical Heritage*, eds Lawrence Graver and Raymond Federman (London 1979), p. 156. But Davie was less than forthcoming in explaining these.

9

AUSTIN CLARKE: SATIRIST

It is one of the curiosities of Irish literary history that the nineteenth century is deficient in satire. Certainly the century opened with one of the classics of Irish satiric invention, the damning indictment of irresponsible landlordism, Maria Edgeworth's *Castle Rackrent* (1800). But for many subsequent decades it was as if the Irish writer, who had in the past so relished the mode, was no longer visited by the satiric muse. In his pioneering study *The Irish Comic Tradition* (1962) Vivian Mercier suggests that the explanation for this must be sought in the facts of social and political history. The majority of the population in that desperate century, he argues, were too emotionally involved in the miseries of their country to achieve the ironic detachment necessary to satire, and the Anglo-Irish, with their energies directed towards the maintenance of English power in the country, could not risk satirizing the authority (and authority is the customary object of satiric assault) upon whom their privileged position depended. The point is well made, and certainly has persuasive force when one considers how satire in general has often been the artistic resource not of repressed majorities nor of privileged and powerful elites, but of radical conservatives confronted by emergent democratic power. Pat Rogers indeed, in his book *The Augustan Vision*, argues that precisely such a response to social change accounts for the satiric flowering in poetry of the early eighteenth century in England. And it is quite possible to construct a case whereby the last great moment of satiric verse in the Irish language in this country can be seen as the consequence of very similar processes. He writes:

The period was one in which major social changes took place; for example, the growth of public credit and government financial institutions,

127

with a consequent realignment of 'money' as against 'landed' interests. Satire is usually engaged in detecting infractions from a norm: and one common theme is the picture built up of 'new men', the invaders of established society, the pretenders to taste, the *nouveau riche*, the pushing outsiders. They lie at the heart of this issue.[1]

As they lie, readers will remember, at the heart of much seventeenth and eighteenth-century Gaelic satire where Clan Thomas is excoriated as a revolting and barbarous *parvenu* by poets who had lost their patrons in the new social order which had emerged after the Cromwellian and Williamite wars.

The disdainful voice of radical conservative satire sounds again in Irish verse through the scornful satiric accents of the Yeats of *Responsibilities* (1914). Paudeen in his shop, the Catholic middle classes, their fingers in the greasy till, betraying an heroic Parnell, are certainly things we might expect to pre-occupy an imagination driven by radical conservative outrage to satiric utterance. And in like manner there is something of a middle-class urban repugnance for the vulgar pretensions and cultural absurdities of the rural Michael Cusack in Joyce's famous *tour de force* of satiric invention in the Cyclops episode of *Ulysses*.

Since Irish independence in 1922 there has been much satirical writing. Perhaps none of it has been as scarifyingly personal as eighteenth-century English and Gaelic satire (the modern libel laws have induced a necessary caution) but nevertheless the period has provoked much satiric fire directed at institutional and societal targets. A post-revolutionary society established an official ideology compact of conservative Gaelic and Catholic versions of Irish identity that many writers experienced as a simplification of the rich human variety of Irish reality. That many members of the Anglo-Irish community felt themselves excluded from political and cultural power by a new petit-bourgeois state and its ideology certainly accounts for some of the satire of the period, of which Denis Johnston's *The Old Lady Says 'No'!* was the most brilliant example. And it is possible to see the even more famous Abbey trilogy of Sean O'Casey as a satiric attack (among other things) on the complacent post-revolutionary middle-class society which had adopted a nationalistic ideology to buttress its own social control of a country in which all forms of dissent and protest were to be rendered ineffectual.

Austin Clarke, one of the principal satiric writers of independent Ireland, was not of course a product of any kind of Anglo-Irish background. Indeed, in many respects his credentials, for one who might have played a definitive role in the new order, were impeccable. He had learnt the Irish language and studied with such as Douglas Hyde and the martyred Thomas MacDonagh. He had commited himself intellectually to the Gaelic tradition and was profoundly influenced by the heady cultural nationalism of the pre-independence years. But instead of playing some part in the new Ireland, as many of his contemporaries were only too ready to do, Clarke became an isolated outsider, the writer who would eventually produce a searching satiric diagnosis of the ill-fare state which in his view betrayed the dreams of the revolution.

One supposes that Clarke's personal experience of the forces of Irish puritanism must have had a decisive effect in souring his attitude to the new state. In 1921 he lost his job at University College, Dublin (he had been appointed assistant lecturer in English to replace Thomas MacDonagh) apparently because he had chosen to marry in a civil ceremony without benefit of clergy. This event is often passed over in accounts of Clarke's life and career as if the occurrence was merely one more unfortunate development in a youth and young manhood that had brought mental illness and sexual trauma. But how different might Clarke's career have been had he been allowed to occupy the post in the National University of the newly independent country, one for which he was eminently qualified (a first class honours degree and a thesis on the English dramatist John Ford) and to which he was surely entitled. Instead he was to spend the rest of his life in the essentially precarious situation of the man of letters, for whom the small cheque and wearisome hack-reviewing were an inadequate resource and an uncongenial activity in an era when the civil list pension had not been replaced by Arts Council support or the cnuas of *Aosdána*. It can also be pointed out that his action for divorce was heard in a London court the year after a free Dublin parliament had chosen not to speak of divorce in its chambers. That the young Clarke became an Irish outsider for whom issues of sexuality and religion were to be aspects of an almost obsessional alienation from much in modern Ireland, is scarcely surprising. Accordingly there is in Clarke's satiric assault on Irish society a curious blend of the disappointed hope of the republican idealist and the radical conservatism of one who senses himself as a natural inheritor of the new state, denied his due by the corrupt, venal mediocrities who exploit a narrow definition of nationalism for their own less than idealistic ends.

Clarke's artistic response to the dilemma in which he found himself, and his riposte to the society so much of a disppointment to him, was to highlight in his poetry a version of the Gaelic past which he thought had more authenticity than anything so sedulously cultivated as *echt*-Gael by the new puritans who elevated their own prejudices into universal Irish principles. Instead of a society where people lost their jobs for disobeying Church law, where censorship of publications became a statutory duty and a parliament forbade itself discussion of social reality, Clarke proposed a version of the Gaelic past which might represent a norm for a society dedicated to realizing a truly Gaelic form of human identity. *Pilgrimage and Other Poems* (published in 1929, the year of the Censorship of Publications Act) evokes the Hiberno-Romanesque period of the Irish past, not with a romantic's nostalgia for a pre-lapsarian mediaevalism, but with a classicist's sense of norms by which a society might measure its own manifest deficiencies.[2] The title poem itself offers to us a mediaeval Ireland when, as Clarke believed, the country almost had a religion of its own. This, it seems from the poem, was altogether a more integral part of a whole sense of life than anything the present could afford. Art and piety, Christian and pagan, were not so absolutely at odds with one another in the Irish past:

> Grey holdings of rain
> Had grown less with the fields,
> As we came to that blessed place
> Where hail and honey meet,
> O Clonmacnoise was crossed
> With light: those cloistered scholars,
> Whose knowledge of the gospel
> Is cast as metal in pure voices,
> Were all rejoicing daily,
> And cunning hands with cold and jewels
> Brought chalices to flame.

Here the intricate verse pattern suggests an integrated poetic world, where form and matter were one, and religion and craftsmanship embodied a harmonious synthesis. In this volume, too, a proper sense of piety does not involve a disavowal of the joys of the flesh, for 'The Young Woman of Beare' asserts her proud sexuality despite all those who would say her nay, without embarrassment or *pudeur*:

> I am the bright temptation
> In talk, in wine, in sleep.
> Although the clergy pray,
> I triumph in a dream.

There was a note of genuine respect for the mediaeval Irish experience in *Pilgrimage and Other Poems*. But it was to be many years before Clarke would be able to use the norms which he had established in his imaginative recreation of a vanished world as a measure of the deformed social and psychological conditions of contemporary Ireland. First, he had to wrestle with his personal past in his remarkable volume of conscience and intellectual self-release, *Night and Morning* (1938). From these poems of mortal anguish in which the mind confronts all those things which would defeat its powers – superstition, guilt, fear of punishment – the poet emerged, after the years in which he sought to express himself in the poetic drama, as the voice of individual, learned, Irish good sense. An appreciation of an Irish humanist tradition allowed him to find in all about him those deviations from a norm which must be recorded with a kind of weary, ironical anger. He responds to the new Ireland of the Grocer's Republic in the name of Gaelic enlightenment, the in-jokes, the puns, the complex verbal effects functioning as the embodiment of a learned tradition. And however affronted he may be, he also knows that vulgar puritanism and crass nationalism are merely unhappy aberrations in the Irish experience. In 1955 he published *Ancient Lights, Poems and Satires*, gathering stray poems and pamphlets together under a title that signalled his mood. Here anger, usually fairly muted, could be roused into momentary savagery by such events as the burning to death of orphans in a Church-controlled orphanage, which occasioned a peculiarly offensive clerical response. But the poem 'Three Poems About Children' is the most scathing, in a collection where the general effect is one of mature distaste for the Ireland he knows to be inauthentic even as it prates about its holy Gaelic identity. Overall, the technique does not in fact seem characteristic of satire. There are few individual objects of his poetic ire – there are no Shadwells or Valentine Brownes here; no individual is so vituperatively and comprehensively lampooned as to become a grotesque, a terrifying principle of dullness or a byword for inhospitality. And there is none of the black-minded fury of the Gaelic tradition, where the power of the poet's words are such that they can bring blisters to a man's face. The tone in Clarke's satires by contrast is one of careful, even lucid, questioning and description. Contemporary follies are less flayed and laid bare for horrified inspection than presented for commonsensical examination, as the victims of society's ills are afforded quiet pity, a compassion that is all the more convincing for its lack of stridency. Some of the time these poems scarcely earn their keep as satires at all. Clarke himself in fact adverted to this lack of bite when he wrote in a note to *Too Great a Vine*, the second series of *Poems and Satires* which he published in 1957: 'In their notices of *Ancient Lights: Poems and Satires, First Series*, a few critics suggested that some of the pieces were too mild to be called satires. I hope I have made amends.'[3]

In the second and third series of satires, he does to some extent. There is more anger than in the first; the tone also at times achieves the satirist's lofty disdain for the objects of his invective, as in 'Abbey Theatre Fire'. In this poem the Yeatsian occasion provokes the Yeatsian tone, that of the Yeats of 'September 1913', 'Paudeen' and 'To a Shade'. And there are, too, bitter satiric squibs, as in 'Irish Mother':

> 'My son will burn in the Pit,'
> She thought. Making his bed
> And glancing under it:
> 'He slept last night,' she said.

The rather better-known 'Irish-American Dignitary' is in the same mould, as is 'Intercessors', both combining contemporary reference with satiric comment. But the controlling mood is expository even when the level of indignation rises. The tone remains descriptive, compassionate, wry; sometimes, to use Clarke's own word, it seems unduly 'mild', preparing us for the rather journalistic procedures of the later poetic manner, where he can appear like a tedious editorializer with a few over-active bees in his bonnet. It's as if nothing can happen without the

Templeogue chronicler recording an opinion.

The topics of his poetic commentary are predictable enough: the sexual oppressiveness of an inhibited religion; the miseries of virginity and of too-fertile marriage; the indignity of procreation where fear rules in the absence of contraception; the power of a middle-class Church with its indifference to the poor; sectarianism in what to all intents and purposes is a confessional state; theological casuistry, which can allow nuns to take the pill when faced by possible rape in the Congo while denying family-planning facilities to mothers whose lives are threatened in child-birth; suburban sprawl; *nouveau riche* pretensions; the consumerist temptations of the Common Market. It all amounts to a rather depressing picture of a society where politicians lack even the compulsive energy of true corruption and kow-tow to a Church which averts its gaze from reality where

> We destroy
> Families, bereave the unemployed.
>
> ('A Simple Tale')

It's easy to make too little of this aspect of Clarke's career; the fact that many of the things about which he berated his society are now part of conventional liberal opinion or on the reformer's agenda tends to make us take for granted the poet who kept resolutely on as a social critic when he was almost a lone voice, or when others had wearied at their posts. Poetically, though, there was a price to pay. In Denis Donoghue's words: 'As a "local complainer" he was tireless and therefore tiresome. Thank God he was a poet too.'[4]

But both his complaint and his poetry are the most obvious expression of a sensibility grounded in a satirist's sense of things. And I believe Clarke's poetic vision must be so identified, despite moments of controlled lyricism (such as the well-known 'The Planter's Daughter' or his equally familiar Ossianic version of 'The Blackbird of Derrycairn') and despite the absence of some of the aspects we most readily associate with satire – personal lampoons, vituperation and savage anger (indeed when Clarke does rarely attempt savagery he can seem simply silly, or peevish, or unpleasantly ill-natured, as in 'Living in Sin').

Clarke's imagination is a satiric imagination in as much as he possesses an ineradicable sense of margin and centre, and a conviction that the poet's proper location is at the margin, utilizing

133

his art as a subversive instrument. Whether this controlling assumption in Clarke's poetic derives from his own experience of marginalization or was a matter of his basic nature, it is the settled conviction from which his art proceeds. Indeed he seems to require a centre to allow him the peripheral role in which he feels most artistically at ease. In his poety that centre is of course the Irish Catholic Church, whose doctrines, authority and dominance of the state, deny the possibility of that very marginality, which the poet assumes as his prerogative. As centre it must seek to achieve hegemony, to totalize, to deny that reality can exist outside its purview. By contrast, and in subversive opposition, the poet as satirist proposes a version of life which offers marginality as the truest mode of being.

There is something of this understanding of the nature of the satiric imagination in the origin of the word 'satire' itself. The Latin word *satura* is derivative of *satur*, meaning 'full, a "medley", full of different things' (*Oxford Classical Dictionary*); a mixed stuffing with which one might fill a sausage (indeed *satura* was used to denote just such a stuffing in the kitchen). Now what usually gets put into a stuffing are left-overs, bits and pieces, mixed ingredients of marginal culinary worth. And sometimes it is wise not to inquire too closely what a sausage contains. For to do so would be to realize how curious are the facts of human appetite and consumption, how much we are intimate with offal, left-overs, fleshy organs of beast, bits and pieces of dead creatures, all things we normally like to relegate to the margins of our awareness as we eat. Satire as a mixture of coarse humour, colloquial language, ironic wit, personal statement and familiar topicality is the literary equivalent of such culinary scavenging.[5]

Clarke, in his medley of poetic perceptions, his mixed stuffing of poetic ingredients, takes us to the margins of our consciousness in the same way that as poet he occupies a marginal social role. His poetic entertains aspects of human experience in ways that are not central to everyday consciousness. So he is a poet who examines sexual experience in original and oddly off-centre, subtly unconventional fashion. And while we might wish to describe him as an erotic poet it could not be in any simple sense that we might use that word. There are moments of delicate, idealistic eroticism in his work but these often co-habit with a frank acceptance of the fact that sexuality is a matter of bodies, organs, glands, secretions of various kinds. Such

134

poems as 'A Student in Paris', 'The Healing of Mis' and 'Tiresias' make this palpably evident. At moments, too, there is something of the giganticism and grotesquerie in Clarke's treatment of sex which we associate with the subversive satiric perspectives of Swift. For sexuality and exaggeration are twin allies of the satiric imagination:

> Our crookshank godlet –
> Shows what he has in store with nod and tod.
> From temple steps, along a marble pavement,
> Processions hymning under tilt of tower,
> To forest worship, bear a gigantic dildo
> Carven in ebony.

('From A Diary of Dreams')

Elsewhere it is the delight of the body which he emphasizes, but it is the body as a delicious marginality that he celebrates, the body as compact of things which we normally don't allow at the centre of our consciousness, in our sense of ourselves. In a poem like one of Clarke's 'Eighteenth Century Harp Songs' (free variations on Gaelic songs by Turlough O'Carolan), the exquisite 'Mabel Kelly' is more than an elegant erotic tribute to a desirable young woman; rather it highlights how in erotic experience customary modes of bodily and mental awareness are subverted. Normally we think of ourselves as beings for whom mind is the central and controlling power. In sexual desire we become aware of the other as body in quite surprising and even sometimes shocking ways (and in what we call normal social intercourse we scarcely ever look at each other in any really intimate way). The first stanza of 'Mabel Kelly' observes a young woman in an apparently conventional fashion, as the poet imagines the joys which await a fortunate husband. Hair is unplaited, breasts released; but the celebration of Mabel's beauty from 'dimple to toe-nail' is an odd touch. For the toe-nail is infrequently an object of erotic attention in the more conventional of literary sexual occasions. And a toe-nail seems curiously separate from a person as normally perceived. Oddly marginal. So the poem subtly suggests in its progression, as it oscillates between conventional tropes of sexual desire and strangely unexpected perspectives, how in desire what we feel marginal or peripheral to ourselves becomes central to an act of attention. In stanza three the poet advises:

> Gone now are many Irish ladies
> Who kissed and fondled, their very pet-names
> Forgotten, their tibia degraded.

The introduction of the medical and scientific term here is distinctly unsettling, as it reminds of the fact that the body which is so desired in sexual longing is made up of various detachable parts (the fact, too, that there is a scholarly game being played is also a shade unnerving, for a tibia is also a kind of ancient flute, fashioned from an animal's leg-bone, an association of satiric impact in a poem which exploits musical metaphors). Such a perspective suddenly alerts us to the fact that the erotic moment and the satirist's perception of the human body are closely related. It would take only a twist of syntax or a trick of diction in the final stanza to transform an erotic celebration into something reminiscent of Swift's 'A Beautiful Young Nymph Going to Bed'. And the presence in the mind of such things as toe-nails and tibia keeps that possibility open, even at the moment of transport:

> No man who sees her
> Will feel uneasy.
> He goes his way, head high, however tired.
> Lamp loses light
> When placed beside her
> She is the pearl and being of all Ireland.
> Foot, hand, eye, mouth, breast, thigh and instep, all that we desire.
> Tresses that pass small curls as if to touch the ground;
> So many prizes
> Are not divided
> Her beauty is her own and she is not proud.

Such perception undermines normal consciousness and one senses that Clarke is recruiting the erotic principle, with its disordering perspectives, to subvert what authority would wish to maintain. As he has it in another of the harp songs, 'A lawless dream comes to me in the night-time'.

The same process is at work, too, in those poems where Clarke introduces cloacal matters to his verses. The digestive and excretory functions of the human body are of course grist to the satirist's mill (Pope, Swift and Rabelais were all notable taxonomists of privy matters). And such literary exploitation of bodily processes, like the attentiveness to our sexuality, involves an awareness of the strangely peripheral and marginal aspects of human existence. As bodies we defecate, urinate, bleed, give off scales of skin, hairs, nail-clippings, vomit, semen, ear-wax, saliva, sputum, smegma, sweat, none of which we associate fully or readily with our essential selves. It is as if this human waste exists at the very edge of our consciousness, beyond even our awareness of flesh, bone and soft tissues, which constitutes a fundamental aspect of our existence. The satirist with his cloacal awareness and preccupation with bodily processes makes such things central to his vision. And he accordingly disrupts our conventional sense of ourselves as social, intellectual and spiritual beings, who would like to suppose that such things can be kept in their place. Clarke invokes Swift as his master on the exploration of this subversive poetic territory. In 'A Sermon on Swift' the great Dean's blessing allows him to summon 'Our Lady of Filth, Cloacina, soiled goddess / of paven sewers' to assist his labours. But his own poetry shows that in his peculiar, quiet, scholarly way he had made his own studies of the facts and the language of bodily processes.

'Martha Blake at Fifty-one' is perhaps the most telling occasion on which Clarke sets the variousness and copiousness of bodily functions against the controlling forces of piety and a repressive belief system. This remarkable poem recounts the pitiful story of an Irish cousin of Auden's Miss Gee, but where Auden subjected his pious Church of England spinster to a degrading pathological examination which denied her dignity more than it indicted the repressive exploitation which she had suffered, Clarke makes the physical sufferings of Martha Blake central to the poem, itemizing them with unrelentingly diagnostic, yet compassionate, accuracy. Language enacts indigestion, flatulence and diarrhea as realities, in the face of which the claims of religion and of pious authority seem simply impertinent and fantastic:

> She suffered from dropped stomach, heartburn
> Scalding, water-brash
> And when she brought her wind up, turning
> Red with the weight of mashed
> Potato, mint could not relieve her.
> In vain her many belches,
> For all below was swelling, heaving
> Wamble, gurgle, squealch.

> She lay on the sofa with legs up,
>   A decade on her lip,
> At four o'clock, taking a cup
>   Of lukewarm water, sip
> By sip, but still her daily food
>   Repeated and the bile
> Tormented her. In a blue hood
>   The Virgin sadly smiled.

Through the poem images of her narrow piety are overwhelmed by the experience of pain, with its sweat, phlegm, palpitations, soiled sheets, purgatives, toilet, bed-pan, greasy food, eructation, until:

> Unpitied, wasting with diarrhea
>   And the constant strain,
> Poor Child of Mary with one idea,
>   She ruptured a small vein,
>   Bled inwardly to jazz.

A similar fusion of compassion and unsentimental accuracy of observation is at work, too, in 'Mnemosyne Lay in Dust' a poem that takes us to the margins of society and confronts us with unthinkable truths about human experience. For in the mad-house the satirist encounters images of the mortal conditon that it seems wise in normal life to relegate to the farthest reaches of consciousness. The mad-house and the gaol, where society incarcerates its victims and villains, contain compelling imagery of subversive marginality, and in 'Mnemosyne Lay in Dust', Clarke's account of mental breakdown and recovery in St Patrick's Hospital in Dublin, that imagery is one where the physical life of the body is overwhelmingly noxious. In the hospital Swift founded 'for fools and mad' the distressed Maurice Devane endures extremities of physical loathsomeness that are Swiftian in their precise intensity. The material world becomes alien to the body, the body alien to the mind in a universe where the image of God has died in human kind:

> Poor Mr Prunty had one fault
> In bed. Nightly he defecated.
> Warder great-handed, unbolted his vault,
> Swept sheet and blanket off in a rage
> At 'Murder! Murder!' dragged the body
> Naked along the corridor.

> Trembling beneath the piled-up bedclothes,
> Maurice could hear bath-water pouring.

> Far doors were opening, closing
> Again. The corpse was clumping back.
> The warder stuck it on the close-stool,
> Laid out clean pair of sheets and blanket.
> Soon Maurice waited for his turn,
> Whenever he wet the bed; sodden
> Sheets pulled off, the warder called him 'Dogsbody',
> Christened his ankles with the key-bunch.

This is a world where words like 'spew', 'shent', 'rack', 'prick', 'chill', 'spill', 'shriek', 'drag', 'pissed', 'dribble', 'yard', 'cock', in their unremitting reductionism, insist on the undeniable physicality of existence in a way which undermines human pretension. At the end of the work the reader is left with a chastened sense of the fragility of awareness, of the way consciousness itself can be set at nought and reason brought low. The poem enforces the essentially Swiftian lesson that Man is less a reasonable creature than one capable of reason when the circumstances permit. And it is to this bleak truth that Clarke bears witness from the edges of human experience in 'Mnemosyne Lay in Dust'.

There is, too, a satiric quality in the kind of language which Clarke habitually employs. The way Clarke exploits the punning possibilities of words reveals the essentially satiric nature of his sensibility. For his characteristically learned pleasure in the way words suggest two meanings from one sound in a pun, highlights his sense of how the world is composed of centres and margins, authorities and subversive peripheral facts. Denis Donoghue alerts us to the significance of such linguistic ploys in Clarke's verse when he notes:

Homonyms are crucial in Clarke's poetry because he loves to find one sound releasing two words; all the better if one word stays at home and obeys the rules while the other one runs wild and makes love upon whim and desire. This points to the dominant motif in Clarke's work, the life of freedom and impulse set against the law of institutions.[6]

The very language, it seems, disallows what all authorities would wish – that words should have one meaning and one meaning alone. For it is always possible that at the edge of one meaning waits another subversive thought undermining the language as an instrument of control. And, as Donoghue points out, a poem as a whole can function like a homonym, one meaning being shadowed by a second which subverts the first in a carnival of clerkly satiric irreverence:

> Burn Ovid with the rest. Lovers will find
> A hedge-school for themselves and learn by heart
> All that the clergy banish from the mind,
> When hands are joined and head bows in the dark. ——

('Penal Law')

Here the double meaning of the final line is like a word which subverts its own meaning. The centre cannot hold. And the satirist makes us glad of it.

NOTES

1. Pat Rogers, *The Augustan Vision* (London 1978), p. 171. Declan Kiberd in an unpublished article draws many interesting comparisons between eighteenth-century English and Gaelic literature.
2. For a study of Clarke which treats Clarke as a classicist, see G. Craig Tapping, *Austin Clarke: A Study of His Writing* (Dublin 1981). In a note to his *Later Poems*, which he published in 1961, Clarke remembered that the future of the country had seemed hopeful when, in exile, he wrote the poems in *Pilgrimage*. By the time the book was published Clarke had involved himself in the ineffective opposition to the Censorship Bill and the future must have seemed more problematic.
3. Austin Clarke, *Collected Poems* (Dublin 1974), p. 549.
4. Denis Donoghue, 'Austin Clarke' in *We Irish* (Brighton 1986), p. 245.
5. I am significantly indebted in my understanding of satire in general to a remarkable series of lectures on the subject delivered by Dr Valentine Cunningham of Oxford University and by Professor Rawson of Yale University at the annual meeting of the Brazilian Association of University Teachers of English in February 1988.
6. Denis Donoghue, *op. cit.*, p. 248.

10

GEOFFREY TAYLOR: A PORTRAIT

In the second volume of Frank O'Connor's autobiography, *My Father's Son*, there is a remarkable portrait of the young Geoffrey Phibbs who, O'Connor tells us, 'loved poetry as no one else I have ever known loved it, and he rapidly turned me from a reader of anthologies into a reader of poetry – a very different thing'. For the young O'Connor, Phibbs, apparently, represented the very epitome of the iconoclastic avant-garde poet whose disregard for orthodoxies of all kinds was a necessary condition of true poetic inspiration:

When he was self-conscious, as he usually was for the first quarter of an hour, particularly if there was someone else in the room, he was stiff, curt and mechanical; but when he relaxed he had all the grace of a thoroughbred. The long lanky hair hung over one eye; the thin lips softened, and you saw the thick, sensual lips of the poet, and he paced round the room with his hands in his trousers pockets, bubbling with boyish laughter. Later, when I read Proust, I knew exactly what Saint-Loup must have looked like.

And Phibbs certainly obliged in providing colour, vitality, recklessness, providing in fact what O'Connor as a youth from Cork clearly took to be an object lesson in the ways of Bohemia, a liberating glimpse of a life lived for poetry's sake alone. Poetry was to remain Geoffrey Taylor's ruling passion throughout his life.

Geoffrey Taylor was born Geoffrey Phibbs in 1900, the eldest son of Basil Phibbs and Rebekah Wilbraham Taylor. His was a Co. Sligo Anglo-Irish family on his father's side. His mother was English. Phibbs' early experience was that typical of his class. An idylically happy childhood spent mostly in the company of his mother and of his English nurse (who began his instruction in natural history) gave way to unhappy schooldays in England, first at a preparatory school and then at his public school, Haileybury. At his preparatory school the boy's interest in science and natural history (possibly inherited from his great-grandmother Maunsell, who had been an enthusiastic amateur geologist*) was encouraged by a Welsh master, himself an ornithologist and antiquary. An introduction to the science of archaeology bore worthwhile fruit when in 1914 his father inheritied Lisheen, the family home, and Geoffrey discovered some prehistoric remains on the estate. It was in the house at Lisheen, in his grandfather's library, with his great-grand-mother's collection of fossils to hand, that Taylor's later intellectual interests began to form. Amidst many volumes of forgotten Victorian pieties (his grandfather had been a Plymouth Brother) were books which addressed themselves from the theologicial viewpoint to the challenge of Darwinism. 'I was confronted with the opinions of Darwin, Tyndall, Spencer, and Huxley at second hand, as they appeared to outraged or frightened or bewildered clergymen whose defence of orthodoxy, not over-skilful, did nothing so much as to sow seeds of doubt in an adolescently impressionable mind.' So Taylor became a convinced Darwinian, an enthusiastic convert to 'a crude, but so far as I could see an unanswerable materialist gospel'.

Taylor was reasonably fortunate in his public school for there two of his masters encouraged his interests in natural history and the life sciences. One master, F. W. Headley, published a book on evolution and an important work on ornithology, *The Flight of Birds*. In the nearby gravel pits 'exposing strata of the late Tertiary period', Taylor explored the mysteries of fossils, and minerals with their intimations of geological time spans, confirming the boy's increasingly truculent dismissal of orthodox religious faith.

* 'In her younger days she had been a rather remarkable and intelligent woman. She was, among other things, an enthusiastic geologist, and she made a collection of minerals and fossils – mostly, I should think, obtained on her travels abroad – of which she compiled a careful catalogue, written with a crow quill and tied with green tape; she also bought and read all the important geological books of the period.' Unpublished autobiographical fragment, 'A Natural History'. I am most grateful to Mrs Mary Taylor who generously gave me access to Geoffrey Taylor's unpublished poems and papers. I am also grateful for her thoughtful criticism and advice.

Upon leaving school, Taylor (still Geoffrey Phibbs) was packed off to an Officer's Training Corps attached to Queen's University, Belfast, where he insisted on bringing a copy of Shelley's verses on parade. He returned to Sligo, without seeing any action, as soon as the Armistice was signed in 1918. It was about this time that his interest in things scientific began to take second place to his developing passion for poetry.

A.E. published a number of Taylor's earliest poems in *The Irish Statesman*. These were written while he was at the Royal College of Science in Dublin, where he began a brief career as a scientific demonstrator. When that institution closed he worked as an organizer for the Carnegie Libraries under Sir Horace Plunkett (his immediate superior being Lennox Robinson). He was Frank O'Connor's immediate superior in Co. Wicklow at this time, when they became close friends. He married the painter Norah McGuinness in 1924.

Taylor's earliest poems were mellifluous exercises in a Romantic mode, idealistic and superficial, but he quickly turned, in a manner A.E. may well have found alarming, to cynical fantasies, bravura extravaganzas in a precocious, self-indulgent manner. The Hogarth Press published two collections of his verse in the 1920s. The first, *The Withering of the Fig Leaf*, was published in 1927, the second, *It Was Not Jones*, in 1928. Taylor made efforts to have the first volume withdrawn from publication, and the second was published under the pseudonym 'R. Fitzurse'. Later he himself categorized the two books as 'in their way typical of the notorious nineteen-twenties outlook. They were witty and cynical in an undergraduate mode, their symbolism perverse and their technique licentious'. Taylor came to dislike their contents very much, but Samuel Beckett insisted in 1934 that he had in fact 'performed a very diverting ballet away from the pundits'. And despite the poetry's obvious faults (too many coterie witticisms, too little verbal control in all the high-jinks) there is an energy, a tone of delicious disrespect, a fine aristocratic explosive rudeness in these books which set them apart from the poetry being often so earnestly composed in 1920s Ireland. And from time to time a genuine note of actual personal experience enters to disturb the avant-garde display of sequined modishness. Such is 'Late October' in *The Withering of the Fig Leaf* (is it the first Irish poem to treat unselfconsciously of a car journey?):

At Glencullen all the beech trees were golden
And crossing the Scalp a cold wind followed us;
Again at the Glen-of-the-Downs all the beech
trees were golden
And one willow tree an apollonian shower of gold,
One poplar tree a brazen caryatid;
And in the glen, spanning the road gleaming
silver in the sunlight,
A spider's web, and we broke it.
At Kilpeddar the wind had fallen.
It was here that the girl beside the driver
began to go mad.
The rest of the journey was night, and rain
in the night, with hardly
anywhere a star.

In 1928, when Taylor's marriage broke up, he left Ireland to settle for a time in London. There he met Nancy Nicholson, daughter of the painter Sir William Nicholson. With her he moved to Sutton Veney, Co. Wiltshire, where they founded and ran the Poulk Press. He had recently changed his name from Phibbs to the maternal Taylor, listing on a printed card two reasons: 'General Dislike' and 'Particular Dislike'. There was a brief foray to teach English in Cairo, but he offended a local dignitary there and so his teaching career was stillborn. It was to Cairo that A.E. wrote in reply to one of Phibbs's letters:

The objectionate 'Superior Race' attitude you refer to is not because you are white but because you are Geoffrey Phibbs and it is innate in you. You have been superior to Yeats, myself and everybody else you talked to, not in any objectionable way, but it is quite innate.

To have been superior to Senator Yeats represents quite an achievement.

So in 1930, at thirty years of age, Taylor had two volumes of verse behind him; he had published in the avant-garde pages of *transition* in Paris; he had changed his name, had been married and had ceased to be married. He settled in Wiltshire and in the countryside there turned again, dissatisfied with his verse, to his amateur interest in natural history. He slowly began to combine his love of the countryside and the natural kingdom with his ruling passion for poetry, now sensing that

A love of poetry adds something to an eye trained in observation, and

an accurate eye contributes something to the least as to the most penetrating poetic vision. A naturalist who is also a poet, or a poet who is
also a naturalist, will get more than he who is only one or the other,
by the sight of spring flowers and butterflies above six inches of extraordinary snow in May, by the bowing down of Lombardy poplars into
giant fern-shapes under the weight of frozen sleet, by a Kingfisher
crossing a snowy field in January.

He became aware of the poets associated with the Wiltshire landscape and involved with the broad ranges and forgotten valleys
of English landscape-poetry.

At the same time his sense of life began to alter as his temperamental iconoclasm waned to be replaced by a chastened sense
of the natural mystical tradition and of the limits of human
knowledge. '*The Prelude* had come to take the place of *The Origin
of Species* as the most influential of books.' Life was happy and
busy. There was study and printing work; there were trips to
France and adventures with William Nicholson; there were
friends and the poems which now were alive to the natural
world about him:

> On a brittle morning;
> Smell of nasturtium leaves in passing gardens.
> The which bright beam unhardens,
> Brushed bruised crushed
> By fierce first white frost.
> Peace past, war raged, war lost;
> All the warm synthesis undone,
> Cold, cold the analysis begun.
>> Fair and fragile the friend that undeceives
>> Hope of a thousand green nasturtium leaves.
>>> ('Frost Came')

This was an important period in Taylor's life. He began to put
the traumatic experiences of his twenties behind him. His
relationship with the Nicholson family was enhancing and
stimulating. It was also the period in Taylor's life when he read
widely and deeply in English poetry. He had always been an
avid reader of poetry but now in the calm of the countryside his
taste became catholic and his sensibility attuned to minor as well
as to major work. So when he returned to Ireland in 1940 with
his wife and child (he had married Mary Dillwyn in 1935) it was
entirely appropriate that he soon became the poetry editor of

The Bell, the new cultural and literary journal Seán O Faoláin had begun to edit in 1940.

Taylor's first family home in Dublin was Airton House, Tallaght, which he rented for six years, and it was while living there that he became acquainted with John Betjeman, who was in Dublin as the British press attaché (though the title lapsed due to Betjeman's dislike of it) for the duration of the war. It was a fortunate friendship for both men, since, with their attachment to the English countryside and their devotion to the highways and especially the byways of the English poetic tradition, they were highly congenial company for one another. Indeed their association was to result in two anthologies: *English, Scottish and Welsh Landscape Verse* (1944) and *English Love Poetry* (1957). It is an interesting speculation (for which I am indebted to Mr John Jordan) that Austin Clarke may have come upon William Allingham's verse on the Surrey landscape in their first collaborative volume, which influenced his own long topographical poem 'Beyond the Pale' (published in *Flight to Africa*, 1963). Taylor would certainly have been pleased by such a possibility, for he often regretted that there was so little natural history and topographical poetry of the Irish landscape in the Irish poetic tradition. He himself attempted to fill the gap, publishing such poems as 'Boat-Haven, Co. Mayo', and 'Memory of a Ruin', descriptions of an Irish house and a ruin in their landscapes, poems in an essentially English mode set in Ireland with Irish subject matter:

> That house a stone's throw from the shell-strewn shore,
> Now nearly swallowed by encroaching trees
> That creep upon it from the hill behind,
> Itself a shell like any of these, gaping
> And broken but still beautiful, was built
> By smuggler Jordan in seventeen-twenty or so
>   Gable and wings towards the crimpled sea,
> With vacant door and window, yet look out
> Through unkempt hair of overgrowth – The door
> And lower windows all but blocked by nettles –
> In the spare sunlight and tart air of autumn
> What once were lawns remain like lawn, kept clipt
> By sandhill-warrened rabbits, to high tide,
> While of the garden, one exotic fig-tree
> Still struggles strangled by black-fruited brambles.
>   (from 'Boat-Haven, Co. Mayo')

Taylor spent the rest of his days in Ireland (he died in 1956). This was a full, stimulating time in Taylor's life, fifteen years of reading, writing reviews, critical essays for *The Bell*, and editing poetry, preparing articles and occasional broadcasts on natural history and, in his last two years, acting as poetry editor for *Time and Tide*. From these years also came his books on British insects and on English nineteeth-century gardeners, *The Victorian Flower Garden* (now a collector's item) and his anthology *Irish Poets of the Nineteeth Century* (published in 1952). This last volume is perhaps Taylor's most significant published literary work. His deep interest in minor verse of the past allowed him to select a substantial body of poetry from forgotten or neglected Irish poets. His selections from Mangan, Allingham, Ferguson and lesser figures are useful, while his introductory remarks to each of the selected poets are uniformly judicious. He appreciates his poets' weaknesses but he has an exact eye for their strengths, their overlooked successes.

In 1946 the Taylor household moved to another house, Hilton in Ballinteer. At Hilton Taylor set to work restoring the garden, applying his knowledge of gardening traditions while his home became a retreat for numbers of Irish poets and writers in a post-war Dublin where there was precious little patronage offered to the aspiring poet. John Hewitt and W. R. Rodgers have each testi-fied to the encouragement they received from Taylor in his home where poetry was assumed to be life's most serious yet delight-ful activity. In his editing, both for *The Bell* and later for *Time and Tide*, Taylor spent many hours replying to poets well-known and unknown, hinting occasionally at possible improvements, often writing lengthy words of advice and encouragement to new writers whose work as yet did not merit publication. Under-lying all these letters, which represent a contribution to literary history of a kind which so often goes uncelebrated, is a tone of zestful, exuberant certainty that poetry is not only its moments of great utterance but also the miniature, the delicate, the witty and epigrammatic, the accomplished, the refined and humor-ous. It is a sense that without a rich compost of minor verse a culture will not nourish the earth in which large talents can flourish.

It is this belief that the apparently insignificant, the forgotten, the superceded, the unsuccessful, are important that underlay much of Taylor's life. One senses that it was this temperamental distaste for a vision of life which stressed the necessity for the survival of the fittest that accounts for his eventual antipathy for Darwinian evolutionism which he attacked in articles in *The Bell* and the *Catholic Review*, opposition to which in his later years he took quite seriously. As an amateur scientist he found much to suspect in the philosophic and scientific assertions of the evolutionary humanists; as a man he felt a real regret and respect for vanished species, including eighteenth-century poet-parsons. One of Taylor's unpublished poems, 'Earl and Frogs', touches this centre of feeling with a genuine note. A mode of life and artifice is at an end. The manner is fabulous, the regret real.

> An old earl sat in a moated grange and played
> All day long on a single note
> With such incredible sadness that he made
> The frogs weep in the moated grange's moat.
>
> And between sunset and moonrise he began to sing
> How of all the illustrious and all the noble
> With their crowns in encrusted clusters and
>   their little cloaks of sable
> He was alas the last, and this was a melancholy thing.
>
> Thus hearing him the frogs on the waterlilies wept
> So greatly at his misery that water grew
>   and crept
> Up the high embattled walls and filled the
>   little room
> Where the old earl played, singing in finality
>   of gloom.

One would not wish, however, to create the impression that Geoffrey Taylor, custodian of the byways of the English poetic tradition and anti-Darwinian, was himself a nostalgic exile from the contemporary world. There was much in it that displeased, indeed disgusted him, but Taylor had a great zest for everyday experience, a sensibility alive to the sensuous immediacy of the world about him. He was responsive, indeed possibly hyper-sensitive, to physical and emotional states, to the particulars of countryside and city.

From time to time Taylor allowed this aspect of his sensibility free-rein and produced first-rate mood pieces, poems actively involved in the texture and tone of the world about him. Such is 'Black-Out':

> A crowd of people in the morning street,
> Here shuffling slowly, stopping there to gaze
> Through the shop window and slow passing on;
> Some hastening out along their various ways,
> Some meeting friends with a well-feigned surprise
> Chaos of talk; small newsboy's piercing cries;
> The hum of tram cars and of motor cars;
> The rattle and the clangour of iron wheels;
> The metalled, measured beat
> Upon the cobble stones of horses feet
> Till hardly the brain feels
> And fades the mind –
> Then suddenly gone the sunlight and the city;
> All round
> Old mountains with their cataclysmal scars;
> A wood park-hung with mystery;
> No sound
> But the uneasy breathing of the wind:
> And in the sky such cold terrific stars.

Taylor was aware of the contemporary world in a further, more important way. He sensed the importance of science in twentieth-century culture. Indeed his attacks on evolutionism were efforts to counteract what he considered were certain malign aspects of science's influence on modern culture. But he was no simplistic Luddite. His essays and his criticism are woven through with analogies and metaphors from scientific thought and there are attempts to employ scientific matter in his own poetry. He clearly felt that a modern poet might well be expected to help absorb scientific and technological ways of thought into the mainstream of literary culture. 'The Graph' is a moderately successful example of one of these:

> This is how the matter stands so it appears:
> Two thousand, ten thousand years
> The wheels have been in placing,
> The spring in the winding:
> No achievement, but
> Now a dark achieving of
> A new potential to achieve,
> Achievement's chance.
> Now, as we understand, spring fully wound,
> Must expand, scattering
> All gathered history

149

To unnamed fragments of nostalgia, or
Begin to turn the wheels, drive wheels round,
(Here, gentlemen, the graph at length leaves ground)
It is a question of how to engage the gears
Or so as the matter stands, still it appears.

The difficulty about taking metaphors from science, is , as is evident even from this comparatively simple piece, that such metaphors do not have readily accessible deposits of evocation and resonance lodged to their credit. They will tend towards the abstract, the conceptually particular, lacking general emotional significance.

Abstraction was one of Taylor's weaknesses as a poet. His gifts were for baroque choreography, for simple lyrical verse movement, for the accurate observation of the physical world. But he couldn't often leave well enough alone. No editor could have been more open to the virtues of minor verse, but as a poet he seemed unable to accept for himself the minor gifts of the muse. He was poetically ambitious beyond those gifts.

For the biographer and the critic Taylor's relationship to poetry, his large ambitions, represent a central problem. Undoubtedly he was convinced of the absolute superiority of the poetic life over any other. It seems that he took the decision to be a poet early on and that a sense of himself as poet remained with him to the end. It was a basic ingredient of his self-understanding and yet there are no published collections after his thirtieth year and precious few poems in the journals. An easy solution of this puzzle would be to suggest that for the young Phibbs poetry provided a bohemian escape route from the confines of a family background, with its expectations of a conventional career of one kind or another, that he found distasteful. Many a young man of his class has affected the arts in his twenties before settling for something more humdrum later on. But Taylor kept writing into middle-age, when he died, with an evident seriousness of purpose and discipline that would belie such a simplistic thesis. He believed implicitly in poetry, finding deep satisfaction in his editing responsibilities, relishing the discovery of new or overlooked talent, taking great personal pleasure in the act of writing his own poems.

He chose, however, not to involve himself much, in the way many poets must, in the business of publication either in the

150

journals or in volume form. Perhaps he feared that the process of seeking editorial support, the attention of the public eye, would threaten an independence that he valued second only to the art of poetry itself. Be that as it may, the absence of many published poems in a career so devoted to poetry, together with the sudden untimely death, means that a certain poignancy must attend his last years when his *own* editorial work brought him such intense satisfaction. And that just before he died he had accepted the poetry editorship of *The Listener* in London, makes that sense of the poignant irresistible.

Throughout his life Taylor wrote many, many poems, but a sad number of them fail because too weighty abstractions, too self-conscious an interest in content, drown out the inevitable music which true poetry must possess. Yet many individual lines, stanzas and images, and often enough complete poems, reveal a vital talent, whose contribution as a poet to Irish letters demands judicious selection to allow it its due.

So in the absence of a *Selected Poems*, we must remember him in the brilliant O'Connor impression of the poet as a young man, in the lyrical Nicholson portrait; we must remember him as editor, bibliophile, gardener, naturalist, host and man of letters whose encouragement meant much to the young poets with whom he talked and corresponded. We must remember him as a minor figure in Irish literary history akin to those English poet-parson-naturalists of the eighteenth century for whom he felt such sympathy; and as poetry editor of *The Bell* who played a small but crucial role in the history of modern Irish poetry.

11

C. S. LEWIS: IRISHMAN?

On 23 May 1918 a young Ulsterman, recovering from war wounds in Liverpool Merchants Mobile Hospital in Étaples, France, wrote to a friend back in his native Belfast. He had been hit by the shrapnel of an English shell which had exploded behind him at the battle of Arras and his service with the Somerset Light Infantry had come to an abrupt end. His letter home tells of a bomb attack on the hospital and concludes with a poem entitled 'Song'. This is a slight piece of Georgian fancy which suggests that the author had not allowed the experience of the front to invade his art in the way it had the work of his better-known poetic contemporaries, Wilfred Owen and Siegfried Sassoon.

> Fairies must be in the woods
> Or the satyr's merry broods,
> Tritons in the summer sea,
> Else how could the dead things be
> Half so lovely as they are?
> How could wreathed star on star
> Dusted o'er the wintry night,
> Fill thy spirit with delight
> And lead thee from this care of thine
> Through a land of dreams divine
> To the dearest heart's desire,
> Unless each pale and drifting fire
> Were indeed a happy isle
> Where eternal gardens smile
> And the golden globes of fruit are seen
> Twinkling thro' orchards green
> Where the Other People go
> On the soft sward to and fro?[1]

152

But what such a poem, which was to appear in rewritten form in the poet's first volume, *Spirits in Bondage*, published in 1919, also suggests, with its fairy folk and land of heart's desire, is that the young soldier had been reading his Yeats. As indeed he had. For the young Clive Staples Lewis (later to be known to the world as C. S. and always addressed by his family as Jack) had read Yeats with excitement since his schooldays and was surely stimulated in his desire to be a poet by the work of his elder compatriot.

C. S. Lewis, of course, was never to achieve any real fame as a poet, even though he published two volumes as a young man and continued to write occasional verses through his career as a distinguished mediaeval scholar, fantasist and Christian apologist. His poetic ambitions, seriously nurtured in his young manhood, went underground in the same way as one might be tempted to see his nationality being suppressed in an adulthood in which he seemed to many the quintessential English don of his generation, so at home in Oxford as to seem a manifestation of its spirit. 'Going native' in England in one way or another is always a ready possibility for the Ulsterman or woman who finds the local northern Irish environment stifling or restrictive. We are perhaps more used to that variety of Ulsterman, like George Russell or James Cousins, who finds protective colouration in the various shades of Irish nationalism than in the bolder hues of English conservatism, just as we are familiar with Irishmen like O'Casey, James Stephens, even Shaw himself, who make England their home without ever abandoning their Irish distinctiveness. Absorption, to a greater or lesser extent, into the life of the neighbouring island has always been a possibility for the northern Protestant who seeks broader horizons than those offered by his native province. And it has been so since the Unionist north of Ireland affords straightforward access to what it conceives of as the mainland of the United Kingdom in the way Dublin and the south of Ireland, with their instinctive nationalism and separatist politics, do not. For such, however, the years of the Great War and of the rise of militant Irish nationalism presented peculiar challenges.

The Lewis family was of English and Welsh as well as Scots descent. The religion of their people was, in the main, a moderate Anglicanism. On the Lewis side the family had been industrious self-improvers, and Lewis's father had risen to the point where, as a successful solicitor, it had not been impossible for him to have won the hand of Florence Hamilton, daughter of a Church of Ireland rector, whose typically Anglo-Irish family had the customary links with aristocracy, Church and state.

Jack Lewis was reared in the suburbs of east Belfast. The family resided first in a semi-detached villa until they removed to the large Edwardian house Jack's father built and named 'Little Lea' in Strandtown, near St Mark's parish church (where his father-in-law was rector) in 1905. Jack's childhood was entirely typical for his generation and class. Indeed reading his autobiography one is struck by the similarities between his experience and that of another Ulster child who was to spend his childhood a few years later on the other side of the Belfast Lough that so entered into both their imaginations. For Lewis's *Surprised by Joy* (1955), like Louis MacNeice's *The Strings Are False* (1965), describes the isolated life of the Protestant upper-middle classes of the period, the only relief for the children from the private worlds of reverie and escapism being found in contact with the maids and nurses in whose charge they were so often left. And that both families endured the loss of a mother when the children were still young increases one's sense of parallels. Louis MacNeice's father remarried soon after his wife's death, and the new mistress of the house insisted Louis be sent to school in England, like his sister Elizabeth. ('My stepmother thought it high time she should lose her Northern accent.'[2]) One must assume some similar instinct to that which began Louis MacNeice's complex involvement with the life of the neighbouring island was at work in the Lewis household. For he was despatched to a kind of Edwardian Do-the-boys Hall in Hertfordshire in 1908. Lewis's father had been a pupil at Lurgan College and his wife had graduated in Mathematics and Logic at Queen's College in Belfast, so there does not seem to have been any family tradition of English education or disdain of local opportunity (and in due course Lewis was to spend a short time at Campbell College in Belfast, before his health seemed to counsel a change and he was sent to Malvern College). But, whatever the reason, Lewis's English education was to change the direction of his life. He has left us a memorable record of his first glimpse as an Irish child of the country in which he was to spend his entire adulthood:

No Englishman will be able to understand my first impression of England. When we disembarked, I suppose at about six next morning (but it seemed to be midnight), I found myself in a world to which I reacted with immediate hatred. The flats of Lancashire in the early morning are in reality a dismal sight: to me they were like the banks of the Styx. The strange English accents with which I was surrounded seemed like the voices of demons. But what was worst was the English landscape from Fleetwood to Euston. Even to my adult eye that main line still appears to run through the dullest and most unfriendly strip in the island. But to a child who has always lived near the sea and in the sight of high ridges it appeared as I suppose Russia might appear to an English boy. The flatness! The interminableness! The miles of featureless land, shutting one in from the sea, imprisoning, suffocating! Everything was wrong; the wooden fences instead of stone walls and hedges, red brick farmhouses instead of white cottages, the fields too big, haystacks the wrong shape. Well does the *Kalevala* say that in the stranger's house the floor is full of knots. I have made up the quarrel since; but that moment I conceived a hatred for England which took many years to heal.[3]

There was much in Lewis's subsequent experience of schooling and army life to intensify that hatred of England, before a fellowship at Oxford and the life of a don teaching English made of him the man whose Irish background scarcely obtruded upon his enlarging reputation. And indeed his association with the famous 'Inklings' club at Oxford, with members such as J. R. R. Tolkien, Owen Barfield, Charles Williams, Lord David Cecil and John Wain, and his polemical, somewhat muscular, orthodox Anglican Christianity, his archaic sense of chivalry and apolitical, essentially reactionary cast of mind, made of him in the public view a figure indisputably English, even in some respects the stereotypical Englishman of popular expectation.* One senses an untold story here of how the frightened, unhappy Ulster schoolboy became the figure he did when he might so easily have played a role in the history of modern Irish literature. For from such early alienation from an English schooling, together with the characteristic Irish distaste for the landscape and manners of England, could be born, as we know from the case of Yeats himself, an interest in things Irish of a life-determining kind.

*Witness Peter Medawar: 'C. S. Lewis was a great Englishman in an intolerant Johnsonian sort of way.' (*Memoir of a Thinking Radish*, p. 84)

As it happens we have the materials now to hand which enable us to consider in some detail how this intellectual and social pilgrimage took place, and to identify those moments when the decisive events and experiences occured which made Lewis the curious man he was. His brother Warren Lewis has edited some of his letters; we have the useful if narrowly focussed biography by Roger Lancelyn Green and Walter Hooper; and the remarkable six hundred-page volume of letters (scrupulously edited by Walter Hooper and entitled *They Stand Together*, published in 1979) which Lewis wrote throughout his life to a Belfast friend, Arthur Greeves.

Arthur Greeves was the son of a prosperous and hardworking family which long had had interests in the linen trade. Lewis always thought of him as his first true friend. He had been astonished when he met him (they were both still in their teens) that 'there do exist people very, very like oneself'.[4] The likeness, however, was one suspects only a matter of early shared interests for Greeves, who suffered from a weak constitution and a hypochondriacal disposition, was to spend almost all his days in Belfast, enjoying a life of dilettantism and artistic dabbling of a kind quite foreign to the energetic and industrious Lewis. He painted in a desultory sort of way – the portrait of his friend the Ulster novelist Forrest Reid, which hangs in Reid's Belfast school, The Royal Belfast Academic Institution (Inst.), is by his hand. Lewis in 1935 supplied a vignette of his friend which summed up his aesthetic nature as follows:

Until I met him, and during my frequent absences, his position was much the same as that of an imaginative boy in one of our public schools. Yet he never showed any inclination to revenge himself after the fashion so familiar among our modern *intelligentsia*. He continued to feel – indeed he taught me to endeavour to feel with him – at once a human affection and a rich aesthetic relish for his antedeluvian aunts, his mill-owning uncles, his mother's servants, the postman on our roads, and the cottagers whom we met in our walks. What he called the 'Homely' was the natural food both of his heart and his imagination. A bright hearth seen through an open door as we passed, a train of ducks following a brawny farmer's wife, a drill of cabbages – these were things that never failed to move him, even to an ecstasy, and he never found them incompatible with his admiration for Proust, or Wyndam Lewis, or Picasso.[5]

It was with this Ulster stray from an Arnold Bennett novel that the quickly developing C. S. Lewis shared such innermost thoughts as he was unable to communicate to his emotionally repressed and remote father and his elder brother.

What Lewis shared with Greeves in the early years of their friendship (a friendship which was to keep Lewis in touch with his native province throughout his life) was an imaginative sympathy with the Nordic mythology which Lewis found irresistible and which he associated with moments of mystic longing and a wide range of imaginative experience. His early letters to Greeves accordingly express a delighted enthusiasm in discovering someone with whom to share a taste for Wagner, William Morris, the Icelandic sagas and Malory, as well as works on the Nordic pantheon. Two things emerge from these letters and from Lewis's own account of his spiritual development in *Surprised by Joy*: that Lewis associated his sense of a 'Northern' quality in literature and myth with the Irish landscape and that he found the same inspiration in Celtic legend as he did in Nordic. In his youth and young manhood, when he aspired to be a poet, he was just the kind of Ulsterman who might have been recruited for the Literary Revival which was changing the modern literary map in Dublin. At his first encounter with Wagner he cycled round County Wicklow 'involuntarily looking for scenes that might belong to the Wagnerian world'.[6] At sixteen he was asking for a book on Celtic legend as a Christmas present (Charles Squire's *Celtic Myth and Legend*), was writing to Greeves on the derivation of the word 'Shee' and telling him, 'I am reading at present, for the second time, the Celtic plays of Yeats. I must try and get them the next time I am home.'[7] He also hoped to turn his attention to 'the composition of an Irish drama'.[8] At the same time he was confessing to his friend how much he missed the landscape of home. Soon he is comparing Sidney's *Arcadia* to James Stephens's *Crock of Gold*, and in the summer of 1917, just before he went in the autumn to join his regiment for action in France, he declared of his poetic ambitions: 'If I do ever send my stuff to a publisher, I think I shall try Maunsel, those Dublin people, and so tack myself definitely onto the Irish school.'[9] And in a subsequent letter he spelt out his attitude to Ireland and literature in some detail:

Á propos de Maunsel, you say that the patriotic motive could have no influence on me. Well perhaps that may be deserved; 'tis true I have no patriotic feeling for anything in England, except for Oxford for which I would live and die. But as to Ireland you know that none loves the hills of Down (or of Donegal) better than I: and indeed partly from an interest in Yeats and Celtic mythology, partly from a natural repulsion to noisy drum-beating, bullying Orange-men. . . . I begin to have a very warm feeling for Ireland in general. . . . Indeed, if ever I get interested in politics, I shall probably be a nationalist.[10]

A year later, wounded in action and recuperating in Bristol, a sea-change takes place in Lewis's attitude to Irish writing and Ireland. Greeves has just spent time in Dublin where he met many many interesting people on whose acquaintanceship Lewis congratulates him. He adds:

So you are inclining to the New Ireland school are you? I remember how you used rather to laugh at my Irish enthusiasm in the old days when you were still an orthodox Ulsterman. I am glad you begin to think otherwise: a poetry bookshop for Ireland, in Dublin, would be a most praise-worthy undertaking: it might bring out some monthly journal on Irish literature, containing reviews of contemporary books, articles on classical Gaelic literature and language, and a few poems and sketches. The idea is fascinating: if you could get some big man to take it up.

Here I must indulge my love of preaching by warning you not to get too much mixed up in a cult. Between your other penchant. . . and the Irish school you might get into a sort of by-way of the intellectual world off the main track and lose yourself there. Remember that all the great minds, Milton, Scott, Mozart and so on, are always sane before all and keep in the broad highway of thought and feel what can be felt by all men, not only a few. . . .

It is partly through this feeling that I have not begun by sending my MS to Maunsels: it would associate me too definitely with a cult and partly because their paper and binding are rather poor.[11]

This advice recurs through Lewis's letters to Greeves (he knew that Greeves was a closet homosexual, had an instinct for coteries and that he was inclined to nervous disorders). But there is in the earnestness of the counsel much of Lewis's own ambivalence of feeling about such matters. For these odd letters reveal that the resolute Christian moralist of later reputation in his youth was much troubled by sado-masochistic temptations and stirred by a curiosity about and attraction to the occult (the latter of which he was never entirely to lose). In his autobiography Lewis, in fact, recounts how at preparatory school what he calls 'the passion for the Occult'[12] was awakened and admits that it was something with which he had 'plenty of trouble since'[13] And later in his youth the passion became almost uncontrollable:

There is a kind of gravitation in the mind whereby good rushes to good and evil to evil. This mingled repulsion and desire drew towards them everything else in me that was bad. The idea that if there were occult knowledge it was known to the very few and scorned by the many became an added attraction. . . I was already acquainted with the more depraved side of Romanticism; had read *Anactoria* and Wilde, and pored upon Beardsley, not hitherto attracted but making no moral judgement. Now I began to see the point of it. In a word you have already had in this story the World and the Flesh; now came the Devil. If there had been in the neighbourhood some elder person who dabbled in dirt of the magical (such have a good nose for potential disciples) I might now be a Satanist or a maniac.[14]

Intriguingly, the catalyst of this stirring of the passion for the occult was the poetry of Yeats.

As we saw, Lewis was reading Yeats's 'Celtic plays' in his sixteenth year. By the time he was up at Oxford, waiting for his call-up to fight in France, he had become a convinced Yeatsian, remarking in a letter to Greeves: 'I am often surprised to find how utterly ignored Yeats is among the men I have met: perhaps his appeal is purely Irish – if so, then thank the gods that I am Irish',[15] and back in Oxford in 1919 we note him attending a meeting of a literary club named the Martlets discussing Yeats. Part of Yeats's attraction for the young Lewis was the Irish poet's magical beliefs and wizard-like powers. Indeed the Lewis who read Yeats assiduously as a schoolboy early recognized what many more mature critics failed to credit at the time: that magic was central to Yeats's poetic achievement:

Among all the poets I was reading at this time. . . there was one who stood apart from the others. Yeats was this poet. I had been reading him for quite a long time before I discovered the difference, and perhaps should never have discovered it if I had not read his prose as well (things like *Rosa Alchemica* and *Per Amica Silentia Lunae*. . . to put it quite plainly, he seriously believed in magic.[16]

And when a few years later Lewis got to meet the poet in Oxford, his early impression was confirmed and in letters to Greeves and to his brother Warren he has left us compelling pen-portraits (Lewis was skilled at such) of Yeats in full magical flight:

His house is in Broad Street: you go up a long staircase lined with pictures by Blake – chiefly the 'Book of Job' and the 'Paradise Lost' ones, which thus en masse, have a somewhat diabolical appearance. The first time I came I found a priest called Father Martindale, his wife and a little man with a grey beard who never spoke, sitting with him. It was a very funny room: the light was supplied by two candles, two of them in those six-ft candle-sticks that you see before the altar in some English churches. There were flame-coloured curtains, a great many pictures and some strange foreign-looking ornaments that I can't describe. The company sat on very hard, straight, antique chairs: except Mrs Yeats who lay on a kind of very broad divan, with bright cushions, in the window.

Yeats himself is a very big man – very tall, very fat and very broad: his face also gives one the impression of vast size. There would have been no mistaking which was THE man we had come to see, however many people had been in the room. Grey haired: about sixty years of age: clean shaven: glasses with a thick tape. His voice sounded rather French, I thought, at first, but the Irish shows through after a bit. I have seldom felt less at my ease before anyone than I did before him: I understand what the Dr Johnson atmosphere is for the first time – it was just like that, you know, we all sitting round, putting in judicious questions while the great man played with some old seals on his watch chain and talked.

The subjects of his talk, of course, were the very reverse of John-sonian: it was all of magic and apparitions. That room and that voice would make you believe anything.[17]

Lewis was sufficiently impressed by the magical Yeats to attempt a portrait of him in 'Dymer', the poem he published in 1926 under his pseudonym Clive Hamilton, and the figure of Merlin in his novel *The Hideous Strength* may have been based on the poet. But an incident occured in Lewis's life in 1923 which may account for the resolute way in which he turned away from the occult, to which he was so attracted, to a dogmatic orthodox Christianity. And in rejecting the occult he may also have been rejecting the Ireland of nationalism and literary cult for the broad safe paths of secure cultural tradition. It was Lewis's misfortune in that year to spend a fortnight in close contact with a man who went mad shortly before he died (it was at this time that he began urging Greeves to hold onto sanity in all things and to counsel him against cults – 'We hold our mental health by a thread and nothing is worth risking it for'[18]). The experience affected him profoundly, as he later acknowledged in a passage of his autobiography that explains much about the writer's conversion to orthodoxy as a kind of principle:

He was a man whom I had dearly loved, and well he deserved love. And now I helped to hold him while he kicked and wallowed on the floor, screaming out that devils were tearing him and that he was at the moment falling down into Hell. And this man, as I well knew, had not kept the beaten track. Had he not flirted with Theosophy, Yoga, Spiritualism, Psychoanalysis, what not? Probably these things had in fact no connection with his insanity, for which (I believe) there were physical causes. But it did not seem so to me at the time. I thought that I had seen a warning; it was to this, this raving on the floor, that all romantic longings led a man in the end. . . . Safety first, thought I: the beaten track, the approved road, the centre of the road, the lights on.[19]

One suspects that much in Lewis's imaginative life was repressed following this dreadful incident and his youthful flirtation with 'romantic Ireland' was probably only one of the aspects of his personality which were sacrificed to safety at this time. That his friend's madness may have had its sources in war experience (Lewis described his affliction to Greeves as 'war neurasthenia') was an added reason why the experience significantly affected Lewis. For one senses that his own memories of the horrors of war were acute. And that the war indeed may have been a further element in that complex of events, impressions and encounters which made of the young Ulsterman a curious kind of Englishman.

Warren Lewis has suggested about his brother's almost total, life-long disinterest in politics and contempt for politicians, that these may have had their source in the family home. There, as Warren records, 'Politics and money were the chief, almost the only subjects of grown-up conversation: and since no visitors came to our home who did not hold precisely the same political views as my father, what we heard was not discussion and the lively clash of minds, but rather an endless and one-sided torrent of grumble and vituperation.' And Warren concludes: 'The long-term result was to fill him with a disgust and revulsion from the very idea of politics before he was out of his teens.'[20] But before then he would nevertheless enlist in the forces of the Crown, see action in France and receive a wound in service of the King of England with the Somerset Light Infantry. Even in one disgusted by arid political discussion in his native Ulster, it is surprising that we find no direct reference to Irish political events in any of his letters in the decade in which the world went to war and Ireland asserted its right to independence in arms. In 1915 we find him writing to Greeves that it is only the possibility of letters going astray because of the 'submarine nonsense' which reminds him of the war, adding, 'Though I do not usually take much interest in the war, yet it would be unpleasantly brought home to me if I had to spend my holydays [sic] in England.'[21] By November 1916 he is sufficiently stirred by events in Ireland and the world to tell Greeves, 'it seems pretty sure that CONSCRIPTION is coming to Ireland. I for one shall be jolly glad to see some relations of mine (and some of yours) made to behave like men at last'.[22] But as the time for his own test of manhood approached there was a sign of some ambivalence of feeling about the future. In Oxford in 1917, where he was waiting for the call in the Officers' Training Corps, he made the acquaintance of an Irish nationalist (Theobold Richard Fitzwalter Butler – who was to achieve distinction as a lawyer in later years). In a letter to Greeves of 17 May he wrote:

To-day (Sunday) Butler had brekker with me and afterwards we bathed. We had a long talk on the rival merits of Keats and Swinburne, the improbability of God and Home Rule. Like all Irish people who meet in England we ended by criticisms on the invincible flippancy and dullness of the Anglo-Saxon race. After all there is no doubt, ami, that the Irish are the only people: with all their faults I would not gladly live or die among another folk.[23]

And from Plymouth in November he wrote to Greeves again, telling him that he would be in Ireland before shipping for France and would be billeted in Holywood, Co. Down, near his Belfast home. He writes, 'I now regard a Tommy whether wounded or not as an abominable sight, especially among the scenes of home.'[24] What he didn't tell Greeves was that rumours had been circulating in his regiment that they might be posted to Ireland to fight Sinn Fein or the Germans who, it was also rumoured, had landed there. So the war must have occasioned in Lewis some personal qualms. But it was in France that he was to see action and it is that experience which he recounts in *Surprised by Joy*.

His brother, and Lewis himself, both make a point of treating the effects of warfare on the young soldier/scholar rather lightly. Reading his account in the autobiography a quite different impression occurs. There we sense a diffident, bookish and shy schoolboy quickly coming to appreciate his fellow officers and the other ranks. The pain of lost friends and the tragedy of a generation sounds through these pages. And his account bespeaks trauma and alienation from experience too acute to recount in great detail.

I came to know and pity and reverence the ordinary man: particularly dear Sergeant Ayres, who was (I suppose) killed by the same shell that wounded me. I was a futile officer (they gave commissions too easily then), a puppet moved about by him, and he turned this ridiculous and painful relation into something beautiful, became to me almost like a father. But for the rest of the war – the frights, the cold, the smell of H.E., the horribly smashed men still moving like half-crushed beetles, the sitting or standing corpses, the landscape of sheer earth without a blade of grass, the boots worn day and night till they seemed to grow to your feet – all this shows rarely and faintly in my memory. It is too cut off from the rest of experience and often seems to have happened to someone else.[25]

Such writing has a numbed objectivity, an air of disassociation, which suggests experience that cannot be comprehended, which must be suppressed.

In maturity Lewis scarcely ever referred to Ireland. His writings bear no obvious trace of his Irish origins nor of preoccupations which we might ascribe directly to an Irish sensibility. But throughout his life he maintained his steady correspondence with Greeves, visited Co. Down on holidays, and in later years sought out his brother Warren who like a homing-pigeon made for Ireland on those alcholic drinking bouts which made Jack Lewis's later life such a trial. But there is perhaps in his monumental scholarly work, in his allegorical novels and children's fantasies, in his baroque theological systems which have allowed some of the commentaries on his work to read him as a neo-Platonist, a sense of desperation, a sense of something constructed against the odds, against the spirit of the age that makes him kin of Yeats as well as Tolkien, Chesterton and George Mac-Donald.[26] There are indeed moments in his work (one thinks especially of *A Grief Observed* and *Till We Have Faces*) where the imagination is forced to confront reality without all the circus animals of system, dogma and public mask on show. At such moments it may not quite be the foul rag-and-bone shop of the heart that we encounter, but something similar – the fear of the small boy who in his Belfast childhood recognized on his mother's death in the lonely, isolated Edwardian house, 'no more of the old security. It was sea and islands now; the great continent had sunk like Atlantis'.[27] And like Yeats, too, perhaps Lewis's deepest attachment to Ireland (like so many others of the Protestant Irish in the period) was in a relationship with its landscape. It does not seem unduly fanciful therefore to reflect that the land of Narnia owes much to Lewis's memories of the Holywood Hills in Co. Down, the Castlereagh Hills and the Belfast Lough. In 1934 Lewis had in fact written to Greeves as he read Agnes Romilly White's novel of Dundonald life, *Gape Row*: 'The scenery is quite well described, and it is probably the only chance you or I will ever have of seeing that landscape described in fiction – except our own fiction of course!'[28] And in *Surprised by Joy* he described that scenery at length, contemplating it as 'the thing itself, utterly irresistible, the way to the world's end, the land of longing, the breaking and blessing of hearts'.[29] But it was also an Irish landscape. And, as he admitted in a poem of 1920 (echoing Yeats and anticipating the MacNeice of 'Valediction' and section XVI of 'Autumn Journal'[30]), the landscape of Ireland was one whose 'colourless skies' and 'blurred horizons'

> breed
> Lonely desire and many words and brooding and never a deed.[31]

NOTES

1. Walter Hooper (ed.), *They Stand Together: The Letters of C. S. Lewis to Arthur Greeves (1914-63)* (London 1979), pp. 215-16. Henceforth this volume is referred to as T.S.T.
2. Louis MacNeice, *The Strings Are False* (London 1965), p. 62.
3. C. S. Lewis, *Surprised by Joy* (London 1955), pp. 25-6. Henceforth this volume is referred to as S.B.J.
4. S.B.J., p. 106.
5. T.S.T., pp. 24-5.
6. S.B.J., p. 66.
7. T.S.T., p. 59.
8. *Ibid.*, p. 55.
9. *Ibid.*, p. 195.
10. *Ibid.*, p. 195-6.

11. *Ibid.*, p. 229.
12. S.B.J., p. 53.
13. *Ibid.*
14. *Ibid.*, p. 142.
15. T.S.T., p. 202.
16. S.B.J., pp. 140-1.
17. T.S.T., pp. 286-7.
18. *Ibid.*, p. 292.
19. S.B.J., p. 163.
20. W. H. Lewis, 'Memoir of C. S. Lewis' in *Letters of C. S. Lewis*, ed. with a Memoir by W. H. Lewis (London 1966), p. 6.
21. T.S.T., p. 65.
22. *Ibid.*, p. 148.
23. *Ibid.*, p. 187.
24. *Ibid.*, p. 201.
25. S.B.J., p. 157.
26. John Wilson Foster has suggested in his *A Changling Art: Fictions of the Irish Literary Revival* (Dublin 1987) that it might be possible to consider fantasy (with its frequent mediaeval focus) in the works of writers like Lewis and Tolkien as transposed theology. He further suggests that the parallels between such fantasists and the 'Celtic writings of the Protestant revivalists may be worth pursuing' (*op. cit*, p. 375).
27. S.B.J., p. 23.
28. T.S.T., pp. 470-1.
29. S.B.J., p. 126.
30. See my 'Louis MacNeice's Ireland' in *Tradition and Influence in Anglo-Irish Poetry*, where I compare Lewis and MacNeice in greater detail. Lewis himself recognized how similar his own experience was to that which affected the generation of poets to which MacNeice belonged. In *Surprised by Joy* he wrote, 'Looking back on my life now I am astonished that I did not progress into the opposite orthodoxy – did not become a Leftist, Atheist, satiric intellectual of the type we all know so well. All the conditions seemed to be present. I had hated my public school. I hated whatever I knew or imagined of the British Empire. And although I took very little notice of Morris's socialism. . . continual reading of Shaw had brought it about that such embryonic political opinions as I had were vaguely socialistic.' (S.B.J., p. 140.)
31. T.S.T., p. 270.

12

DONOGHUE AND US IRISH

Denis Donoghue is our foremost critic. Easy to say. Most people would agree, mindful of his reputation as a commanding lecturer, his Henry James Chair of Letters at New York University, the reviews in *The New York Review of Books*, the Reith Lectures, the key-note addresses here and there, the distinguished list of publications. But what on earth does it mean to be a literary critic these days, and an Irish one to boot? Easier to ask than to answer. But the answer is slow in coming not because it would not be possible to offer various traditional definitions of the critic's role but because the contemporary condition of literary culture in the English-speaking world and the political realities of this country make the question especially problematic. Indeed the experience of anyone who aspires to the avocation of literary critic in Ireland must be to endure crisis in some form or other in the interests of the literary imagination. For the critic who conceives that imagination as involving moral responsibilities, political burdens, the sense of crisis can be particularly severe. The career of Denis Donoghue affords therefore a fascinating opportunity to observe the effects of crisis on one of the most subtle intelligences of his generation.

The crises in which Donoghue has found himself caught up are two: the disintegration of the humanist consensus in literary studies in the Anglo-Saxon world and the increased politicization of critical writing, under the pressure of terrible events, in his native country. Either could have overwhelmed a weaker intelligence. Donoghue has sought to confront both.

Denis Donoghue made his critical reputation as an elegant, suggestively eloquent reader of poems, plays and novels. As such he was the exemplary New Critic, his sensibility acutely tuned to the verbal structures of complex modernist poetics. At a time when such criticism as existed in Ireland tended at best to be biographical when it was not naively anecdotal, his presence was a remarkable stimulus. I still remember the pleasure and relief with which I read *The Ordinary Universe* (1968). Here was a work which took seriously the revolution in thought which modernism had effected but which did not wholly succumb to its siren voice. Here too was an Irish critic who took it for granted that he should attend to contemporary writing with as much concentration as other university dons gave to the literature of the past. And to the New Critic's dedication to the autonomy of the work of art he brought a humane concern for the felt life of a poem, its relationship to the ordinary universe of shared, common experience. His stance was that of a Leavisite concern (Leavis himself never really seemed an enabling critical voice in Ireland) without the puritanism, the rancour, the sense of embattlement. Indeed the problem of such early work as *The Third Voice* (1959) and *The Ordinary Universe* might be seen as a too easily achieved urbanity, a hint of the grand manner too readily adopted by a youthful conservative.

In subsequent works that innate conservatism developed into something altogether more formidable: a defence, in the face of post-modernist critical theory and an assault on the privileged status of authorship by Marxist and Deconstructionist alike, of the individual imagination and its creative power. His work has been a defence of the human, of art as a mystery of circumstances rather than a product of conditions, of poetry as personal expression rooted in individual experience rather than free play of linguistic possibility. There has been a kind of nobility about this, or to use one of Donoghue's favourite words, an exorbitance. For the very titles of the books – *Connoisseurs of Chaos* (1966), *Thieves of Fire* (1973), *The Sovereign Ghost* (1976), *Ferocious Alphabets* (1981) – suggest an exorbitance of mood and manner bred of the desperate situation in which a critic of Donoghue's persuasion now finds himself. So the nobility is not without poignancy.

For conditions are indeed desperate for a Donoghue in the world of the post-modernist academy in which he makes his living. Theory is all. Literary discourse reflects upon itself in proliferating jargon, increasingly opaque to any conceivable common reader. Deconstructionists deconstruct a small literary canon of works amenable to their method while Marxists indulge in their sectarian disputes in an environment of New Right complacency, remote from any real engagement with the actual social order. The specialization and professionalization of literary studies (the kind of things literary humanists used to find repugnant about sociology) takes place, to speak of the United States, in an enviroment where one-fifth of the population is functionally illiterate, where general publishing is increasingly a matter of the conglomerate and the blockbuster, and where books of fundamentalist piety and propaganda far outsell the titles which make *The New York Times* best-seller's list. The Alexandrian metaphor presents itself as an image appropriate to such a baroque spectacle of simultaneous decadence and barbarism. Works of reflection, even those as eloquent and assured as a Denis Donoghue's assaults on the excesses of contemporary theory, make little impact on the academy, where publishers' contracts, tenure, sabbaticals, professional advancement and the opulent comforts of the North American suburb depend more and more on theoretical novelty and assumed sophistication of critical methodology. On any wider audience they make almost no impact whatsoever.

The New Critical Theorists rarely if ever write for the literary periodicals in which the remains of a general literary culture can be discerned. Such organs as *The New York Review of Books, The London Review of Books, The Times Literary Supplement, The New York Times Book Review*, are where such critics as Helen Vendler (the best reviewer, along with Edna Longley, of contemporary poetry now writing), Hugh Kenner, John Bayley, Christopher Ricks and Donoghue himself attempt a last ditch stand in the essay/review of new works of literature and criticism. Their writing assumes, in face of much contrary evidence, that an audience still exists for literate, comprehensible, broadly humane reflection, in terms both social and aesthetic, on twentieth-century writing. Indeed it is perhaps an illusion sustained by the excellence of these critics' writings, that such a community does in fact still exist, that some form of cultural health can still be imagined in the midst of what sometimes seems the terminal phase of cultural disease.

In such high literary journalism, where Donoghue excels, he is of course much more than a simple formalist, a product of the New Critical era. From the strict standards of that by now antique critical school his criticism is impure; in its wide-ranging, speculative social and moral concern, Trilling seems more the model than Blackmur. But its primary strength remains its capacity to experience poems, plays and novels as *données*, as things realized and achieved as well as things expressed. So in his 1986 collection of essays and reviews on things Irish (curiously, even portenously entitled, *We Irish*[1]), some of the most illuminating moments are when Donoghue alerts us to the distinctive textures of a poem (he has an excellent essay on Austin Clarke) or to the peculiar aesthetic satisfactions offered by a short story (of Frank O'Connor: 'His stories are always implicit in the characters to whom they happen.'). These moments are practical criticism at its best, warm, evaluative, suggestive, sending one back to the works; raising, too, moral and social questions, giving pleasure, giving one pause.

Many modern critics have been attracted, as Morris Dickstein has reminded us in an article on 'Journalism and Criticism'[2], to 'the fragmentary dynamics of the essay for the way it accords with our fractured sense of contemporary reality'. In *We Irish* Donoghue collects (with a few exceptions) his essays and reviews on Irish matters composed over the last two decades. And, God knows, fracture has been the dominant experience of that period for most of us. In a somewhat enigmatic introduction to his book Donoghue reminds us of what may be the distinctive Irish experience, which allows talk of the 'we Irish' kind and which our writing – creative and critical – must negotiate:

If there is a distincitive Irish experience, it is one of division, exacerbated by the fact that division in a country so small seems perverse. But the scale doesn't matter. At various times, the division has taken these forms: Catholic and Protestant, Nationalist and Unionist, Ireland and England, North and South, the country and the bloated city of Dublin, Gaelic Ireland and Anglo-Ireland, the comfortable and the poor, farmers and P.A.Y.E. workers, pro-Treaty and anti-Treaty, child and parents, the Irish and the English languages, the visible Ireland and the hidden Ireland, landlord and tenant, the Big House and the hovel. To which it is now necessary to add: a defensive church and an increasingly secular state, Irish law and European law.

It is of course a measure of the distance Donoghue has travelled, under the pressure of events one assumes, that he permits such extra-literary matter, 'the gross conditions under which poems, plays, stories and novels are written', to stand at the head of his book. It was not the way with the New Critics. There are essays collected here, however, ('Yeats: The Question of Symbolism' and the essay of 1965, 'On the *Winding Stair*'), which seem generally disengaged from such immediate reality, reminding us of the Donoghue who made the world his critical oyster before the native condition more directly engaged his attention. So essays of great tactical assurance rub shoulders with reviews and articles where the tone is much less adroitly controlled. For the fractured quality of our contemporary Irish crisis challenges Donoghue as profoundly as the current crisis in criticism in the academy. And he brings to contemporary Irish experience and to the critical comprehension of our present distresses a conservatism of mind and feeling as unfashionable among his likely Irish audience as his theoretical stance must be at Yale, Johns Hopkins or Duke University, North Carolina (where the theorists have established an influential curia). Perhaps awareness of this accounts for the variously remote and condescending mannerisms which mar some of its paragraphs.

Donoghue's *We Irish* is, to varying degrees among its several parts, a somewhat fragmentary, oddly hesitant, even belated contribution to the debate in Ireland about traditions, essence, existence. But where Field Day, for example, is impatient with ideas and ideals of Irishness, Donoghue hankers for such possibilities, is half a believer. The political stance implicit in much of this book, visible in the poise of a sentence, a gesture of mind here and there, is that of a traditional Irish nationalist. Ireland's cause is just, partition unjust, the northern state irredeemable, the British must go eventually, violence is deplorable but can be understood. In cultural terms such nationalist feeling expresses itself in a distaste for the Ascendancy, its privilege, its pretension. Poor John Synge is dismissed in terms which even Daniel Corkery might have found surprising: 'But his constitution was determined to be gloomy. Delicate, morbid, and after a few years, nearly always ill, he made himself a writer by imagining forms of life as different as possible from his own.' Trinity College, Dublin, is a 'bizarre institution' (we aren't told why exactly but it seems to be an unforgiveable capacity to survive and adapt when it should have done the decent thing and accepted extinction), 'still in many respects, a remarkably defensive and inward-looking college'. In fact Donoghue quotes a former President of University College, Dublin, saying to him that 'Trinity was an irrelevance to Ireland and its development, it was merely an appendix to the country' without recording any demurral.

For Donoghue Trinity's vice has always been complacency. A vice the nationalist critic does not always avoid. So he can set our minds at rest about Joyce's exile, in a passage remarkable for its complacency and maladroitness of phrasing. Here Donoghue sounds like a front-bench spokesman:

So it was only inevitable that Joyce would choose not any of the Irish ways of being a genius, but the European way. I have never felt inclined to lose much sleep over Joyce's exile, or the conditions which allegedly drove him from Ireland. The truth is he was not driven, unless we mean that he was driven by a fretting and chafing sense of any conditions offered him.

Donoghue, however, is far too alert to the revisionist and sceptical mood of current Irish intellectual life to allow himself to be read simply as some kind of eloquent Irish reactionary. He attends, therefore, somewhat fitfully to the contemporary cultural debate – to the Field Day critique of Yeatsian mythologizing, for example. He confesses, of the less than full-bloodedly nationalistic history upon which teachers in Irish schools are now encouraged to concentrate their minds: 'I have entertained the revisionist version of our history and do in part believe it.' Yet he pays these developments the kind of attention which suggests his discomfort in the Irish context where crisis has generated intellectual commitments and engagements which Donoghue finds uncongenial. In face of such risky intensity of feeling and thought Donoghue affects to represent balance, the long view (conservatives are always good on that), a superior point of judgment which allows him the luxury of an aphorism, an agreeable digression, the consolation of style. In a key essay, unpublished until it appeared in this collection, 'Yeats, Ancestral Houses and Anglo-Ireland', Donoghue avers: 'I am describing a political judgement imposed upon poetry, and glancing at some of its consequences. My own stance is that of a latitudinarian, and I would hold to its concessiveness until a particularly extreme outrage makes me ashamed of it.' Latitudinarianism can draw the charge of equivocal blandness, and at moments Donoghue's characteristic form of engagement with ideas does prompt the reader to enter such an indictment. For Donoghue

171

in his writing tends to arrive at a point of necessary commitment and then he subtly changes the subject, enlarges the context, shifts tonal register. The overall tone remains, it is true, assuredly concessive, but the effect can be disconcerting. Though it should also be noted that in some passages which seem vitiated by concession important and illuminating things are being said, even as the reader's desire for explicit authorial commitment is frustrated. The passage in the essay entitled 'Together', where Donoghue reflects on Conor Cruise O'Brien's anti-republican, anti-romantic revisionism, is a good case in point:

His arguments may be vindicated in the end but meanwhile the spirit of acceptance which he espouses is attractive mainly to people who are disgusted with the Irish question and want to be rid of it; or to people who are weary, indifferent, interested only in getting on in the world. There are men and women who dispise the notion of a plural society and who are ready to kill and be killed for the sake of national purity. O'Brien does not understand such people, or the aboriginal loyalities which mean far more to them than a contemptible liberal peace. He answers that his policy will not cause a single death; it is true. But a Republican will assert that there are things more glorious than liberal tolerance – a martyr's death for instance. So the old rhetorical battle starts up again.

In such writing there are commitments disguised rhetorically as even-handed assessment, and the reader awaits their clarification. Instead, real life and death arguments are disengaged from in an allusion to the tiresome rhetorical debates they often generate. The next paragraph begins: 'The real trouble is that our national experience has been too limited to be true. Our categories of feeling have been flagrantly limited; our history has been at once intense and monotonous.' A brilliant, typically suggestive Donoghue insight which dissipates the reader's irritation at the preceding paragraph's shifts and stratagems. Elsewhere Donoghue gets neither himself nor his readers so easily off the hook. Rather his characteristic inclination to disengage at the moment when matters get really difficult or troubling is productive only of frustration.

What we would really like to have from Denis Donoghue is something on his Irish experience and our contemporary imbroglio as sustained and as formidable as his protracted defence of the literary imagination which he has given to the international academy. I believe that a full engagement with Irish reality as he has known it might give the coherence to Donoghue's career, which, remarkable as it has been, at present I sense it lacks. The New Critic and practical critic of the moral imagination in the decadent barbarism of North America has no full community or audience outside the pages and readership of *The New York Review of Books*. A less than wholly engaged conservative mind is on the other hand not likely to command much attention in an Ireland where the running is now made by the followers of the Frankfurt School. What we need from this remarkably gifted writer is a definitive book, an *apologia pro vita sua*, a complete work of criticism or reflection which makes as whole as possible the fractured Ireland which he has known. The conservative moralist should not make do with fragments. His burden is the vision of wholeness rooted in clearly realized commitments of mind and heart. There are moments of autobiographical revelation in *We Irish* which suggest that Donoghue has an important tale to tell, the story of a Catholic RUC man's son from Warrenpoint, Co. Down, who became an internationally renowned literary critic. One suspects that were Donoghue to tell such a tale the concessiveness of a latitudinarian would be tested in interesting ways.

NOTES

1. Denis Donoghue, *We Irish, The Selected Essays of Denis Donoghue, Vol 1* (Brighton 1986).
2. Morris Dickstein, 'Journalism and Criticism' in *Criticism and the University*, eds Gerald Groff and Reginald Gibbons, *Triquarterly* Series on Criticism and Culture, No. 1 (Northwestern University Press 1985), pp. 147-58.

13

SHOW ME A SIGN: BRIAN MOORE AND RELIGIOUS FAITH

Brian Moore has always been a Catholic writer. Happily not in the sense in which, for example, Graham Greene can be said to write Catholic novels, where characters who seem to all intents and purposes much like the rest of us suddenly admit to religious scruples of a mysterious kind. There is none of that rather off-putting sense that one gets in Greene or Evelyn Waugh of faith as some arcane blend of cult and hobby, or as a club whose peculiar constitution makes sense only to its members. Rather, in Moore's fiction the Catholic faith is as undeniable as the weather, with its prevailing winds of depressed feeling and moral demand affecting the psychological temperature of almost all his protagonists. Catholicism is a given which the fiction takes for granted even as it steps out into the secular world of modern, rootless, relativistic consciousness. Indeed, one always sensed that Moore's readings of late twentieth-century life in many of his novels of the late 'sixties and 'seventies as shallow and lacking in fundamental authenticity, was predicated on a sense of absent faith. So perhaps it has not been all that surprising that this most assuredly realistic chronicler of contemporary secular experience in the North American cosmopolis that we all inhabit to greater and lesser extents should have produced in recent years three novels which treat directly of religious faith and experience. It is as if Moore, having tested the secular reality of the modern world and found it wanting, since it afforded his protagonists nothing secure to live by, has turned to the issue of belief to find in Catholic faith a compelling example of the human capacity for conviction, which can, for the fortunate individual who possesses it, sustain a life.

But from another perspective this recent development in Moore's career may, initially, appear very surprising indeed. For throughout his very productive life as a novelist Brian Moore has appeared and appealed to many as the quintessential realist whose occasional forays into fantasy or parable (one thinks of *Fergus, The Great Victorian Collection* or *Catholics*) only served to confirm a sense of his sure hold on the palpable world of empirical reality. His work had in fact seemed to accept the basic philosophical premises which underpin the realistic enterprise: that the physical, empirical world exists and is explicable in its own terms without recourse to transcendence; that human consciousness is similarly explicable in terms of a psychology which likewise requires no transcendental validation; that human culture is an arbitrary construct, a matter of relativities, and that this reality of world and consciousness is most appropriately and accurately rendered by a prose narrative which is transparent in its eschewal of self-reflexive techniques. Such a fictional mode is obviously well-suited to the literary exploration of various forms of pathology, whether of belief or disbelief or of cultural dislocation, and some of Moore's most memorable novels have been works of this kind. His first remarkable novel, *The Lonely Passion of Judith Hearne* (1955), was a *tour de force* of psychological realism in which religious faith could not withstand the pressures of frustration and disappointment; *I Am Mary Dunne* (1968) was a harrowing portrayal of a faithless mind at the end of its tether, unable to achieve any integrity of being in the absence of personal convictions, while some of the power of *An Answer from Limbo* (1962) derived from its sense of a deracinated personality finding a personal point of reference in a destructive obsession.

But for all the energy and empirical density of Moore's realism throughout his career there was often something unsettling about this writer's presentation of his fictional world. One often sensed an author ill-at-ease with the various philosophical implications of his method. One sensed a mind conscious of metaphysical absence employing with great skill but some ruefulness a method that assumed the complete sufficiency of such presence as the world possesses. So his characteristic protagonist was a personality finding the quotidian, normal existence unsatisfactory or unbearable in one way or another. His novels were novels of crisis when this chronic awareness of dissatisfaction or distress becomes acute for his almost uniquely harassed gallery of misfits, failures and malcontents. The dominant mood was one of a depression which seemed at least to some extent that of the author as well as that of his creations. The world never seemed to afford enough for Moore's many victims of circumstances to transcend their predicaments. And those moments in the work when they long to do so likewise seemed as much an authorial *cri de coeur* as an exigency of the literary matter in hand.

So Judith Hearne is obsessed with the reality of symbolism in a way which suggests an authorial pre-occupation. For in a novel so realistically grounded in the particulars of a Belfast of dismal weather, grim interiors and a suffocating social climate, Judith experiences an *angst* which has only something to do with any of these things. Her dilemma, did she but know it, has its ontological aspect. For her problem is not just whether Belfast can give her a husband, but whether being can give her a sign, an earnest of transcendence. And the novel at its most compelling moments forsakes the immediacies of realism for a dialectic between sign and silence, sacrament and insignificance.

She stood up, bowed her head to the tabernacle, genuflected and went quickly down the aisle to the door. She made the Sign of the Cross in dirty Holy Water (if it is only ordinary water and the priest is wrong. . .?) and went out of the church, hearing the swinging door slap shut.

Outside the church gates, people passed. People busy with the immediate things of life. People making a living, bringing up children, planning, talking, sharing each other. Alone, Miss Hearne looked back at the church, an unhaunted house of God, an empty place stripped of the singing, the ritual, stripped of men; men who brought it to sudden glorious life.

Empty. And above her, the night sky . . . nothing beyond it but the stars, the planets, with the earth spinning among them. Surely some great design kept it all moving, some Presence made it meaningful.[1]

'Show me a sign,' prays the distracted Judith Hearne, but no sign is given unto her. Rather intimations of emptiness, absence, which give to Moore's realistic evocations of a grimly provincial Belfast an eerie, insubstantial quality. Realism breaks loose from its material in a vision of unreality:

Miss Hearne stood up, drink in hand, and went to the window. She
pulled aside the heavy curtains and looked out. Here, in the best hotel
in the middle of Belfast. Me. But Royal Avenue was asleep, a wet grey
belt studded with garish street lamps. A policeman turned his back
against the wind and huddled in a doorway. A lonely tramcar clattered
by, bright-lit, empty, its conductor standing alone on his platform, fare-
less and forlorn. Traffic lights flashed red, amber, and green in empty
futility. Two late-goers passed below on the pavement, the voices loud,
unreal in argument.[2]

Judith Hearne finds the solid empirical world inadequately significant (Moore has her live, as in the quoted passage, in a world
of signs which say nothing, the Sacred Heart of Jesus as
inarticulate as the traffic lights in the street).

In others of Moore's realistic novels it is the stuff of consciousness itself that unravels, as if faith in mind is as difficult for this
master of realism as faith in matter. In so many of his novels
human personality seems only a residue of a past which haunts
the present in dream, neurosis, anxiety, guilt and obsessional
shame. His characters, inhabitants of the realist's world, seems
products of their histories, locked in the prison of the self's
determinism. Their experience of themselves is almost invari-
ably depressed. No Moore protagonist is happy with himself,
as ease with his past. They almost all live with the unfinished
business which provokes the crisis of a novel. There seems no
escape from the treadmill of consciousness, no way to transcend
the awful inevitability of personality. This knowledge is unbearable for some of Moore's protagonists, and, one senses, for the
author himself. The consciousness of the arbitrary significance
of selfhood induces the same vertigo that the empty universe
does. As Ginger Coffey, for example, in *The Luck of Ginger Coffey*,
endures his trial for indecent exposure before a Canadian judge
this Irish exile is overwhelmed by a sense of the insubstantiality
of his own history and being:

Coffey looked at them: the judge grinning at his witticism, the lawyers
looking up to laugh with the bench, the spectators lolling back in their
seats like people enjoying a joke in church. Seven years in prison and
yet they laughed. But why not? What was he to all these people except
a funny man with a brogue, not a person; an occasion of laughter. His
whole life, back to those days when he ran past the iron railings of
Stephen's Green, late for school, back through the university years, the
army years, the years at Kylemore and Coomb-Na-Baun, through

courtship, marriage, fatherhood, his parents' death, his hopes, his humiliations – it was just a joke. All he was this morning, facing prison and ruin, was an excuse for courtroom sallies. So what did it matter, his life in this world, when this was what the world was like? Unsurely but surely he came to that. His hopes, his ambitions, his dreams: what were they but shams?[3]

For Ginger the experience is a liberating one, the knowledge of the stuff of his life occasions a kind of joyous freedom for a moment: 'For one liberating moment he became a child again; lost himself as a child can, letting himself go into the morning, a drop of water joining an ocean, mystically becoming one.'[4] But for most of Moore's protagonists after such knowledge there is neither forgiveness of the self nor of the world. There is only the anguished despair of a Mary Dunne in *I Am Mary Dunne* or the literally broken heart of Fergus in *Fergus*. For at the moment when the self unravels, no principle of significance can be discovered in the dimension of consciousness which the realist knows so intimately. It is not in the script of selfhood that selfhood necessarily sustains itself, regenerates, re-establishes meaning when meaning has been lost. So *Fergus* ends with an image of bleak repetitiousness, the universe and the human soul at one in a single truth – mere continuance: 'In the east, dawn came up. Breakers slammed on the morning shore, monotonous as a heartbeat. He walked toward the house.'[5]

Moore has allowed his realism the luxury of travel. His novels have had settings as far apart as Cork and California. Accordingly, culture is a theme as well as character. Indeed, from the beginning, with the arrival of the returned Yank James Patrick Madden in Belfast to disturb poor Judith Hearne, Moore has been interested in the way cultures clash in the modern world. The archaic encounters the contemporary, the religious the secular, the repressed the liberated. In *An Answer from Limbo*, for example, the hero's mother has been summoned from Belfast to look after her son's children to allow the work on the great novel to proceed uninterrupted, while Brendan's wife goes out to work to support the improbable *ménage*. The ghetto meets the secular city in the presence of Brendan's wife, Jane, part-Jewish Swarthmore graduate and conscientious agnostic, with a taste for Zen interiors. Brendan's mother inspects her new home with alarm and mystification:

She had never seen a room quite like this, with its canvas and wood chairs, its long black modernistic sofa, its gooseneck lamps like a dentist's surgery, and enormous painting of potato-headed creatures on all the walls, painted by Jane. Who signed her maiden name Jane Melville. (Was that a Jewish name?) Books galore and magazines, ashtrays every place and three half-empty bottles of spirits on a side-table. But for all the untidiness, all the objects strewn about, the room made her think of a room on a stage: it was not real. There was not one thing in it from their family homes, not one thing which looked as if it had belonged to some one else before them.[6]

In his account of cultural clash Moore as realist maintains a cool, detached neutrality. Culture seems a product of economic and social development (in *The Great Victorian Collection* a culture is most fully present to itself and posterity in its artefacts) and the values it expresses are relative, not absolute. Moore's most memorable treatment of this theme came in his parable-like novella *Catholics* in 1972. This work explored the theme in a futuristic tale of ecclesiastical *realpolitik*. Set some time in the approximate future (in 1972 the current revanchism in the Roman communion would have seemed an unlikely development), the Church has abandoned almost all its mysteries for a gospel of secular hope and eirenic ecumenism. The young Father Kinsella is dispatched to bring a recalcitrant abbot on a remote island off the west coast of Ireland to the heel of the new discipline. The abbot and the emissary meet and argue, their debate representing an encounter between two contrasting modes of life. Kinsella is at ease in the secular world, an adept of progressive hope, the abbot by contrast is faithful to traditions, not because they are immutably sacred, but because they work. What was most striking about this text was the way Moore maintained his neutrality of tone and attitude throughout the book. Neither mode of consciousness, the secular and progressive optimism of Father Kinsella nor the depressed local pragmatic piety of the abbot, was valorized in the book. Instead, each was subjected to a cool, almost ironic, inspection, implying that to expect sustaining transcendental value in something as artifical and relative as human culture is a form of naivety. And to highlight this ironic mood which pervades the work, Father Kinsella, shallow and ingenuous as he is, in fact possesses faith of a kind, whereas the abbot is a sceptic with a constitutional fear of change. Throughout the novel, however, Moore intimates that in the sphere of culture only change prevails. The novel in fact suggests, in its imagery of wind, rain and sea, minor apocalypses that presage change until the following passage casts its cold, despairing light over all that has gone before. The moment is almost Yeatsian (it echoes Yeats's great poem of apocalypse, 'The Second Coming', which the Father-General of Kinsella's order has quoted earlier in the book):

Kinsella woke at seven. In the rectangle of window above his bed, the sky was already light. Gulls rode that sky, kites held by an invisible string. When, dressed and shaven, he opened the guest house door and stepped outside, he met the rush of breakers on shore, a long retreating roar of water. Obbligato of gull cries overhead, their harsh, despairing scream seeming to mourn a death. Winds whipped like penny tops, spinning in the long grasses this way and that. The sky, immense, hurried, shifted its scenery of ragged clouds.[7]

But where Yeats's vison of historical inevitability is charged with exhilarated, if horrified, anticipation. Moore's by contrast is touched with nostalgia, even grief (one is reminded of the melancholy roar of the retreating tide of faith in Matthew Arnold's 'Dover Beach'). It is as if for a moment the detachment of mind, which has set two opposed world views in conflict in the novel and ironically observed the outcome, gives way to an elegiac regret for lost faiths of all kinds (we must remember however that in the novel the new world's emissary is the agent of faith). No faith, no human culture, the realist writer understands, is the equal of that wind, that immense sky, with its turbulent cloud.

If, therefore, much of Moore's fictional output can be seen to test the limits of realism and to imply an authorial dissatisfaction with the philosophical implications of that method, one can the more easily account for his recent work. For this has explicitly explored the dimension of faith in human consciousness and has further subjected the philosophical underpinnings of realism itself to a fictional critique.

In 1983 Moore published *Cold Heaven*. Nothing in his previous work had, however, quite prepared his readers for this work. Moore had employed fantasy before, in *Fergus*, in *The Great Victorian Collection*, in *The Mangan Inheritance*. But whatever the dissatisfaction with realism and its implications these and other works might have suggested, in all of them it was possible to understand the fantastic method as a means of exploring a mental or personal problem of an individual psychology. *Cold Heaven* was something else.

The book begins in an entirely recognizable world, one in which realism seems securely at home. A young American couple is enjoying a few days' break in the south of France after a medical conference at which the husband has participated. He is killed in a dreadful accident while swimming and his wife, Marie Davenport, seeks to cope with the shock and the bureaucratic details of disposing of the remains. But the body mysteriously disappears with scary signs that her husband may not have died after all. Eventually Marie catches up with Alex, who if not dead is certainly not alive either. He is holed up in a Californian motel with a horrible wound in his head and inhibited life signs. At moments he seems to recover only to relapse again. What are we to make of this perplexing plot? We have learnt that Alex's accident was ironically timed, for his wife had recently determined to end their marriage and to leave him for another man. A rational psychological explanation for Moore's fantasizing presents itself to the reader. The plot is a bizarre, literal working out of the death of a marriage. Marie Davenport, as she emotionally withdraws from her husband, is responsible for the dreadful condition which afflicts him. As she seeks to take account of his well-being, he appears to 'recover'. But this realistic reading of the book doesn't really fit with the facts of the case. Alex's condition seems altogether more miraculous than this rather too simple parable of marital disintegration would suggest. And Moore introduces a complication in the plot to increase the sense of miraculous powers at work in the novel. Marie Davenport is a secular woman, although she has had a Catholic girlhood in her native Quebec. So a secular mind is confronted in the novel with the possibility of the miraculous, not only in the strange occurrence of her husband's 'death', but in an encounter with visionary experience. For Marie has been afforded a vision of the Virgin in whom she does not believe and must come to terms with that otherworldly experience which challenges the very basis of her customary mode of consciousness. At one level this strand in the book, like Alex's illness, is capable of a psychological interpretation. Moore is exploring the essentially psychological problem of what it would take to convince a secular mind of the miraculous and in that sense is writing of a personal, if rather unusual, crisis of faith in the way he had done before. But there's more to the novel than that. Throughout Moore has tantalized the reader too with the problem Marie must solve. Are her experiences merely some kind of aberration from the normal, perhaps mere delusions, the product of a disturbed mind? Or are they some kind of sign which suggests that the material, daily world we take entirely for granted is in fact a script to be read for its implicit messages? For the world in this novel is never simply the world which realism explores with the absolute conviction that it is self-explanatory. Rather the world is presented as a hermeneutic puzzle, a text composed of ambiguous signs. But the skill of the work means that we are also introduced to locales and ambiances realized with all the particularity and credible detail that we expect from a work of realism and especially from a Moore novel. The world may be alive with messages or it may simply be the familiar place that usually tells us nothing. We are left as readers with a semiotic puzzle as tantalizing as that Thomas Pynchon sets us in *The Crying of Lot 49*, where the existence or non-existence of the Tristero remains in radical doubt throughout the book.

We are alerted early to the fact that semiotics will be a fictional concern in this book. Marie, en route in the ambulance to the hospital with her injured husband, sees 'a sign on a street lamp: HÔPITAL, and an arrow pointing to the right.'[8] The French and the capitalization highlight the strange arbitrary quality of such signs. But we soon learn that Marie has seen a sign which may not be arbitrary at all, but may bear transcendental messages. Increasingly, events in the natural world seem to take on the significance of portents, warnings, in her confused and fearful mind: 'Rain spattered against the opaque glass pane of the bathroom window. The sound reverberated a second time, directly overhead, seeming to shake the room. It was a knell. Or a coincidence?'[9] Thunder rumbles through the book like a visitation, ambiguous, undeniable. Signs are taken for wonders. But she hopes signs are just signs and that the threatening sky is simply sky. As she arrives at the Point Lobos Motor Inn, where her husband has gone to ground, a living corpse, she comforts herself with a sign:

There were no secrets in these neat new rooms; there was no hidden purpose behind the sign she could see from her window, a sign lettered on a redwood marker, the lettering announcing Cliff Walk. And yet as she looked at the sign she felt that she was being summoned. She left the room, locked the door, and went down the outdoor staircase to the graveled driveway. Like a somnambulist she turned toward the redwood sign.[10]

Suddenly the world of signs has become the world of undesired significance. Marie is 'led' to the convent near the motel where she encounters a group of five nuns at work in the convent garden:

They did not see Marie, and as she looked at them it was as though, in their medieval clothing, working under this harsh high sun, they were a representation of reality rather than reality itself, peasants at harvest in a Breughel painting rather than real nuns at work in a convent garden. And yet this scene was contemporary.[11]

The realist's world has dissolved in a vision of artistic meaning. Accordingly, the rest of the novel is haunted by the possibility of presence in the signs which in *The Lonely Passion of Judith Hearne* had intimated the full horror of absence: 'But now, in this church, she feared the doll's stupid eyes as she feared the naked sky, thunder, and the jumbled rocks and the twisted cypress tree. There was a presence here.'[12]

Marie is as aware as the reader that her visions may be all in the mind, that she may be suffering from some kind of paranoia. But a strange encounter with an old nun leaves both her and the reader in real perplexity. For one of the nuns in the convent exudes a genuine sanctity and love that seem associated with the experiences Marie has been undergoing. Moore descibes this mysterious encounter thus:

Then Mother St Jude raised her bowed head and looked Marie full in the face, her dark luminous eyes intense, her expression one of overwhelming reverence joined to a complete and enveloping love. It was as though, in Marie, she saw one she had waited for all her life and now, praying for her wish to be granted, she gazed in supplication.[13]

Even at this resonant moment ambiguity remains in that syntactic scruple 'as though'. But what the novel has been exploring is the possibility that the world in which realism seems an appropriate literary tool there may be things of which it cannot take account. And Mother St Jude's holiness may be an even more problematic reality than the miracles to which Marie is an unwilling witness. As Michael Paul Gallagher has suggested: 'My own hunch is that Brian Moore intended us to recognize another dimension in the soliciting to faith – the eyes of the saint and their impact on Marie.'[14] Those eyes may be the truest sign in a book of signs, human, fully present, an invitation to belief. And the world may be read as more than self-referential text. It speaks volumes. It proffers occasions of faith and love.

Cold Heaven seemed to address the question of faith in the realm of being. Its concern was ontological as it rendered the world as ambiguous text. *Black Robe*, which followed it in 1985, presented that question in the context of culture. The familiar Moore theme of contrasting cultures in conflict found expression in a darkly powerful, gripping adventure story which took a seventeenth-century French Jesuit Father to his private heart of darkness in colonial Canada. Father Laforgue is on a mission into the Indian interior to relieve a fellow priest in danger of his life. He travels with a group of Algonkian Indians and a young companion who is attracted both by one of the Indian girls and by the Indian way of life in the great forests in which they seem so at home. Unlike the earlier novel *Catholics*, which had explored two inadequate forms of life and belief, *Black Robe* allows us to see how certain kinds of belief can give meaning and dignity to human life. And they do so not simply as functional codes but because, as aspects of a living culture, they express values that may have their sources in a relationship with the world that reason cannot fully understand. The Indians are by no means sentimentalized as noble savages, in this book of quite horrendous violence. Nor is Father Laforgue, the Jesuit missioner, presented simply as a life-denying puritan imposing an alien creed upon a free people. The Indians have their nobility, to be sure, but their savagery is a sadistically cruel kind. Yet as Moore presents them in this novel they possess a dignity, an ability to adapt to their environment and a capacity for a kind of divination, an instinctive reading of signs, that makes them representatives of a sophisticated and profound culture. This becomes completely clear in Moore's treatment of an Indian death towards the end of the novel. Chomina, who has stayed with Father Laforgue despite the danger to himself and his surviving daughter (the rest of his family have been tortured and killed by the Iroquois), sickens with his final illness. He know that death is upon him, recognizes from dreams a break in the forest as his last resting-place:

'I must be alone. I have dreamed this. As I brought the canoe into this place, it was as though I had come home. That rock there, that line of trees, even this mound where I sit, all of it has been in my dreams for many years. Often I have asked myself what this place means. But it is not granted to us to know what some dreams mean.'[15]

Such faith allows Chomina to die with pagan stoicism, a man true to his animistic sense of reality and to a human culture that touches a kind of truth. 'What shit you speak,' he tells Laforgue when the priest bears witness to the Christian hope of salvation in the world to come:

'Look around you, the sun, the forest, the animals. This is all we have. It is because you Normans are deaf and blind that you think. . . the world of the dead is a world of light. We who can hear the forest and the river's warnings, who speak with the animals and the fish and respect their bones, we know that is not the truth. If you have come here to change us, you are stupid. We know the truth. This world is a cruel place but it is the sunlight. And I grieve now, for I am leaving it.'[16]

But great as the testing is which Father Laforgue must undergo in the forests of the night, he too keeps the faith, a faith which survives the near-martyrdom which the novel asks of him. Something beyond what reason might comprehend sustains this Jesuit Mister Valiant-for-Truth:

And there, among the faint sounds of the river, the slap of paddles, the canoes gliding through the chill morning mists, he was filled with a strange exaltation. In France, in the cloister, after a long and painful night's vigil of prayer, or at humble or disgusting tasks in the kitchens and sickrooms of the Order, he had, on rare occasions, known this feeling. It was as though Paul Laforgue no longer existed on this earth but, instead, a body and mind made for Jesus did Jesus' will.[17]

In the Author's note to the book Moore had made clear that his intention had been to explore a tragic cultural clash, a conflict of world-views. The tale itself suggests that his imagination told him, more profoundly, that human cultures and the belief systems which sustain them are rooted in a mystic ground of being. That such an intimation comes in a novel whose realism is so persuasive that the reader feels the wind and the rain, hears the whispering of the trees and the hiss of arrows, gives it the kind of truth status that one does not normally expect in a work of such a kind.

While he was reading for the novel which eventually appeared as *Black Robe*, Moore remarked in an interview that he had begun to see and feel 'that the great lack of modern life is the lack of a belief in something greater than ourselves.'[18] *Cold Heaven* had suggested that that something might be found in a world that opens its meanings to the receptive heart, *Black Robe* that human culture with its myserious truths offers values to live and die by. Moore's most recent work, *The Colour of Blood* (1987), considers the possibility that it is in the secret places of the psyche, that final focus of the realist's art, that rumours of angels, hints of transcendence, may be overheard. But the music of the spheres is a strange silence.

The hero of *The Colour of Blood* is another faithful priest, but this time a Cardinal, no less, in an imaginary eastern European Communist state. Cardinal Bem undergoes a testing as severe as that which assailed Father Laforgue. He is caught up in a plot spun by two of his bishops to launch a counter-revolution, thereby risking the concordat of Church and state which he had so skilfully set in place, and preciptiating civil war. In a plot of Le-Carré-like complexities Cardinal Bem, at the cost of his life, averts the crisis and maintains the peace. But where Laforgue in his time of trial was sustained by the rituals and traditions of his Church and by his commitment to and dependency on the Jesuit rule, Cardinal Bem is cast back completely on himself in a world where the very existence of human identity seems in question. He lives in a land of appearances, Hamlet's Elsinore with courtiers in Lada cars and secret police raincoats. Signs here only seem to disguise meanings. Seem, seem, seem; the word recurs through a novel of distrust and suspicion. Human identity seems a matter of masks, portraits, in which true personality is absent. A dead face is 'pale and composed as though a skilled surgeon had removed the intelligence behind it'[19]; it is difficult to put a face to a voice on the telephone; the 'pale pear-shaped face, with large unfocused eyes' of the head of the secret police seems 'less like a human face than a child's unfinished drawing.'[20] Respect for a man is granted and withdrawn as he dons and discards the robes of office, priest or doctor, politician or soldier. Bem constantly catches sight of his own face in mirrors as his involvement in the clandestine world of plots and *real-politik* strips him of accreted identity and casts him out like Lear on the wilderness of invisibility, his hold on identity tested to the uttermost. And in the depths of self Bem finds something greater than self, something which transcends a world of appearance, making this taut, skilled thriller a more direct religious statement than any Moore has provided before. Bem is a reader of St Bernard and that mystic source helps put him in touch with a dimension in the self where he might 'withdraw into that silence where God waited and judged.'[21] In a country of deceptive signs, of identity cards and false identities, of surveillance and a fear as palpable as the streets, fields, cars and lorries, rooms and buildings in which Bem endures his trial of faith, we are reminded of the country of the spirit where the political state is challenged by a transcendent state of consciousness, where a different authority is established: 'As always in prayer, in the act of prayer, he sought to open that inner door to the silence of God, God who waited, watched and judged.'[22] When that door opens we leave behind the world of signs for the presence of truth. For now we see through the glass of realism, darkly. But then face to face.

NOTES

1. *The Lonely Passion of Judith Hearne* (London 1965), p. 104.
2. *Ibid.*, p. 155.
3. *The Luck of Ginger Coffey* (Harmondsworth 1965), pp. 190-91.
4. *Ibid.*, p. 195.
5. *Fergus* (London 1983), p. 189.
6. *An Answer from Limbo* (Toronto 1977), p. 47.
7. *Catholics* (London 1983), p. 79.
8. *Cold Heaven* (London 1985), p. 14.
9. *Ibid.*, p. 36.
10. *Ibid.*, p. 69.
11. *Ibid.*, p. 75.
12. *Ibid.*, p. 78.
13. *Ibid.*, pp. 86-7.
14. Michael Paul Gallagher, review of *Cold Heaven*, in *The Irish University Review*, Vol. 14, No 1 (Spring 1984), p. 133.
15. *Black Robe* (London 1987), p. 170.
16. *Ibid.*, p. 169.
17. *Ibid.*, p. 14.
18. Brian Moore, in *Education and the Arts* (Dublin 1987), p. 86.

19. *The Colour of Blood* (London 1987), p. 3.
20. *Ibid.*, p. 128.
21. *Ibid.*, p. 2.
22. *Ibid.*, p. 54.

14

POETS AND PATRIMONY:
RICHARD MURPHY & JAMES SIMMONS

James Simmons's collection of poems, *Constantly Singing* (1980), contains in 'Cloncha' a wryly self-aware assessment of his cultural and social patrimony. Ironically distancing himself from a past self, he asserts:

> Our hero's Arcady was here
> with the bleak moors and strands,
> for forty years near enough,
> the Derry hinterland
> between Foyle and Swilly
> from Malin to Buncrana
> to Greencastle to Shrove
> Moville and Carndonagh.[1]

The topographical imperative here, the almost talismanic recitation of place-names is, were irony not present, recognizable as a recurrent reflex response of poets of Protestant background to the vexed question of their possession of an authentic Irish identity. Allingham's claim on the Ballyshannon district, Yeats's on County Sligo, MacNeice's on the West as a whole, Hewitt's on the Glens of Antrim, even Longley's on Mayo and Richard Murphy's on Connemara and on High Island off its coast, all can be read as insecure assertions of an Irish identity established through association with place that a man or woman of Catholic nationalist stock feels no need to make. Simmons in 'Cloncha' wittily reflects on this defining stratagem in relation to a poetic career that bears a partial resemblance to his own while serving a more general representative function:

> The Anglo-Irish boy adores
> broken demense walls
> empty condemned cottages
> moorlands littered with boulders
> gold-braided thinly with lichen,
> sheeps' wool coarse and grey
> from Lear's theatrical beard
> on the rusted barbed wire,
> the dried-blood red of rust,
> the fragile brilliance of fuchsia
> dancing dolls, a Japanese theatre
> in country hedges grown native
> and deserted like Yeats's plays,
> pale water agile on slatey beds
> of mountain streams, rain
> on hotel windows, the pale gold
> of whiskies set on the wine-dark
> wood of country bar counters.[2]

Such topographical claims in Anglo-Irish poetry (using the term here to denote the work of poets of Protestant origins) sometimes co-exist with familial and dynastic piety. It is as if a claim on a district, locale or region, and a rich, variegated, yet deeply rooted family tree, can give the lie to any suggestion that the species is not native to the Irish soil and climate. Simmons has his say on such dynastic celebrations too, recognizing how falsely they would ring in 'our hero's' case:

> Today he searched for anecdotes
> to establish his rights there,
> retailed his mother's world of Moores,
> Montgomerys, the Royal School,
> Raphoe where young Magillicuddy of the Reeks
> boarded, the names of her father's
> two friends, Peter Sauce and Darby Toye,
> the aunt from Manorcunningham
> who wouldn't inherit
> a moneyless Scottish title,
> Cunninghams, Rentouls, Kings, Craigs. .
> Nothing of this was his or him.[3]

In the case of Richard Murphy much of this does engage his imagination in a direct way, obeying as he does both topographical and dynastic imperatives in his verse. In an essay entitled

'The Pleasure Ground' published in 1963 (the year in which his first full collection, *Sailing to an Island*, appeared) Murphy gave us access to the constituents of his primary imaginative world. It is one compact of almost legendary places and family history.

The 'pleasure ground' of the title is the garden of his grandfather's house in the west of Ireland. The place is remembered as a realm of privacy and delapidation, its mystery and its joy dependent on the sense of things having run to seed, permitting freedom and disciplined action within its constraining wall.

The whole garden was surrounded by an Anglo-Irish wall, a great wall of pride and oppression, liberally overgrown with romantic ivy. For years the place had been neglected. Many things had improved in Ireland, but this garden of the ascendancy had declined like the family fortune. A laurel forest now covered the lawn except for a patch kept trimmed by rabbits round the trunk of the beech tree. The yew hedge, where the daughters of high sheriffs had decorously flirted, was now a dark row of trees, and the walks were impassible with briers. My mother devoted herself to restoring this pleasure ground.[4]

In this world the young boy received his early education, which his mother hoped would fit both him and his brother for civil service careers; but the poet confesses, 'We were much too wild. Our life went from one extreme to another, from discipline to anarchy.'[5] It is clearly implied here that the enthralling disciplines of restoring a pleasure ground and acquiring education could not master the essential anarchy of the place, however deeply nurtured it might become.

Visits to the Connemara coast initiated the growing boy into an awareness of his caste's alienation from the 'truly Irish'. He and his brother longed to belong: 'They seemed sharper, freer, more cunning than we were. Stones, salmon-falls, rain-clouds and drownings had entered and shaped their minds, loaded with ancestral bias.'[6] Then the poet recollects: 'Twice before, much earlier in my life, as far back as I can remember, we ha⁴ lived in the Connemara hills, first by a lake and later by the se that greatest of all pleasure grounds.'[7] And the essay ends with gnomic suggestiveness: 'As I grew older the garden grew wilder, losing its form as trees were felled . . . so I searched more and more into the origins of that garden till I found them finally in the sea.'[8]

As I read this essay, Murphy placed his trust in the sea as 'a pleasure ground' in which the discipline required to travel upon its waters will never overcome its absolute anarchic power. It is a pleasure ground upon which a man may employ his powers of strength and skill in the knowledge that no ordering principle can ever exercise complete dominion over its spirit. Conversely it will never subside into mere shapeless chaos. A garden lacking a 'masculine energy in the place, to mend walls, plant new trees, sow and cultivate and labour'[9] may decline into irreversible chaos, in which no exhilarating dialectic between discipline and anarchy can be experienced. The sea is therefore the ultimate pleasure ground because it will always offer itself as an arena for such experience, its anarchic power always challenging to disciplined engagement. And it does so in its terrifying disinterested fashion in a way that renders caste distinctions, between Anglo-Irishmen and native Irishmen, of no import. Offshore in a storm men are simply men.

Three long poems in *Sailing to an Island* relish the sea's mysterious 'pleasure ground'. Each of them is almost too deliberately attentive to the lore of sea-craft and to the arts of boat-building, making for what Seamus Heaney has called 'clinker-built poetry'[10] in recognition of the 'finish of the verse, the eccentric stress of the metric, the conscious wording'.[11] The best movements in these poems, therefore, are not those where the poet's shaping skill is too obtrusively identified with boat-builder's trade and the sailor's ancestral knowledge, but where we sense the turbulent energies of the sea (the Old English poems, 'The Wanderer', 'The Seafarer', Hopkins' 'The Wreck of the Deutschland', seem present to the poet's imagination here) and distinctions between men lost in an elemental struggle:

> Now she dips, and the sail hits the water.
> She hoves to a squall; is struck and shudders.
> Someone is shouting. The boom, weak as scissors,
> Has snapped. The boatman is praying.
> Orders thunder and canvas cannonades.
> She smothers in spray. We still have a mast;
> The oar makes a boom. I am told to cut
> Cords out of fishing-lines, fasten the jib.
> Ropes lash my cheeks. Ease! Ease at last!
> She swings to leeward, we can safely run.
> Washed over rails our Clare island dreams,
> With storm behind us we straddle the wakeful

Waters that draw us headfast to Inishbofin.
                    ('Sailing to an Island')

But it is in a later collection, *High Island* (1974), that Murphy provides us with his most evocative celebration of the sea as pleasure ground. Here, in 'Seals at High Island', the deliberative quality of his earlier verse and the too ready identification of the poet's making with masculine, almost Conradian tests of skill and nerve upon the waves are quite absent. Instead male and female luxuriate in a hauntingly plangent, sexually explicit veneration of the processes of creativity, in which the sea's final erotic power is acknowledged.

> At nightfall they haul out, and mourn the drowned,
> Playing to the sea sadly their last quartet,
> An impoverished requiem that ravishes
> Reason, while ripping scale up like a net:
> Brings pity trembling down the rocky spine
> Of headlands, till the bitter ocean's tongue
> Swells in their cove, and smothers their sweet song.[13]

The dynastic aspects of an Anglo-Irish Protestant sensibility are as fully present in Richard Murphy as the topographical impulse. *Sailing to an Island* contains his touching memorial to his grandmother, Lucy Mary Ormsby, with its quiet insistence that in specific individuals the Ascendancy tradition in Ireland expressed itself with humane, even gentle, dignity:

> The bards in their beds once beat out ballads
> Under leaky thatch listening to sea-birds,
> But she in the long ascendancy of rain
> Served biscuits on a tray with ginger wine.
>
> Time can never relax like this again,
> She in her phaeton looking for folk-lore,
> He writing sermons in the library
> Till lunch, then fishing all the afternoon.[14]
>   ('The Woman of the House')

The Battle of Aughrim (1968) contains 'The God Who Eats Corn', a portrait of the poet's father, a member of the British Colonial Service in retirement in Rhodesia, still maintaining family traditions in his efforts to create and sustain order within the confines of his 'plantation'.

> Tall in his garden, shaded and brick-walled,
> He upholds the manners of a lost empire.[15]

It is here, as in the title poem of the volume, that Murphy most fully confronts his patrimony. 'The Battle of Aughrim', a pageant-like historical meditation on a crucial military engagement of the seventeenth century, does much more than merely re-create the events and atmosphere of the day of battle (which as a radio piece commissioned by the BBC it was, one feels, obliged to do), but tries to establish the poet's own relationship with an ambiguous inheritance. The inheritance is ambiguous not only because the poet is a scion of the Ascendancy which held sway in Ireland for more than two centuries following Aughrim's great disaster, but because Patrick Sarsfield, the poem's hero who fought on the losing side, was also one of the poet's ancestors.[16]

Consequently, the disturbing question with which the poem opens, 'Who owns the land where musket-balls are buried?'[17], reverberates through it towards a doubtful present. That's not a question a dispossessed native would ask; nor is it one that a planted occupant dare ask as he validates possession by work and improvement. But it is the sort of question a poet perplexed about his contemporary social position can, particularly when he knows that in attempting an answer he will summon up a impressive array of ancestors to help authenticate his own identity.

One of the things some of those ancestors did of course was to call 'architect and artist' in that they might 'rear in stone /The sweetness that all longed for night and day'. For Anglo-Ireland was a splendid colonial caste which built heroically, amidst a somewhat dishevelled landscape, monuments to its own magnificence. Clearing a demense and building a great house were claims to possession and permanence. Murphy too has been a builder, and not just of poems. First he built a house for himself in Cleggan, County Galway, and then he bought a small offshore island where he renovated a room in a miners' cottage where he might sleep overnight.[18] In comparison with the earlier architectural exploits of Anglo-Ireland what strikes one about Murphy's activities, especially as they surface as matter for poems, is their solitariness. The Anglo-Irish demense had in the past, for all its historic ambiguity, and isolation from the majority population, the potential for intense relationships.[19] Murphy's poetic world is a strikingly lonely one. Colour, energy, sociability seem the privilege of a past which has given way to present solitude. Indeed Murphy's contemporary social canvas is remarkably underpopulated. Some fishermen, sailors, tinkers, other solitaries ('The Philosopher and The Birds; In Memory of Wittgenstein at Rosroe', 'The Poet on the Island; To Theodore Roethke') share a world of sea, air, storm petrels and the ubiquitous stone.

Murphy's most recent work was not surprisingly, in view of his obsession with building, entitled *The Price of Stone* (1985). In this carefully constructed volume the poet allows a collection of buildings their say in a series of architecturally compact sonnets. In various houses and buildings a life, an autobiography of feeling, are hinted at, but the overall effect remains one of isolation, solitude, and stoical loneliness. At moments in the book the strategy seems a little desperate, tellingly of a piece with the poet's earlier work. For one senses that what the stones have to offer is an objective retrospection; the life they possess is the life they have enshrined. In the least successful of these poems a slightly programmatic obviousness of tone is not rescued by the arcane vocabulary to which the poet has rather strained resource. The price of stone seems costly in terms of poetic feeling, and is not made less so by the ostentatious verbal chiselling. But the best of the poems in this ambitious volume, some part of the titular sequence, others part of an introductory selection of recent work, manage to suggest the pain of the solitude now experienced as impoverishment in comparison with the emotional intensities of the past. If the poet's life is a construction of words and metres, it is a building which, whatever the current silence, chill and stony emptiness, has known the cries of children, the voices of lovers and friends, the sounds of passion. And all of these things, so insubstantial when set against the apparent durability of stone, of art, are in fact the truest things the poet has known, his own obsession with construction a kind of betrayal of the real. Accordingly the autobiographical significance of *The Price of Stone* is a self-scrutiny which includes a recognition of the life-rejecting impulses of some kinds of art. To build for permanence loyal to a patrimony is to ignore the perishable significance of the passing moment:

How much it hurts me to have neglected all this Summer
    the friends whom I might have seen,
But for my mad obsession of building more rooms
    to entertain them in time to come:
Because these times are apt to elude us, we die, or our
    Friends drop dead before we can say
I'd love you to see and enjoy the house whose construction
    has kept us apart entirely.[20]

                                      ('Stone Mania')

The waifs and strays, the lovers and remembered friends, who people this book as much as anybody does, are reckoned to have possessed a wisdom of a more full kind than anything that inspires the poet. Principal of these temporary visitants to the poet's stony chamber (and the poet's loss of so many of them is the true price he has paid for the stone structures of his art) is his dead friend Tony White, for whom there are a number of chaste, tender elegies in the book. In 'Tony White' his very life has the strength of a building: 'His granite chimney breast / Warmed friend or stranger at its open fire'. But he knew that attachment to income, house and family was a disease 'Nothing but unpossessive love could cure'. His warm presence haunts this chill collection, drawing the expression of subjective feeling from this most objectively reticent of Irish poets. A dead friend's commitment to integrity of feeling encourages the poet, even as he shelters behind the facade of his architectural *dramatis personae* to confront the truths of his own nature. And in a number of shockingly honest poems the poet manages to set down the facts of a dual nature, Anglo-Irish, oddly androgynous, cold and yet deeply emotional, in an art which, objective and subjective simultaneously, is the convincing embodiment of a kind of controlled, self-aware encounter with a rigorous patrimony – the solitude of being human:

    No worse pain could be borne, to bear the joy
    Of seeing you come in a slow dive from the womb,
    Pushed from your fluid home, pronounced 'a boy'.
    You'll never find so well equipped a room

    No house we build could hope to satisfy
    Every small need, now that you've made this move
    To share our loneliness, much as we try
    Our vocal skill to wall you round with love.

This day you crave so little, we so much
For you to live, who need our merest touch.[21]

('Natural Son')

'All he could offer honestly', admits James Simmons in 'Cloncha'
reflecting on his lack of a personal Anglo-Irish mythology,

> was a private childhood, secrecy,
> a boy drifting alone through fern
> forests and alder groves, smoking
> his first woodbine above Carrig Cnoc,
> a consciousness apart from ancestors
> and local inhabitants, a stranger
> at home in the present moment
> happily, then as now.[22]

That sense of a cultural void is of course a fairly common northern Protestant experience for those who grew up in the post-war
period, beneficiaries of the Education Act which took them to
state-supported grammar school and university. James Simmons's route to the university job, the poetry reading tour and
the slim volume was not wholly typical (Campbell College and
Leeds University), but his awareness of a signally insubstantial
imaginative inheritance, when set against the kind of thing to
which a Richard Murphy can lay claim, is entirely so. Few northern Protestants in the period were permitted by education to
enlarge the diminished social reality of middle and lower-middle
class surburban experience by an involvement with Irish literature, history and mythology. The professions, medicine, law,
the civil service, scientific and managerial success, were
presented to the ambitious young as the most esteemed escape
routes from provincial confinement. The past, where it wasn't
simply boring, was sectarian, politically idiotic and to be
eschewed in favour of upward social mobility. By comparison
with the southern Protestant, regretting or redefining a heritage,
the northern Protestant was characterized by an impatience with
such roots as he did possess and an anxious concern to embrace
a more stimulating future in which power of various kinds
would be his to exercise and achievement, financial and social,
the appropriate reward. It is such a poetically unpromising social
milieu that James Simmons has courageously entered as a poet,
making his art amenable to a world apparently without any of

the mythological and historical resonance which so many Irish poets have exploited in an absorption with personal and communal pasts. Cutting himself loose from the past in the manner of his generation, he embraces its insecure freedoms if he does not seek its power or rewards.

Apparently lacking a myth, Simmons's most obvious expedient as an artist has been to mythologize selfhood through absolute candour. The self, lacking any remarkably significant social, historical or mythic dimensions, is rescued from insignificance by reason of the excruciating honesty with which it can address its primary concerns. Accordingly one of Simmons's predominant themes has been sexuality, in poems which have explored the subject with almost alarming directness. Marriage, seduction, adultery, masturbation, jealousy, lust, sexual ennui, erotic delight, bravado and failure, tenderness, violence, disgust, loss, divorce, renewal of sexual energy, have all received poetic treatment in Simmons's *oeuvre*, have been the vehicle of a view of things whose tenor is that integrity to self is a primary good.

Such integrity often, this poetry insists, involves irony, wry self-mockery, admission of ridiculous self-importance, which invest the work with much humourous good sense. This self is not only absolutely candid, it is also likely to get things in proortion:

> Reading old letters I see it's always myself
> I've been watching, an old maid on the shelf
> as far as life is concerned; not but what
> a prospectus might kid you I'd done a lot.[23]
>
> ('These I have loved')

But pretending not to take oneself too seriously is to take oneself very seriously indeed; and knowing it complicates the ironies, sending them rippling through poem after poem in which the self, without history or myth, comes to possess its own history and myth, its own recognizable dramatic presence in tone and attitude.

It would be wrong, however, to make too much of Simmons's dependence on candour to invest selfhood with significance, to mythologize the self. For a more fundamental aspect of his poetic faith is that everyday experience requires no metaphysical, religious or mythic justification to render it authentic. The quotidian miracle is miracle enough for a poet who believes ecstacy, pleasure, worth, are gifts life offers anyone. Simmons in fact felt strongly enough about this attitude, which informs so many of his poems, especially his tenderly grateful love poems, to make it the explicit matter of his longest work. 'No Land Is Waste, Mr Eliot' is therefore an aesthetic statement as well as a witty, deeply felt riposte to the poet of *The Waste Land*. Simmons latches onto the fact that Eliot's poem had its autobiographical origins and accordingly casts his reply in largely autobiographical terms, establishing that Eliot's 'lurid vision' does not 'touch reality', that well-bred nihilism, 'the up-tight quality in us all',[24] is a betrayal of life's ordinary plenitude.

> Alone in London in my latest teens,
> educated in all the shoddy dreams,
> exposed in an unjust society
> (though less unjust than England used to be)
> I felt, and still feel, life was good to me.[25]

Like *The Waste Land*, too, Simmons's poem is about living in London, but where Eliot, the brahmin provincial from St Louis by way of Cambridge, Mass, found in London a deeper kind of provincial horror (London as province of hell), 'No Land Is Waste, Mr Eliot' has a provincial middle-class young Irishman find both his feet and a kind of faith in the metropolis, as well as his poetic vocation. And he does so in the sort of seedy social ambiance that Eliot's poem renders with disgust. Simmons renders it with a zest which does not blind him to its pains, poignancies and disappointments.

These latter are mostly endured by the cast of characters who inhabit the poem in the same way as Eliot peoples *The Waste Land* with his contemporaries. But Simmons treats them as authentic individuals rather than as manifestations of metaphysical malaise. Perhaps one of the most successful of these vignettes is his portrait of a typist in 'Tiresias got it wrong' (poem 13 of the sequence). This is no fire sermon in which a young man carbuncular and his mechanical copulation are dismissively set in mythic context, but a real encounter between two real people, actual, only partially successful, fully human:

> Later he talks about being over-sexed
> and bores her visibly and is perplexed
> to see her change. Again he starts to hate
> her accent, thinks he will be desperate

> before he comes again, yet really misses
> the tenderness that touched him in her kisses.
> She puts a record on the gramophone,
> but he is going. When she is alone
> she wonders should she be more hard to get
> and wonders what he's thinking on his wet
> walk across London, and sits down to take
> the last half glass of wine, enjoy the ache
> inside her where the young man lately toiled,
> then bed-time cocoa when the milk has boiled.[26]

The crowded social canvas of 'No Land Is Waste, Mr Eliot' is obviously meant to remind of Eliot's populous poem. But the emulation is effortless which is, initially, surprising, until one remembers how Simmons's poetry as a whole is socially hospitable. Lacking a large inherited governing myth, Simmons is open in an engagingly democratic fashion to all-comers. Indeed the variety and interest of the *personae* he adopts, the individuals of whom he writes, and the personages he celebrates, would render rather ridiculous any claim that the lack of an northern Irish Protestant patrimony has been disabling to Simmons as an artist. Rather it has permitted an engaging eclecticism in which figures of canonical respectability (Donne, Yeats, John Clare) rub shoulders with the wicked uncle, Judy Garland and Jelly Roll Morton. By contrast with Murphy's rather attenuated sense of the present, Simmons's work has a richly variegated social awareness, its range of contemporary reference being one of the principal pleasures it affords. Almost everybody welcome, it announces; only bores and prigs stay home.

Nor has a lack of historic or mythic cultural inheritance inhibited the poet in his exploitation of mythic possibilities. Untroubled by necessity or responsibility, Simmons picks up what he needs as he goes along, the journey supplying the adventures. Edna Longley has isolated his primary quality as a poet as a 'special immediacy' which derives from the work's 'authenticity as the fluctuating response of a representatively "flawed" individual to a "chancy universe"'[27] and has perceptively suggested the presence of the 'Ulysses myth as a subterranean point of reference.'[28] Such a point of reference is clearly appropriate to the perennial optimism of Simmons's jaunty poetic embarkations, his ironic landfalls. Also to his celebration of wily survival against the odds, panache under pressure. Also to the figure of the poet as endlessly distractable by a song, a book, a Circe.

> They arrived almost too late
> on the run from insoluble
> complications; but lay down
> in darkness, able to wait
>
> for whatever the morning
> would bring, the house to be all
> they were hoping for,
> and the lakes, and Errigal.
>
> His watch strapped to his wrist
> as he slept. 'What next?
> When do we start?' he was asking,
> turned on like a light switch.
>
> No. He was there already,
> the window before him, a leafy shrine,
> to sunlight and love maybe,
> and all her warmth behind him.[28]
>
>   ('Dunlewey: 1977')

NOTES

1. James Simmons, *Constantly Singing* (Belfast 1980), p. 25
2. *Ibid*,p. 26
3. *Ibid*.
4. Richard Murphy, 'The Pleasure Ground', *The Listener*, 15 August 1963, p. 237.
5. *Ibid*.
6. *Ibid*.
7. *Ibid*.
8. *Ibid*., p. 240.
9. *Ibid*.
10. Seamus Heaney, 'The Poetry of Richard Murphy', *Irish University Review*, Vol. 7,No. 1 (Spring 1977), p. 22.
11. *Ibid*.
12. Richard Murphy, *Sailing to an Island* (London 1963), p. 14.
13. Richard Murphy, *High Island* (London 1974), p. 10.
14. Richard Murphy, *op. cit.*, p. 41.
15. Richard Murphy, *The Battle of Aughrim* (London 1968), p. 62.
16. Murphy is insistent on this point, taking Donald Davie to task when he appeared to associate him with the Anglo-Irish *pur sang*, in *The New York Review of Books*. See Donald Davie, 'Cards of Identity', *New York Review of Books*, 6 March 1975, pp. 10-11.

Murphy wrote to the editors, explicitly to remind Davie that in the poem he addresses 'Patrick Sarsfield, who fought on the losing Catholic Irish side, as my "great uncle", not vainly striving to identify myself with the equivalent of an Apache hero in the wars against the Yanqui conquerors, but precisely talking to the portrait of a man who was an uncle of mine ten generations removed'. The claim, in its very tenousness, seems, to me, rather to confirm Davie's view.

17. Richard Murphy, *op. cit.*, p. 11.
18. The issue of the *Irish University Review* devoted to Murphy's work and career provides a useful biographical chronology. See *Irish University Review*, Vol.7, No. 1 (Spring 1977), pp. 11-17.
19. Elizabeth Bowen has expressed this of the Anglo-Irish Big House in eloquent terms that bear on many of the novels their life has generated. See Elizabeth Bowen, *Bowen's Court* (London 1942).
20. Richard Murphy, *The Price of Stone* (London 1985), p. 27.
21. *Ibid.* p. 92.
22. James Simmons, *op. cit.*, pp. 26-7.
23. James Simmons, *Energy to Burn* (London 1971) p. 41.
24. The phrases are from the briefer though more informative notes which Simmons appends to his poem in the manner of the Eliot of *The Waste Land*.
25. James Simmons, *Judy Garland and the Cold War* (Belfast 1976) p. 41.
26. James Simmons, *op. cit.*, p. 57.
27. *Ibid.*, p. 3.
28. James Simmons, *Constantly Singing*, p. 23.

15

A NORTHERN RENAISSANCE :
POETS FROM THE NORTH OF IRELAND,
1965-1980

The first poem in Frank Ormsby's anthology, *Poets from the North of Ireland* (1979), included a line about a northern poet:

> His rainy countryside didn't, scholastically, exist.

Whether it can be said to exist in any worthwhile poetic or cultural sense is still a question that rouses critical heat. Thomas Kinsella, for example, thought it necessary to introduce his selection from contemporary Irish poetry in *The New Oxford Book of Irish Verse* in 1986 by dismissing the idea of a northern poetic renaissance almost out of hand. Admitting that the idea had 'acquired an aspect of official acceptance and support', he nevertheless reckoned it 'largely a journalistic entity'.[1] The manner of this summary judgement seemed a little too peremptory for comfort. It was as if the anthologist had too much at stake culturally to give detailed attention to the evidence for what he was so ready to set aside. And of course what might seem to be at risk in the idea of a northern renaissance is that unity of tradition (for all that the tradition is a bi-lingual one) that Kinsella's anthology is designed to promote and exhibit. For the emergence of a distinctive poetic in the north of Ireland is a challenge to the idea of Ireland's tradition that Kinsella identifies in his book and which he exemplifies in his markedly limited, even eccentric, choices from contemporary poets from north of the Irish border.

In seeking to discern in what ways recent literary developments in the north of Ireland might properly warrant the term 'renaissance', one is of course aware that there has been a good deal of casual commentary which has accepted the idea with a superficiality which deserves Kinsella's dismissive adjective. It can appear that a media-inspired notion of a renaissance was applied to the work of several distinctive talents in a manner gratifying to local *amour propre* but without much close attention to cultural fact. And the critic of poetry who knows how little the muse attends to political borders and imagined territories is instinctively disinclined to identify schools of English language poetry as if they existed in isolation from poetic activity in the rest of Ireland and the United Kingdom. For the idea of an Ulster renaissance seems to obscure the ways in which literary life in the province is merely a provincial expression of the general Irish and British cultures which considerably determine Northern Ireland's social experience. But it is my conviction that the idea of a northern renaissance is a critically useful one directing us to distinctive features of poetic activity by poets from the north of Ireland in the fifteen years between 1965 and 1980, in the period indeed when Northern Ireland was transformed from a province from which no poetry could be expected, to a place where a Belfast publisher could issue Ormsby's anthology without any sense that his enterprise was notably misguided.

It is in relation to formal and generic aspects of the northern poets' work that I believe it is possible to speak of a northern renaissance. The term is of course readily exploitable in journalistic commentary: it is all too easy to elevate by supposed association the output of contemporary writers at work in a context of political and national crisis, assuming that some kinds of undefined parallels exist between the Irish Renaissance of the 1880s and onwards and the recent proliferation of poets in the north. Desmond Maxwell has caustically advised in a passage where he reflects on the last occasion (in the early forties) when a northern poetic renaissance was, mistakenly, mooted: 'Naissance might in any case have been more accurately the word in dispute. There was no body of regional literature to be re-born.'[2] And despite the pioneering work of W. R. Rodgers and of John Hewitt, and despite the fact that new northern poets could repatriate Louis MacNeice as they cast about for poetic antecedents and turn to John Hewitt as an exemplary survivor, there were precious few grounds for believing in the 1960s that Ulster poetry was being reborn. Naissance might still have seemed the more appropriate word in a province without much of a poetic tradition.

Yet perhaps it is because the word 'renaissance' is so carelessly used in general that the ways in which it can be appropriately and usefully applied to cultural developments in the north are lost sight of. In defining the real parallels which exist between the northern poetic activity of the 'sixties and 'seventies and that of the years of the Irish Literary Renaissance or Revival, these may become clearer. A problem presents itself, however, as one embarks upon this project. For scholars and critics in recent years have in fact begun to cast doubts on the validity of considering even the Irish Literary Renaissance itself in such terms. AE's famous remark about a literary movement consisting 'of half a dozen writers living in the same city who cordially detest one another' is beginning to seem less simply iconoclastic than it once did in the decades when literary scholarship took the Irish Renaissance very much on the terms of its most active propagandist, the poet W. B. Yeats. One can detect a revisionist mood in Irish literary scholarship at the moment, sometimes based less on new historical findings than on boredom at an oft-told tale. But in as much as this revisionism has tried to establish novel explanations for literary developments in Ireland between 1880 and, say, 1940 it has tended to diminish the sense of the period as renaissance. For by proposing a continuity in that period with the Irish literary past, and by accounting for aspects of the literature in political, social and cultural terms, such thinking has seemed somewhat reductionist in effect if not in intent. F. S. L. Lyons's book *Culture and Anarchy in Ireland* (1979) was a stimulating example of this new trend in Irish scholarship, as indeed are the various essays which Seamus Deane has published since the mid-seventies in which the Literary Renaissance has been subjected to astringent demythologizing.[3] While it is certainly proper that the historical myths propagated by the principal Renaissance writers about their own work should be tested against new historical formulations, there may be a risk in such revisionism that the ways in which the Irish Literary Renaissance can properly be described as such will be forgotten. Setting the idea of the renaissance within a more detailed and comprehensive picture of Irish life in the latter half of the nineteenth-century and at the beginning of our own may certainly cut a lot of things down to size, including Yeatsian historiography. What it cannot cut down to size is the fact that, in the period in question, poetry, fiction and drama in the English language were revived. There *was* a literary renaissance in the precise sense that a variety of English literary genres which had seemed defunct, or at best dying on their feet, were wholly reinvigorated in the Irish air in which they found themselves, enjoying a late but nevertheless new lease on life. And it is when one regards it as a renaissance of genres and forms that the Irish Literary Renaissance becomes immune to reductionist critique.[4] For my purposes here it is enough to consider how in the period certain poetic forms were rejuvenated. Yeats inescapably supplies the texts.

Among the several traditional forms of English poetry that come to life anew in the Yeatsian canon are the romantic lyric, the metaphysical lyric and the public poem. The romantic lyric, which by the end of the nineteenth century in the English poetic tradition had evaporated to leave behind only the vapidity of the decadents' quest for the exquisite, was charged afresh with the drama of individual life in Yeats's work. A poem like 'The Cold Heaven', for example, written *circa* 1912, startlingly interjects passionate speech into the kind of poem that had seemed incapable of anything but precious mannerism as the nineteenth century ended. The metaphysical lyric which had seemed lost in the mazes of Tennysonian reflection and Arnoldian doubt, in a poem like 'A Dialogue of Self and Soul', is energized by a commitment to the vitality of abstract thought that distinguishes it from Victorian poetic exhaustion in the face of the demands of the intellectual life, at its most enervated in Arnold. And the public poem, almost disgracing itself in the imperialist verses of Kipling and Newbolt, following 'The Charge of the Heavy Brigade', is altogether redeemed in the poems Yeats wrote in response to public events in Ireland, from the Lock-Out and the Lane Gallery controversies of 1913 to the death of O'Higgins in 1927. In each instance it is striking that the poet in his Irish context felt no need to break with traditional English verse forms and techniques to achieve his purposes, rather attending scrupulously to the rhetorical demands of English poetics, proving to his own and his readers' satisfaction that even where the contents are fresh, 'ancient salt is best packing'. Perhaps indeed it was the very fact that Yeats was working in new territory as a poet that accounts for his perennial dependence on traditional English verse forms. Poets, like explorers, may need compasses when the terrain is new. But be that as it may, a more fundamental question presents itself: Why was it that in Ireland certain English poetic kinds and forms revived in the way they did in the period of the Irish Literary Renaissance?

Of the many answers which might be suggested, two also bear interestingly on the literary history of the north in its current phase. First, and this a fairly conventional view of the matter, the English poetic at the end of the nineteenth century encountered in Yeats's work a language which was novel to its experience. 'The poet's true commitment', the English poet Geoffrey Hill has asserted, 'must always be to the vertical richness of language. The poet's gift is to make history and politics and religion speak for themselves through the strata of language.'[5] And in Yeats, a poet with both gift and commitment, poetry in English had a opportunity to discover the possibilities of a language which history, politics and religion had stratified in ways unknown in England. English poets since Wordsworth had been conscious of the need for poetry to relocate itself periodically in new linguistic territories, and in the career of a Hopkins can be seen how desperate the programme became as that poet sought in the 1870s and 1880s, in Welsh and Old English poetry, in the dialect verse of William Barnes and in philological renovation, a language which would escape the perils of the Parnassian. For Yeats that revivifying language was to hand in the English spoken in Ireland, allowing for the virile dramatic utterance of a poet of major powers.

Secondly, the English poetic's emigration to Ireland in the work of Yeats revived certain kinds of poems because the new linguistic context was charged with new emotional possibilities. For it seemed possible in a culture where myths of personality like that surrounding Parnell's rise and fall combined with an historical myth of aspiration, betrayal and failure, for a poet to project his self-hood in ways that in late Victorian or Edwardian Britain would have seemed impossible, archaic, or merely preposterous. Accordingly, the poet's personal myth of sexual aspiration and failure, in an imaginative context that permitted excesses of self-dramatization, could be expressed without irony or embarrassment in the grandly dramatic manner of, for example, 'No Second Troy'.

It was also possible for Yeats, whose somewhat eccentric Irish education had for the most part shut him off from the humanistic intellectual traditions of nineteenth-century England (Hellenic and Hebraic modes of thought and feeling which could not sustain the assaults of scientific positivism and the Darwinian revolution), to explore alternative systems of occult thought with an altogether freer mind than that possessed by most of his English literary contemporaries. From what to the educated Victorian humanist would have seemed the faddish pre-occupations of the autodidact, he could assemble a body of doctrine so that the mind would not be helpless before its own contents and could express itself in the metaphysical lyric. In this way he again reminds of Hopkins, the only poet of nineteeth-century England who wrote genuinely metaphysical lyrics, and that only when he turned away from the nostalgias of the Oxford Movement and Pre-Raphaelitism for the stark conceptions of a scholasticism that to his contemporaries would have seemed the antithesis of humane culture. So poems like 'That Nature Is a Heraclitean Fire' and 'A Dialogue of Self and Soul' share a fresh energy of argument and structure and a sensuous pleasure in abstract thought absent from poetry in English since the seventeenth-century. And, finally, it was possible for Yeats to revive the public poem, since the ambiguities and tensions of his own social position, in a society that still cherished public life and utterance even perhaps at the expense of private feeling, forced on him dramatic experiments in the nature of the public poem which make works like 'Easter 1916' or 'Meditations in Time of Civil War' force-fields of tensions between private obsession and the public stage of the national event.

In northern poetry of the 1965 to 1980 period, there was a similar regeneration of poetic form, that form being the well-made lyric which has been the hardy perennial of twentieth-century English poetry. At its most successful in the work of Thomas Hardy, the form was the staple of the Georgian Anthology, and it re-emerged at mid-century a little wryer and less assured after the Modernist invasion, in the poetics of the Movement in the 1950s and most successfully in Philip Larkin's *The Whitsun Weddings* (1964). Poems of this kind are easily characterized. They customarily employ traditional metrics, root themselves in quotidian experience and, attentive to empirical fact, proceed through a controlled narrative discursiveness. The protracted spry vigour of this poetic form has, however, shown distinct signs of giving way to terminal decline in the England where until recently it found a very congenial setting. Philip Larkin's *High Windows* (1974), for example, despite local successes like 'The Building', had an air of self-conscious nostalgia in its central attitudes and a suggestion that the poet knew how little his quietly urbane or cantankerous reflections bore on the daily concerns of the contemporary world. And Donald Davie, the critic, who did more than any other to identify even as he was to repudiate the poetic tradition of the well-made poem in the English twentieth century,[6] at a mature stage in his career sought, in more intensive ways than before, to discover a cultural and linguistic setting in which poems not unlike those he most admires, the verses of the English eighteenth-century, could be written and have a meaningful existence. For it is the poet's instinct for what he believes are aesthetic deficiencies in current English usage, and his distress at the paucity of contemporary thought made explicit in such usage, that, one senses, governed Davie's deepening interest in English puritanism.[7] The poet discerns in the puritan tradition the presence of a language that once embodied (in a way unknown to English poets in the present) discipline and passion in an ordered, conservative art, permitting an ennobling relationship to exist between poetry and a possible social order. But since the poet cannot find a credible location for such an art in terms of his own experience, his involvement with anachronistic modes must be seen as a peculiarly frustrated effort to renovate the past in the interests of a present where the poet recognizes

> The Gutenberg era, the era of rhyme, is over.
> It's an end to the word-smith, now, an end to the Skald,
> an end to the erudite, elated rover
> threading a fiord of words. Four letter expletives
> are all of that Ocean's plankton that still lives.[8]

A poetic tradition is overcome with the sense of its own ending, begins to feel the years as it recognizes its inevitable redundancy. And for Davie this is a tragic awareness.

In the north of Ireland since the 1960s the well-made poem discovered a cultural ecology (to expand Davie's image) in which it could not only live but thrive, where the word-smith could still ply a significant trade and the erudite, elated rover thread his fiord of words (almost anticipatory definitions in Davie's poem of Seamus Heaney's gift). As in the revival of poetic forms in the Irish renaissance of the 1880s onwards, the linguistic features of the territory in which the well-made twentieth-century English poem found itself in Ulster can account for the distinct sense of formal revival that one gains from a reading of the poems that were written by northern poets. For since the mid 1960s a form apparently on its last legs in England flourished in a new environment notable for its rich linguistic distinctiveness. The well-made poem, to which most of the poets from the north of Ireland seemed inextricably wedded, found itself required to accommodate a language of a kind unfamiliar to it. In fact Seamus Heaney in his volumes *Wintering Out* (1972) and *North* (1975) made the strata of the north's distinctive linguistic geology the matter of much poetic archaeology, suggesting his awareness of what was afoot:

> But now our river tongues must rise
> From licking deep in native haunts
> To flood, with vowelling embrace,
> Demesnes staked out in consonants.
>
> And Castledawson we'll enlist
> And Upperlands, each planted bawn –
> Like bleaching-greens resumed by grass –
> A vocable, as rath and bullaun.[9]

And sections of John Montague's *The Rough Field* (1972) were deeply absorbed by a pained awareness of Ulster's complex linguistic inheritance.

By a happy chance, the precise nature of that inheritance was the object of sustained contemporaneous scholarly attention. Accordingly, the critic and cultural historian has a good deal of established fact as well as the largely intuitive apprensions of the poets to guide him in his reflections on the relationship of poetry to its linguistic context in the north of Ireland. For concurrent with the emergence of northern poetry in the fifteen years after 1965, dialect scholars and scientific linguists were labouring assiduously to map the linguistic terrain of the northern Irish counties. In so doing they were, perhaps unknowingly, laying the groundwork for what could be a rewarding and possibly unique study in the future: to examine in an extensive and rigorous way how the poetry of the north in the period was invigorated by its specific linguistic hinterland. It might, indeed, prove possible in such a study to demonstrate that what the cultural historian suspects of both the Irish Literary Renaissance and of the poetic renaissance in the north that has produced such a crop of poets, is grounded in the confirmatory facts of a particular case. And if this were done, the sort of speculative theory that critics can so easily take for granted about the vitality of poetic forms being dependent on rejuvenating linguistic challenge and opportunity might receive intensively detailed confirmation.

At a fairly general level one might initiate the enterprise by quoting John Braidwood's characterization (based on detailed analysis) of Ulster Scots' speech, in his essay 'Ulster and Elizabethan English':

In general Ulster speech lacks the exuberance of southern Anglo-Irish. . . over large areas of Ulster native English speakers replaced the Irish, and many of their English speakers were Scots. Medieval Scots is a magnificently expressive and exuberant language, and one has only to read the medieval Scots makers, or browse through the pages of the two Scottish dictionaries now in progress, to realize how extensive and tragic has been the loss and how irreplaceable. The Ulster Scot resembles the modern Scot in being linguistically canny and economical. However reticent the English may appear to foreigners, the Scot and the Ulster Scot regard English loquacity with something almost akin to horror. The Scot may, indeed, on occasion rise to the heights of eloquence, but it takes strong emotion, or strong drink, to move him. His eloquence is rarely so spontaneous as the Elizabethan English or the Irish; he does not love talk for talk's sake. Though prone to argumentativeness he distrusts the gift of the gab. He feels committed to his utterance as no Irishman does. His strong educational tradition, and his linguistic uncertainty caused by the abandonment, for official purposes at least, of his native idiom confirm his linguistic reticence. For this reason he often appears to speak like a book, though, Scots being a slower and heavier speech than English, and more emphatic, he may sometimes, like the American, be accused of speaking more emphatically than he intends.[10]

It may be true that the bluntness of most northerners described here by Professor Braidwood is, as Seamus Deane has caustically put it, 'no more than a kind of demoralised honesty' since 'he feels he might as well have his prejudices gratified, whatever else he may starve'.[11] But what is crucial to my argument is that this relation to one's language, both austerely committed and insecure, conscious ambivalently of linguistic usage in England and in the rest of Ireland that differs from one's own, aware of the logical structures to which language must often be subsidiary, is a complex of feeling provocative of a distinctive poetic discourse. We find such a distinctive discourse at its most exactingly controlled in the poetry of Derek Mahon. His poem 'Gipsies Revisited' supplies a text:

> Sorry, gippos, I have
> watched the dark police
> rocking your caravans
> to wreck the crockery
> and wry thoughts of peace
> you keep there on waste
> ground beside motorways
> where the snow lies late
> and am ashamed – fed,
> clothed, housed and ashamed.
>
> You might be interested
> to hear, though, that on
> stormy nights our strong
> double glazing groans with
> foreknowledge of death,
> the fridge with a great wound,
> and not surprised to know
> the fate you have so long
> endured is ours also:
> the cars are piling up.
> I listen to the wind
> and file receipts. The heap
> of scrap metal in my
> garden grows daily.

On a casual reading this might seem a not especially remarkable empirical reflection of the kind that a Movement poet might have employed to turn a verse or two. However, Mahon's characteristic stance, compact of affirmation and retreat, rendered here in the lyrical pedantry of a precise terminlogy and syntax of reticent emotion, makes of a slight occasion a minor day of judgment, anticipated ironically by a guilty mind. The poem opens with portentous authority:

> I have
> watched the dark police

> rocking your caravans
> to wreck the crockery[12]

but then, as if conscious that such emphatic utterance will weigh too heavily on the matter of the poem, the poet shifts to a conceit which we are directed to read ironically (the irony being against the poet) by the word 'wry'. But despite this ironic grace-note the first movement of the poem is dominated by a slow emphasis which shifts from eloquence to the gravity of moral adjudication:

> and am ashamed – fed,
> clothed, housed and ashamed.

The second movement undercuts that opening with the diffidence of 'You might be interested to hear, though' and of 'and not surprised to know'. Emphatic eloquence nevertheless cannot be long denied as the poet adopts a weightier, more Latinate syntax (Horace by way of MacNeice):

> the fate you have so long
> endured is ours also. . .

Then the word 'foreknowledge', theologically Calvinist in its provenance, suggests a puritan's exactitude of definition and solemnity of judgment. The poem ends unsure of its own emotion, the poet himself and a semi-absurd figure filing receipts against the wind, his garden a semi-surreal disaster area. A linguistic insecurity expressed in tones of emphasis and withdrawal has made for a poem charged with complicated feeling. The peculiarities of a certain kind of linguistic usage can be seen here therefore to have invested what might have been a fairly trite poem with an astingency of emotion not often to be found in English Movement poetry to which it initially seemed to bear a family resemblance.

But it is not only that the well-made lyric in the north discovered a new set of linguistic possibilities in its sea- voyage to Ireland. It was forced to negotiate a different imaginative landscape. It has been a notable feature of the well-made lyrics of modern English poetry, from Hardy to Larkin, that they have all shared an intimacy with landscape. Indeed it might be argued that the idea of landscape with which the poets of this tradition have customarily been absorbed is an expresssion of their conservatism and of their provincial disclination to admit the radical implications of modernism to what they would like to believe is the English consciousness. For a sense of landscape can seem to postpone the need to come to terms with modernism's demand for a new aesthetic for a new age, as well-made English poems, even if only in terms of nostalgia, insist on their continuity with the central poetic tradition of the past for which landscape was a primary reality. But the modern English experience conceived of as landscape has been signally pallid. It is a 'landscape', as Donald Davie avers, 'where virtually all the sanctuaries have been violated, all the pieties blasphemed', in which poetry 'suffers from the loss, or the drastic impoverishment, of the traditional images of celebration'.[13] What is left is a suburbanized scene, as in Larkin, in which the impoverished landscape is a metaphor of social and cultural decline with the poet as 'the saddest heart in the supermarket',[14] bereft of major emotion, subsisting on rue.

In the north of Ireland things were different. Carefully structured empirically rooted poems found themselves required to pick their way through a landscape more akin to a minefield than a suburb or provincial waste. Indeed that northern poets found the well-made empirical lyric so sympathetic a form for their work in the 1970s may in fact derive from their consciousness of the dangerous territory they inhabit. Where English Movement poets sought to discover in the 1950s emotional resonances within the limits of domesticity and the provincial in default of any other possibilities, recent northern Irish poets have treated domestic life with an insecure sense of the horrors outside their front doors, where the northern landscape is charged with atavisms and significances that might overwhelm the imagination. Home for some of these poets is all they dare contemplate directly:

> I have heard of an island
> With only one house on it.
> The gulls are at home there.
> Our perpetual absence
> Is a way of leaving
> All the eggs unbroken
> That litter the ground
> Right up to its doorstep.[15]

In these chilly lines by Michael Longley one senses a careful,

214

crafted art coming to the edge of its competence, recognizing beyond its precise itemizing, reality that might disrupt it entirely if the poet's attention shifted, as those eggs can only survive if we do not lumber into the poem with our weighty presence. So, such a fragile poem achieves an emotional rigour in its intimations of horrific alternatives. And it does so while remaining untouched by any of the elegiac, valedictory notes that tend to sweeten with sentiment even the most austere of Larkin's poems ('High Windows' in the volume of that name, and 'The Explosion' with which that book concludes, for example).

The northern Irish context has therefore, I would argue, charged the well-made, crafted verse of the poets in the 1970s with a tense astringency that represented a renaissance of a poetic form which seemed to have exhausted its possibilities in contemporary England. For many of their poems, so carefully constructed, so rooted in immediate, empirical experience, also managed a cool lack of tonal complacency which absolved their measured art from any charge of evasion in an environment as demanding as northern Ireland has been in its recent past. As various genres and poetic forms were revivified in the linguistic and cultural context of the Ireland of the 1880s and onwards, so the modern English poetic in terms of the well-made empirical lyric found in the northern counties of Ireland a similar new territory in which to be rejuvenated. The Northern Renaissance was a renaissance for a particular kind of poem.

But – and this suggests that the future of poetry in the north will show a development away from the tautly crafted art in which it achieved its surest successes in the 1970s – this was a renaissance oddly dissatisfied with its own procedures. The motif of the car or bus journey, the drive through or to a difficult poetic territory, was a repetitive preoccupation for northern poets in the period and a metaphoric expression of this dissatisfaction.

In one mode, the journey poem allowed poets to widen the horizons of their art without great risk, enabling them to inspect landscapes without involvement, inured by the protective hermeticism of vehicle and poem. Here the poet is prepared to travel beyond the personal world in which he sets his empirical art to admit more disturbing perspectives. But he declines to step into the landscape. Heaney, for example, glimpsed Long Kesh prison camp 'From a dewy motorway'[16] and contemplated the risk of blasphemy in 'The Tollund Man',

> driving,
> Saying the names
> Tollund, Grauballe, Nebelgard,
> Watching the pointing hands
> Of the country people,
> Not knowing their tongue[17]

where the motif of the car journey suggests an effort to maintain the rationality implicit in the restrained, negotiatory articulation of the poem as it is threatened by the powers of 'the cauldron bog' and the archaic atavism of 'our little destiny'. Similarly, Frank Ormsby's poem 'Landscape with Figures' records a scenic observation 'from a bus window' which haunts him but does not disturb the ordered structure of the poem, even as it hints at depths in the past the poet cannot comprehend:

> All lanes and houses
> Secretive in trees and gaunt hills' jawlines
> Turn my thoughts again
> To that day's journey and the thing I saw
> And could not fathom.[18]

By contrast, the journey in another more ambitious mode can be an escape from the haunting landscape of the north or 'the man-killing parishes' out there in Jutland. In 'Westering' by Seamus Heaney we drive away from Donegal as the

> Roads unreeled, unreeled.[19]

In 'Night Drive' by the same poet

> The smells of ordinariness
> Were new on the night drive through France: . . .[20]

Field Work (1979) opens with a drive to a place where a 'perfect memory' can be laid down 'In the cool of thatch and crockery',[21] a memory akin to that which a drive around the Ards peninsula can provide, a dream of freedom which may not start the poems flowing but can supply a new kind of clue to more familiar landscapes:

> When you have nothing more to say, just drive
> For a day all round the peninsula.
> The sky is tall as over a runway,

216

> The land without marks so you will not arrive
>
> But pass through, though always skirting landfall.
> . . . .
> And drive back home, still with nothing to say
> Except that now you will uncode all landscapes,
> By this: things founded clean on their own shapes,
> Water and ground in their extremity.[22]

Such journeys aspire to escape history, to be rid of the weight of an all-too-familiar place and the linguistic depth which preserves that knowledge, for a freer art. Derek Mahon begins one poem:

> I want to be
> Like the man who descends
> At two milk churns
>
> With a bulging
> String bag and vanishes
> Where the lane turns,
>
> Or the man
> Who drops at night
> From a moving train
>
> And strikes out over the fields
> Where fireflies glow
> Nor knowing a word of the language.[23]

But the most ubiquitous journey in northern poetry in the period is neither the journey of self-consciously protected observation nor the escapist day-trip around the peninsula, the voyage away from history, but a drive back to atavisms the poet senses he has in part left behind, or towards energies and forces he knows the landscape contains which may yet overwhelm him. Poet after poet in the north has written poems that imagine the journey back to origins, to the primal place, to Garvaghey, to Belfast, to Derry, to visit home, to make, in the title of Frank Ormsby's beautiful poem of pained home-coming, 'Winter Offerings'. Such poems enforce a sense that the poet knows there are things in the individual and collective past and present which his art must encompass if it is to be true to Irish reality. John Montague made this quite explicit in an interview he gave in 1979: 'Ulster is something we have to come to terms with. Unless we come to terms with it, there will be lack in us *as*

217

writers.'[24] Other poets are less explicit, but the sense is there in many of their poems which employ landscape as a metaphor of poetic progress towards that encompassing art. The poet imagines a journey to a dangerous, imaginative territory of which his art must ultimately take account. Mahon's 'Day-Trip to Donegal' is such a journey into an experience which no empirical, rational art could finally control, to a region beyond the ken of the well-made poem:

> At dawn I was alone far out at sea
> Without skill or reassurance (nobody
> To show me how, no earnest of rescue),
> Cursing my mindless failure to take due
> Forethought for this, contriving vain
> Overtures to the mindless wind and rain.[25]

Common to each of these metaphoric journeys to aesthetically freer or more challenging territories, known or unknown, is the sense of conscious or unconscious dissatisfaction with the limits of poetry as coherent, logical discourse; a conservative art – the poetry of the Northern Renaissance – I am arguing, contained metaphors of its own partiality. Indeed in employing such metaphors it made poetry of a burgeoning aesthetic ambition.

In the 1980s that ambition was realized in the work of two poets of a later generation than that which began publishing in the mid sixties and with whom the idea of northern renaissance is most commonly associated. Paul Muldoon's poem 'The More a Man Has the More a Man Wants', included in his collection *Quoof* (1983), and Ciaran Carson's collection *The Irish for No* (1987) both suggest in the complexity of their handling of content and form that the ready association of the well-made poem with a northern poetic is now a matter of history. But, interestingly, both these collections assume the poetic gains of their predecessors, even if those are sometimes available only as opportunities for parody. Both poets exploit with assured ease the demotic variety of northern Irish speech patterns and vocabulary, and Muldoon especially and to a lesser extent Carson set their arresting sequences of surreal narrative against the ostensible rationality and order of the well-crafted lyric. Muldoon's 'The More a Man Has the More a Man Wants' is in fact a series of forty-nine unrhymed sonnets where the fixed nature of the work's recurrent forms serves as a kind of ironic pointer to the essentially metamorphic activity of the narrative. Carson, in similar fashion, anchors his weirdly mutating narratives in the precisely observed detail of a realistic but vanished Belfast that might have been the basis of an empirical if nostalgic art. But both poets confront the experience of living in the dangerous territory that the north represents for them through an art that suggests the polysemic freedom of dream. Both poets accept the artistic challenge of seeking to encompass in art the horrors of political violence. They do so, furthermore, with a kind of freedom from humanist moral concern which makes their work imaginatively exhilarating when its ostensible subject might be reckoned wholly appalling. And the fact that the northern nightmare can now only be poetically comprehended in terms of the metaphor of metamorphosis, is, when one reflects on the frozen nature of political expression in the province, not without political and social hope.

Muldoon's poem recounts a bizarre narrative which takes a shape-changing hero (betimes Gallogly, Gollogly, Golightly, Ingoldsby, gallowglass) on a cosmopolitan sexual and hallucinogenic trip, which improbably includes the North at war. Gallogly is a wilful, mischievous trickster (the poem draws on North American Indian folklore, as well as on the more contemporary lore of the acid-head and the drug-inspired visionary) whose playful interference with conventional reality can include such japes as bloody murder:

> The U.D.R. corporal had come off duty
> To be with his wife
> While the others set about
> a follow-up search.
> When he tramped out just before twelve
> to exercise his greyhound
> he was hit by a single high-velocity
> shot.
> You could, if you like, put your fist
> in his chest.
> He slumps
> in the spume of his own arterial blood
> like an overturned paraffin lamp.[26]

But it can also include parody of Ulster pastoral and linguistic evasion:

> Gallogly lies down in the sheugh
> To munch
> through a Beauty of
> Bath. He repeats himself, *Bath*,
> under his garlic-breath.
> *Sheugh*, he says. *Sheugh.*
> He is finding that first 'sh'
> increasingly difficult to manage.
> *Sh*-leeps.[27]

The overall effect is of a fictive disassociation between event, language and narrative which serves to suggest the experience of living in the midst of a violence that bears little relationship to the various ideologies which sustain or seek to justify it. The world of Muldoon's remarkable poem is shockingly recognizable in its laconic juxtapositions of folklore, legend, sexual argot and knowing consumerist reference with atavism and atrocity.

A similar, unnerving sense of an entirely recognizable world mediated in a narrative of dream-like, cinematic cross-fades and shifting perspectives is produced by Carson's *The Irish for No.* But where the centre of Muldoon's poem is occupied by the protean antics of Gallogly, Carson's collection has the perpetually adaptive histrionics of the human voice as its strategic principle. Carson's world is the city of the mind, where memory, place and destructive violent change constitute a challenge to the narrative structures of speech itself. Carson's model of such speech is the relentless verbal assurance of the seanachie, but whereas in the past such a figure may have presumed a static world of genealogical inheritance and local legend as matter for his narrative, the Belfast of the eighties demands constant realignments, re-orientations, reformulations, as art seeks to contour speech to the inchoate social experience of a city in disintegration. The tone is exuberantly colloquial, exploiting the rich textures of Belfast demotic, a kind of side-of-the-mouth Irish Chandlerese, interjectory, garrulous, funny, compulsively derisive, elliptical and unstoppable. A constant preoccupation is the vanished city of Belfast now only available in an obsessive memory of a place which has ceased to exist, transformed as it has been into a dream-landscape in which the human voice is the only certainty. In such writing, as in the coolly hallucinatory imaginings of Paul Muldoon, we realize how far contemporary poetry from the north of Ireland has travelled from the empirical, well-made poem in which in the sixties and seventies it had some of its surest successes:

As the Guinness-like chiaroscuro of the cat settled into the
    quickthorn hedge
I had a feeling I'd been there before: in a black taxi, for
    example, when this bullet
Drilled an invisible bee-line through the open window and
    knocked a chip
Off the Scotch sandstone façade of the Falls Road Library.
    Everybody ducked
To miss the already-dead split-second; the obvious soldier
    relaxed back into
His Guinness-and-tan uniform, since to hear the shot is to
    know you are alive.

It is this lapse of time which gives the film its serial quality: the
    next
Episode is about the giant statue of the newly renovated
    Carson, verdigris becoming
Bronze. It is suggested that it might be camouflage – as glossed
    on
In the SF novels of W. D. Flackes, particularly in
    his novel, *The X*
People. And so in the words of another commentator, *the future is
    only today*
Fading into the past – drawing, perhaps, a retrospective dotted
    line on the map

For from here the border makes a peninsula of the South,
    especially in the shallows
Of Lough Erne, where so much land is so much water anyway.

(from 'Serial')[28]

NOTES

1. Thomas Kinsella, Introduction to *The New Oxford Book of Irish Verse* (London and New York 1986), p. xxx.
2. D. E. S. Maxwell, 'Contemporary Poetry in the North of Ireland' in *Two Decades of Irish Writing*, ed. Douglas Dunn (Cheadle Hulme 1975), p. 167.
3. See Seamus Deane, 'Irish Poetry and Irish Nationalism' in *Two Decades of Irish Writing*, pp. 4-22; 'The Appetites of Gravity', *The Sewanee Review*, vol. LXXXIV, no. 1 (1976), pp. 199-208; and 'The Literary Myths of the Revival: A Case for their Abandonment'in *Myth and Reality in Irish Literature*, ed. Joseph Ronsley (Waterloo 1977), pp. 317-29. See also Seamus Deane, *Celtic Revivals* (London 1985), where part of the first of these appeared in modified form, together with a reprinted version of the latter-named essay.
4. This point is suggestively made by Ronald Schleifer in his introduction to *The Genres of the Irish Literary Revival*, ed. R. Schleifer, (Norman 1980).
5. Geoffrey Hill, 'Under Judgement', interview with Blake Morrison, *New Statesman*, Vol. 99, No. 2551 (8 February 1980), p. 214.
6. See Donald Davie, *Thomas Hardy and British Poetry* (London 1973).
7. See also Donald Davie, *A Gathered Church: the Literature of the English Dissenting Interest* (London 1978).
8. Cited in Eric Homberger, *The Art of the Real, Poetry in England and America since 1939* (London 1977), p. 84.
9. Seamus Heaney, 'A New Song' *Wintering Out* (London 1972), p. 33.
10. John Braidwood, 'Ulster and Elizabethan English' in *Ulster Dialects: An Introductory Symposium* (Holywood 1964), p. 82. This volume would make a useful starting-point for the kind of study I am mooting.
11. Seamus Deane, 'The Northern Minority: The Super Teagues', *Third Degree*, No. 1 (1977), p. 9.
12. Derek Mahon, *Lives* (London 1972), p. 29.
13. Cited in Homberger, *op. cit.*, p. 83.
14. The phrase is Randall Jarrell's, also cited in Homberger.
15. Dedicatory poem to Longley's collection *The Echo Gate* (London 1979).
16. Seamus Heaney, 'Whatever You Say Say Nothing', *North* (London 1975), p. 60.
17. Heaney, *Wintering Out*, p. 48.
18. Frank Ormsby, *A Store of Candles* (London 1977), p. 4.
19. Heaney, *Wintering Out*, p. 80,
20. Heaney, *Door into the Dark* (London 1969), p. 34.
21. Heaney, 'Oysters', *Field Work* (London 1979), p. 11.
22. Heaney, 'Peninsula', *Door into the Dark*, p. 21.
23. Derek Mahon, 'The Last of the Fire Kings', *The Snow Party* (London 1975), p. 9.
24. 'Global Regionalism', interview with John Montague, *The Literary Review*, Vol. 22, No. 2 (Winter 1979), p. 166.
25. Derek Mahon, *Night Crossing* (London 1968), p. 23.
26. Paul Muldoon, *Quoof* (London 1983), p. 49.
27. *Ibid*.
28. Ciaran Carson, *The Irish for No* (Dublin 1987), p. 51.

16

REMEMBERING WHO WE ARE

I

In his poem 'After the Summit' in *Liberty Tree* (1983), Tom Paulin reflects plaintively on the northern Protestant's contemporary lack of a significant historical inheritance:

> Boot polish and the Bible,
> the Boys' Brigade is arming.
> This is the album you found
> in your grandmother's sideboard,
> the deedbox with her burial papers,
> a humped ledger and a lock
> of that dead uncle's hair.
> There is so little history
> we must remember who we are.

In view of the recurrent complaint, usually voiced by impatient British commentators on Irish affairs, that Irishmen of all persuasions are invincibly attached to an all-too-palpable historical legacy, Paulin's sense of deprivation might strike one as beside the point. It isn't – rather, it's a perception of poverty grounded in an accurate reading of the northern Protestant's historical imagination. That imagination is one that has in modern times (at least since 1886) had recourse to a vision of the Protestant community's history which is starkly simple in outline and depressingly lacking in emotional range and complexity. In that sense, a community that superficially might appear to be burdened by historical awareness can accurately be said to possess 'so little history'.

The study of historiography, like so many other branches of cultural history, is in Ireland in its infancy. The writing of the modern political history of the country has involved scholars in so many difficulties of approach and emphasis (not to mention the official indifference to documentary evidence with which they have had so often to contend) that any sustained reflection on the writing of history itself in the country and how this activity might bear on the popular consciousness is very hard to discover. Professor Oliver MacDonagh is one who has made some attempts to explore the matter.

Professor MacDonagh has in recent years proposed the thesis that modern Irish historical awareness is the product of developments in early nineteenth century historiography.[1] In the period between 1790 and 1820, MacDonagh notes, Catholic historians laboured to reveal the magnificence of ancient Celtic Ireland while their Protestant contemporaries were assiduous in anti-Romantic reductionism. What they shared, however, was a predilection for eliding time, foreshortening historical chronology, even in a sense annulling it, so that 'the character of druidical Ireland was being treated as validating or otherwise, in some significant degree, the early nineteenth century political and social order'. MacDonagh argues that in the years following the 1798 Rebellion and the period when Catholic Emancipation was a compelling issue, this predilection helped to validate current political actions and assertions. To write history was not to offer a neutral account of sequential events – rather, the historian was the custodian of a sacred, tribal narrative, and this form of historiography became dominant within Ireland. Such a temporal awareness, MacDonagh argues, also infused Irish historiography at its modern commencement, and it continues to shape 'the historical assumptions of most ordinary Irish people'.

If we accept MacDonagh's thesis, the consequences of this sacral reading of Irish history are everywhere to be seen in Irish political life. Since history is not to be understood as a series of events occurring as time passes but as a permanently existing reality to which appeal can be made in order to endorse contemporary political deeds, a sense of historical repetition is inevitable . Events are seen as expressing perennial aspects of an ineluctable condition. And this Irish condition is always reckoned to involve moral and legal absolutes, primordially determined and unaffected by the passage of time. So the Easter Proclamation is profoundly expressive of popular Irish historical consciousness in its reference to six earlier assertions of Irish nationhood in arms with its commitment to a seventh (the number seven possessing appropriately sacred, even mystical resonances).

MacDonagh's thesis is highly persuasive. Less so is his account of the reasons why such an historical consciousness developed in Ireland when it did. He recognizes that the historiography of the late eighteenth and early nineteenth centuries was 'politics by other means' but instead of employing this conception as an analytic tool he has recourse to a speculation which is less that fully convincing. Ireland as a Christian society was apparently fertile ground for a view of history which, in a modulation of Ranke's famous *dictum* 'Every generation is equidistant from eternity', is readily to be accommodated with belief in a supreme moral being who stands 'outside time entirely, without yesterdays or tomorrows, omni- present in an ever-present'.

More credible as explanation, as MacDonagh implicitly accepts in his essay, is that a politically dispossessed people confronted by manifestly greater powers than they knew themselves to possess sought what weapons they could to prosecute their cause. One of these was a historical myth, gratifying in as much as it gave a sense of historic nationalist authenticity to political aspirations and functional in as much as it could discomfort opponents by its implacable moralism. If the religious sensibility of the Irish had anything to do with their historiographical awareness in the nineteenth century (and indeed in the twentieth), it was surely that the generally calamitarian mood of mid- and late-Victorian British society invested an already sacral sense of the past and the present (in which events recur according to a typology) with millenialist expectancy.

So a nascent Irish Catholic nation in the nineteenth century provided itself with the kind of historical awareness it needed both for self-sustenance and for the purposes of propaganda. A myth of the indestructible Irish nation with immemorial rights permanently infringed gave moral impetus to political agitation for specific reforms and for separatism. A vision of the Irish people permanently betrayed by traitorous informers and national apostates accounted for the fact that an historic nation possessing remarkable resources had for so long been in thrall to an alien tyranny. A myth of origins in an heroic past gave conviction, in a cyclical view of things, to the work for a cultural revival which was imaginatively intuited as a re-enactment of the past and a creation of the future (the title of Yeats's essay 'The Stirring of the Bones' captures just the sense of regeneration and repetition that I am suggesting Irish historiographical awareness gave to the Literary Revival). As a reading of social reality this mode of thought and feeling gave to nationalist Irishmen and women a complex, rich, emotional identity. Perennial features of the human condition – suffering, loss, aspiration, daring, rebellion, sacrifice, moral conviction, communal feeling, hope, transcendence of the material world through creativity – are encompassed within it, which fact undoubtedly helps account for its tenacious hold on the Irish mind. There is, to reverse Paulin's poetic formulation, so much history that it can sometimes be difficult for the individual nurtured in Irish nationalism to step outside its complex of emotional ideas and see himself in different terms.

II

The contemporary northern Protestant's sense of history is, I would argue, markedly similar to that of the Catholic nationalist. That his history seems impoverished by comparison with nationalist historical awareness is because that history has had to perform fewer functions and is necessarily simpler. By its nature, it is bound to comprehend imaginatively much less of the human condition. Northern Protestants, as inheritors of those who have prosecuted the political cause of the Protestants of Ireland, have in the last analysis only the one historical requirement – to uphold the Settlement of 1689 and to try to ensure that the principle of Protestant hegemony is recognized and supported. Accordingly, in MacDonagh's words, 'The siege of Derry in 1689 is their original and most powerful myth. They seem to see themselves in that, and since then, as an embattled and enduring people. Their historical self-vision is of endless repetition of repelled assaults, without hope of absolute finality or fundamental change in their relationship to their surrounding and surrounded neighbours.' To this one would only wish to add that this primal sense of siege has, like nationalist historiography, been infused with millenialism (the assaults may be endless but faith must recurrently be placed in the powers of some eschatalogically prescient prophet). And it draws also on a dour blend of the Calvinistic doctrine of election with a Whiggish commitment to a liberty which can only be enjoyed by those possessed of the true faith. As an interpretation of human experience such a historical myth is not without some merit; tenacity, acceptance of suffering, will, are the emotional registers of which it can take account. But there is little else to recommend it for it is disabled by an insecure imaginative exclusiveness. Indeed that the siege was, in the telling of the tale, self-imposed by the Apprentice boys, the temporizing Lundy forced to flee the city, seems metaphorically appropriate to the emotionally exclusive quality of the northern Protestant's historical self-vision. And it may be this emotional narrowness in the northern Protestant's basic self-vision that has led to the literary trope of 'the Black North', with its sense of restriction, bleakness and atrophied possibility which is employed in dozens of poems, novels and plays,[2] and representatively in a poem by Patrick Williams, 'Cage Under Siege' (published in Padraic Fiacc's anthology of 1974, *The Wearing of the Black*).

> This is home. This is the Irish North.
> Where we endure the earth's falling away
> Rivets an iron sky to north and west.
> Where the covetous South darkens, granite
> Rears a grave wall. Eastward the sea recoils
> Toward England, breathless with horror, sobs back.
>
> On our borders the known world ends sheer.
> We've pulled the sea around us like a shawl
> And heaved the mountains higher. The waiting
> South's bog-barbarians starve against a grand
> Squiggle on our map. The sky is closed.
> This is home. This is the Irish North.

Writing in 1699 of the Established Church in Ireland, Sir Robert Southwell (the diplomat and principal Secretary of State for Ireland) referred to 'those English Protestants who have nothing on this side of paradise to adhere to but old England'. For most of the time since the Settlement of 1689 northern Protestants have not been forced to place their trust in heaven alone. This is because British power has in varying degrees and for varying reasons sought to protect their position, allowing them the dubious luxury of permanent dependency in a country where, had such support been definitively withdrawn, they would have been forced to develop a different, ultimately more truly serviceable self-understanding and historiographical consciousness. And British policy in Ireland has accordingly been able to depend for its needs upon one apparent constant in Irish affairs: that whatever internal differences there may have been within the northern Protestant community – for example, between Episcopalians and Presbyterians – that community will unite in oppostion to any threat of domination by Catholic Ireland. With one exception – the years leading to the '98 Rebellion – this has always been the case. And it has been especially apparent since 1886. Indeed, it was the prospect of Home Rule which in the years between 1886 and the Great War forged the modern Ulster Unionist identity, an identity which subsumed manifold differences within northern Protestant society in a fundamental all-embracing opposition to the proposed constitutional change. Since that time, the historical myth of siege has had its greatest social utility as the expression of a primary solidarity of purpose within a community principally defined by a determination to resist.

Yet any detailed consideration of northern Irish Protestanism since the seventeenth century would, of course, easily destroy the myth of perpetual united solidarity. The northern Protestant community has recurrently been riven by contentious disputes, oppositions of class and creed, and theological schisms to a degree which is remarkable, given the almost total contemporary silence on the matter. Only a community with very simple historical needs could maintain such an extraordinary, near-unanimous reticence about the complications of its past. Individual academic historians have, it is true, produced monographs on aspects of history that touch on the Protestant experience in the north of Ireland (an example is J. C. Beckett's lucid, coolly analytic *Protestant Dissent in Ireland*), but almost no awareness exists in the general community of how such works might challenge the dominant self-consciousness of contemporary northern Protestantism. It is only when we consider the works of certain Protestant Church historians that we can find traces of a more general awareness of how complex the north's past has been. There the piously inspired exercises of Presbyterian historians have had to reckon with a social history which is not conducive to a vision of the northern Protestant experience as one of continuous, unified, lawful, rational, disciplined resistance to a papally dominated, terrifyingly irrational nationalism.

III

In terms of modern historical studies the Church historian is in a somewhat anomalous position. He may choose to study the history of a Church or a sect as one phenomenon among many, and to employ that emotionally and intellectually neutral manner which is currently respected in the academy. He is more likely, however, to be drawn to his subject, as a nationalist is to the study of his nation, or a Marxist to the history of a working-class, by reason of faith and creed. The story of the trials and tribulations of those whom he must consider his brethren in the faith is hardly then merely matter for disinterested enquiry, since that historical suffering touches the historian's personal sense of religious values as a living part of the community. For such a historian the study of, for example, the Presbyterian Church in Ireland will, inevitably, involve value judgments and personal commitments in a way which draws historical research out of the library and lecture-hall into the meeting-house and manse where it must more readily affect contemporary attitudes and assumptions.

At least five aspects of the history of the Presbyterian Church in Ireland present the contemporary Presbyterian historian with severe problems because they do not co-exist easily with the dominant Unionist ideological framework which conditions most Protestant thinking. Such historians must frankly face these truths about their Church: the Church had its origins in the crucible of dissent from established authority; it has been involved in direct ways with sedition and revolutionary action, even if only as a last resort; it has traditions of conflict on issues of conscience and has endured schism; it has had an ambivalent and not always mutually accommodating relationship with the Orange Order, and it has been profoundly affected by the dangerously uncontrollable forces of evangelical revivalism. Each of these in obvious ways can be seen to disturb the vision of the northern Protestant as having always belonged to a homogeneous, ideologically monolithic, social group which stands for authority, law, order, loyalty, conformity, social cohesion and reason.

A 1981 collection of essays by a group of Presbyterian historians allows us to see these problems exercising the minds of influential northern Protestants. This volume, *Challenge and Conflict: Essays in Irish Presbyterian History and Doctrine*,[3] makes for more interest than its title might promise. Despite some moments of slightly starchy pedantry, it shows a number of distinguised Presbyterian scholars and teachers making an honest effort to assess the history of their Church in ways which necessitate confronting a highly problematic past. A central issue is, of course, the fact of their Church's history of radical egalitarianism.

A key essay in the volume is 'The Presbyterian Minister in Eighteenth Century Ireland' by the Reverend Principal John M. Barkley (the volume in fact is one presented to this scholar, who has instructed generations of young ordinands in the history of their Church at the Assembly's College, Belfast). It is the most unapologetically partisan of the essays in the book, quite resolutely proud of the Presbyterian heritage. Throughout, Barkley espouses a view of the Presbyterian tradition as democratic:

In many towns, one comes across 'Meeting House Street' or 'Meeting House Lane'. Here stands, or stood in the eighteenth or early nineteenth century, the oldest Presbyterian Church in the district. The term is important because it guaranteed within Presbyterianism the New Testament principle that the building is not the Church. It is simply the meeting house of the people of God. The people are the Church. The local congregation consists of minister and people. The latter elects 'elders to co-operate with the minister' in the governing of the congregation, and to act as their representatives in the higher courts of the Church. The minister and elders form a Court called the Kirk-Session which supervised the whole life of the congregation and its members.

This democratic order allowed central virtues in the tradition to receive social expression: moral order was maintained in the community, charity justly administered and education esteemed. In due course, cultural values were also protected. Indeed Barkley claims that 'had it not been for Presbyterians the music and tradition of the Irish harpers could well have become a lost culture'. And all this was achieved when Presbyterians laboured under legal constraints which, though less severe than those that affected their Catholic fellow-countrymen, were felt to be both injurious and insulting.

A sense of offence recalled surfaces in Barkley's essay as he remembers how some 'episcopalian landlords' refused to permit Presbyterian Churches to be built on their property, 'as in the case of my mother Church, Malin, which was built on the sands of the sea-shore in 1717'. Indeed, the Presbyterian experience of the eighteenth century is associated by the essayist with the social nature of Irish Presbyterianism as a product of two antagonistic forces – their position in law and propaganda treatment of them as 'no-church' by the Ascendancy and 'foreigners' by the Catholics. These tensions, Barkley argues, contributed to the moulding of Irish Presbyterians into a 'closely knit community and were determining factors in the relationship of minister and people, as well as that of Presbyterianism and the community.'[4]

In Barkley's historical vision, democratic impulses, independence of mind and a dissenting tendency which existed both in North America as well as in Ireland, naturally drew Presbyterians to democratic political movements, and even to sedition and violence. How the modern Presbyterian historian handles such a perception reveals his currently anomalous position as a member of a Church which is almost wholly identified with established authority.[5] On the one hand there is an earnest concern to make it clear that Presbterians had no hand in the founding of the Orange Order; on the other the Church Synod's Address of 1798 following the defeat of the Rebellion, where all violence was condemned, is fully endorsed as consistent with a similar Address of five years earlier. The clear implication is that the position which the Church took in 1798 should be normative for its political dealings in the twentieth century:

In the maze of Irish politics of the period the Synod adopted a policy of moral and constitutional leadership. The effect of this in the political and social life of the community may be seen in the fact that it enabled the Synod to build up a people who stood for social justice as is evident from the fact that, with the exception of the Presbytery of Ballymena, every Presbytery in the Synod, in 1813, declared its support for the abolition of political distinctions on account of religious profession.[6]

How such a commitment to social justice might bear on contemporary Northern Ireland the author fails to address. But what Barkley cannot avoid is identification with those, who perhaps wrongheadedly, he suggests, took part in revolution in America and who attempted rebellion in Ireland. 'The names', he declares, reflecting on '98, 'of Neilson, McCracken, Orr, Simms, Drennan, M'Teir and others, deserve to be held in higher esteem within Presbyterianism than they are, though we must still repudiate and reject their methods.'

Yet, despite that last cautious and confused clause, Barkley clearly wishes that the Rebellion had succeeded in its aims. Indeed he gives implicit expression in this section of his essay to a subterranean emotion in northern Protestant, and especially Presbyterian, historical awareness. It might be termed the 'Theory of Ireland's Last Chance'. In this almost unconscious memory of the past, the '98 Rebellion is recalled as the moment when radical, just ideals and demands rooted in the achieved identity of the northern Presbyterian people were overwhelmed by forces of atavistic racial nationalism. Ever since that time this memory has meant that Protestant ideas of liberty have taken second place to *realpolitik*. And for some this suppression of a community's libertarian instincts in the interests of political expediency is a matter for profound regret, their own position, accordingly, a tragic one. The '98 is read, therefore, by Barkley as a just cause betrayed by the forces of Catholic nationalism. The sectarian violence of Scullabogue and Wexford was a symptom of a national malaise which has proved terminal for hopes of a united democratic country:

Had revolutionary 'catholic-nationalism' gloried in the things Pres-byterianism stood for – an independent Irish Parliament achieved by constitutional means and representing all the people and the promotion of Irish culture and music, instead of mythology glorifying the use of violence, the history of Ireland could have been very different.

In one respect such a reading of Irish history is merely a variant on the familiar theme of siege, past betrayal validating contem-porary determination to maintain the Union.[7] In another, how-ever, it suggests the discomfort which that presumed necessity can occasion in the northern Protestant who values a tradition of democratic independence. And in that discomfort may be found the source of some of the aggressive defensiveness which characterizes the rhetoric of Unionism. For the politics of the lesser evil, in which dependency on Britain must unhesitatingly be preferred to the proven dangers of attempted fraternity with Irish nationalists, is an uninspiring creed, hard to celebrate with any dignity. And as such it is conducive to that political lack of generosity which so marks northern Unionism.

How minds accustomed for so long to so depressing a vision of political possibility might be encouraged to consider the politics of the greater good and to forsake the politics of the lesser evil is probably at the root of the national question. Minds like that of Professor Barkley must, if the future is to differ from the doleful present, be enabled to conceive of the Year of Liberty not as a last chance but as an inspiration to those who might wish to see their society develop according to some more magnanimous and more fulfilling political philosophy than the one they have for so long espoused.

The other essayists in *Challege and Conflict* are more concerned with doctrinal matters than Barkley, though the history of doctrine brings contributors face-to-face with the fact that Presbyterianism in Ireland has a highly disputatious aspect in which dissent has recurrently confronted conformity. Debates in the 1720s and the 1820s about the necessity for ordinands to subscribe to the Westminster Confession (the primary theological expression of Presbyterianism formulated in London between the years 1643 and 1647) have resulted in epic personal battles (that in the nineteenth century between Henry Cooke and Henry Montgomery being conducted as a clash of Titans), theological controversy and ecclesiastical schism. In each period of struggle what seems to have been at stake was the purity of Calvinist doctrine as against the need for the Presbyterian Church to take account of contemporary intellectual life, though partisans would undoubtedly have seen the matter more in terms of orthodoxy, heterodoxy and heresy. What emerges of importance for contemporary northern Protestant self-understanding is the fact that Presbyterianism has often permitted fierce and vigorous exchanges of theological ideas. In the theological sphere and where that touches the social (as in the matter of appointments in the early nineteeth century to Belfast's Academical Institution) the Presbyterian heritage is one of robust dispute, where the total intellectual engagement of the participants is naturally assumed to the point where schism is accepted by all as the inevitable and right consequence of genuinely held differences. And such freedom of theological reflection is acknowledged as a good. So the Reverend Dr. R. G. Crawford can accept of the schismatic Arians of the Second Subscription Controversy of the 1820s: 'Many of the principles for which they stood have been vindicated and accepted. Their love of liberty from creeds made them avoid a mental cul-de-sac, and their fearless and free inquiry led them to discover truths which are commonly accepted now.' Indeed modern Presbyterianism has had the melancholy experience of having in 1926 conducted a heresy trial. In that year the case against one of the professors at Assembly's College, Belfast, was thrown out by the Church's General Assembly by 707 votes to 82, despite a fairly general, ill-informed hysteria amongst a vociferous fundamentalist constituency. That sharp divisions among Presbyterians still provoke vigorous disputes in which commitments are made with demanding seriousness was evidenced in 1979 when the General Assembly agreed to withdrawal from the World Council of Churches. The debates then were sustained, tense and outspoken.

One essayist in *Challenge and Conflict* (the Very Reverend Dr A. A. Fulton) raises the question whether the heat of debate in the contemporary Presbyterian Church may be generated by politics, whether theological conflict is politics in disguise. 'Ecumenical activities are under a cloud because they are feared to be fraternizing with the political enemy.' He frankly accepts that theological attitudes are welcomed 'accordingly as they are thought to strengthen or weaken strongly held political positions'. And what is seen to be true of contemporary debate was probably a feature of the conflicts of the early nineteenth century when the highly political Henry Cooke was aligning Presbyterianism with the Tory interest. Nevertheless, what strikes the observer of these debates and the cultural historian as he reflects on the history of Irish Presbyterianism is the contrast between the energy expended, polemical skill employed and quality of mind displayed in Church matters and the extraordinarily debased level of political consciousness expressed by the Unionist Party since the foundation of the Northern Irish state until very recent times. How individuals nurtured in the disputatious atmosphere of Presbyterian life have so readily acquiesced in the monolithic political simplicities of Northern Ireland is surprising – especially if Church conflicts have indeed possessed political significance. For political life is conducted within a rarely challenged homogeneous ideological monolith, while theological and ecclesiastical life (often bearing on political matters) displays vigorous heterogeneity. If the Presbyterian respect for dissent, individual conscience and personal commitment were to be translated into the political dimension one could at the least expect a toughening and sharpening in northern Irish political discourse, and to see the dominant historical myth of Ulster Protestantism subjected to some characteristically cantankerous disrespect. Similarly, the frequently effete and condescending utterances of Official Unionists and of British Secretaries of State on the Union would not be so often accepted without demur as reflecting a regrettable historical necessity. Facing the uncharacteristically timorous political engagement of many of his fellow Presbyterians, the Reverend Fulton suggests that the rise of Ian Paisley has inhibited them from expressing political dissent:

Political and ecclesiastical leaders glance carefully over their shoulders before committing themselves publicly on issues in which Paisley is involved. The Roman Catholic Bishop of Derry is reported in the *Belfast Telegraph* for 21 March 1981, saying: 'Any Protestant churchman or politician who shows any sense of rapproachment or willingness to come closer or work closer with members of the Catholic Church will usually find that is prelude to the end of his career.' If that statement exaggerates, it is only slightly. Paisley's followers seem to invest him with an almost messianic destiny: the defender of the Faith, the Champion of true Protestantism, the guarantor of civil and religious liberty. Others may fear that here is a dangerous threat to the freedoms of Democracy: but their fears are usually muted.

What Fulton doesn't care to reflect on is how Presbyterianism, in the period before Paisley's emergence, allowed its political commitments to become predictably uniform, so that there is no twentieth century Montgomery to oppose the twentieth century Cooke.

If Fulton ignores this particular challenge, there is yet another challenge which the Presbyterian historian has to face, because the Protestant who identifies his creed with order, law, stability and rationality must consider the deep Presbyterian involvement with evangelical revival.

During the nineteenth century an evangelical awakening swept through much of the Protestant world – it affected Scandinavia, Germany, Switzerland, France, Holland, England, Scotland, the United States – and this phenomeon took a particularly bizarre and unnerving form in the north of Ireland. In 1859 a wave of religious enthusiasm spread from Connor in Co. Antrim to inspire thousands of rural Protestants. The revival often affected the poorest sections of the community and was marked by symptoms of violent hysteria which terrified spectators. It stimulated many in their religious enthusiasm and clearly remains an important, if unacknowledged, influence on the northern psyche. Its monuments are the innumerable mission halls and tents, evangelistic crusades, and evangelical associations, that make Northern Ireland an Irish extension of the Bible belt.

Revivalism challenges the Ulster historial myth in two ways – it suggests that an ordered, dignified, disciplined vision of life is no match for the excitements of religious ecstasy and that the northern Protestant is no more immune to irrational forces than the Irish Catholic in the popular Protestant view of him. A Presbyterian historian whose work on the subject is cited with approval in *Challenge and Conflict* reveals a characteristic unease before the emotional violence that was released by the Year of Grace:

There were elements which shocked and puzzled, as in so many similar movements found in the States at the same period; but many strange and objectionable features presented themselves. After all, the movement was a tremendous stimulus to the nervous system of those brought under its power, and, whatever the source of the manifestations might be thought or claimed to be, the overwrought system of many people played them strange tricks in those involuntary phenomena which are today known as automatism, such as trances, kicking, screaming and the like; hysterical evidence of the coming of great and unaccustomed emotion into channels as yet ill-adapted to contain or control it in normal ways.

What precisely such channels might be is not clear, but the fear of abnormality is noticeably present.

The phenomenon of revivalist fundamentalism in present-day Northern Ireland therefore raises doubts in sensitive minds as to how 'normal' their society is. This is because so many of its members seem to require emotional outlets that combine extremes of individualism with the gratification of a mass movement. And for the Presbyterian intellectual there is no ready mechanism whereby he may dissociate himself from a disturbing, threatening awareness. The atavistic celebrations of the Orange Lodges can be held at a distance in the knowledge that

Presbyterians were in general not responsible for their foundation. But revivalism arose in the very heart of Presbyterianism. Accordingly Presbyterian historians tread uneasily between the religious interpretation of revivalism as the outpouring of the Holy Spirit and sociological explanations which regard it as the inevitable outcome of a process of modernization which has created a class of deracinated, lonely, frightened people, ready prey for the exotic emotional appeal of a millenialist eschatology.[8] Neither is supportive of a sense of northern Protestant identity as characterized by a resolute, stable attachment to civic virtue.

Most Presbyterians who know something of the history of their Church and the enduring tensions within it are able to ignore the ways in which that rich and complex tradition challenges the dominant historical myth of the whole Protestant community. That this myth is a disabling one I have suggested earlier, for it excludes a great deal of human experience, so that a lot of life must be lived without communal imaginative support.[9] It is also crucially disabling in the political sphere since all political possibilities are subordinated to the basic determination to maintain the historically authenticated resistance. Temporizers who dally with political revisionism are made immediate victims by appeal to the historical myth.

IV

Essays of the present kind are all too frequently victims of wishful thinking. So it must be said that it is highly unlikely that with the British guarantee to maintain the Union apparently secure, even after the Anglo-Irish Agreement, northern Protestants will to any significant degree begin to reflect on their controlling historical sense of themselves, (though a minority in the new context have shown signs of adaptive thought). It is even less likely that any writer who tried to remind them of their complex historical experience and of how the history of the Presbyterian Church, for example, raises problems of interpretation of past and present which are at odds with their self-understanding will seem pertinent, let alone induce original political and cultural questioning. That, one imagines, will only be attempted when it seems absolutely necessary. What can with some measure of satisfaction be said, however, is that if and when the necessity for a new historical interpretation of the northern Protestant's experience does arise, the material is there for its fabrication. When the British Government finally decides to remove its authority from this island there may not be much history to tell in those circumstances who northern Protestants are, but there may be just enough. A people who have known resistance as well as dissent, rebellion, dispute, religious enthusiasm in the midst of rural and urban deprivation, have an interesting story to tell themselves – one of essential homelessness, dependency, anxiety, obdurate fantacizing, sacrifices in the name of liberty, villainous political opportunism, moments of idealistic aspiration. And in the telling of it they may come to realize at last where they are most at home and with whom they share that home.

One last reflection may be in order. A people without much history, or which feels the need for no very complex historical self-awareness, is homeless in a particularly special way. The visual constituents of the past (within which it makes a home) are all around it, and no matter how indifferent individuals may profess themselves to be they cannot fail to be aware of them, if only subliminally. Indeed, the spate of books of photographs published in recent years on Victorian and Edwardian Ulster bear a kind of mute testimony to the power the past holds even over a people who have suffered a kind of collective amnesia about so much of their experience. But for so historically bereft a people as the northern Protestant community, what the past cannot vouchsafe is the language in which their predecessors expressed their public experience. Consequently the northern Protestant lives without much sense of the modes of thought and feeling that the written records of his ancestors represent. What T. S. Eliot in *Four Quartets* termed 'the communication / Of the dead. . . tongued with fire beyond the language of the living' is rarely heard in Ulster (though northern poetry with its richly compacted linguist strata is one place where it can be heard). With its messages of social complexity, that communication hints at a fuller kind of cultural inclusivenes than the myth of besieged solidarity can possibly allow.

Even in the limited area of Presbyterian history, which has been a principal concern of this essay, voices, tones, ways of addressing political realities echo down from the past and complicate one's sense of a people's history. Contemporary speech is apprehended as an historically generated phenomenon, and the rhetoric of current experience is identified as possessing origins in past struggles. The obsessional, narrowly dogmatic, infuriatingly uncompromising voice of fundamentalist self-righteousness sounds from the seventeenth century to the present, tempered to a steely conviction by the experience of social condescension. The scene is Belfast, 11 August 1636. A Calvinist minister has been summoned to appear before the bishops of Derry and of Down and Connor. Down arrives before Derry and engages the recalcitrant certitudes of Mr Hamilton (the record of the event is an Appendix to Volume I of Reid's *History of the Presbyterian Church in Ireland*) on the matter of kneeling to receive the Sacrament which the Calvinist refuses to do. Derry arrives to observe of the milder Down and Connor:

My Lord of Down, in good faith I commend your charity, but not your wisdom, in suffering such a prattling jack to talk so openly against the orders of the Church. My Lord, it is more than ye can justify yourself in the state.

Derry expresses patrician exasperation in the face of a dissentient obduracy undoubtedly reinforced by class condescension, in a dialectic all too familiar in the present: 'I would you should know that the heaviness of our Church and State hangeth not upon the Atlas shoulders of such as you are.'

From the nineteenth century sound the tones of crude oratorical pomposity and lugubrious solemnity that so often are the rhetorical embodiments of a respectable Calvinist conservatism in the north. The voice is that of Henry Cooke in an address to the General Assembly of the Church of Scotland in May 1836:

Our Scottish forefathers were planted in the wildest and most barren portions of our lands. . . the most rude and lawless of the provinces. . . Scottish industry has drained its bogs and cultivated its barren wastes, has filled its ports with shipping, substituted towns and cities for its hovels and clachans and given peace and good order to a land of confusion and blood.[10]

But from the same century come the sinuously logical, sceptical, satiric accents of Presbyterian disputation that still appeal to the northern intelligence. In one ecclesiastical engagement of the 1850s Cooke accuses his opponents of dealing with the Assembly in a dictatorial manner (the pot calling the kettle black). The Protestant Pope was assailed by the following rhetorical salvo:

Were it not that Dr Cooke has himself lost all power of astonishing, what amazement must it not excite to see him the chivalrous champion of Presbyterian freedom and independence, and that against the assaults of such ruthless tyrants as Dr Brown, Mr Gibson and myself. . . Independently of Dr Cooke's chivalrous devotion to your freedom, he has other motives to preserve you from our claims. He is not the man to allow any other to set foot on his own dominions, or, to adopt illustrations more suited to his taste, and more in conformity with his example; he will allow no other 'cock on his walk' or any other to 'wallop his nigger', whilst he has an arm to wield; therefore we are secure against all other rule – unless, indeed, it may be that of the government. He seems not unwilling to share his throne with them, and he manifestly considers that all 'conditions' imposed on your free-born necks by such allied powers, so far from being 'ignoble', are noble and glorious.[11]

And, as a final example, from 1859 the Year of Grace comes the voice of revivalism, anxious, curiously local, sensing eruptive energies in a familiar place, investing the provincial with the numinous mystery of an egalitarian parish, expressing the communality of the dispossessed. A Reverend J. A. Canning reports on the movement in Coleraine:

Upon the evening of the 7th June 1859, an open-air meeting was held in one of the market-places of the town, called the 'Fair-hill'. The announced object of the meeting was to receive and hear one or two of the 'converts' as they began to be called, from a district some eight or ten miles south of Coleraine. The evening was one of the most lovely that ever shone. The richly-wooded banks of the river Bann, which bounds one side of the square in which the meeting was held, were fully in prospect, and there was not a cloud in the sky. Shortly after seven o'clock, dense masses of people, from town and country, began to pour into the square by all its approaches, and in a short time an enormous multitude crowded around the platform from which the speakers were to address the meeting. After singing and prayer, the converts, a young man and a man more advanced in years, and both of the humbler class, proceeded to address the meeting.[12]

A night of violent emotion ensues, the minister himself is almost victim to an agonized hysteria, both frightening in its intensity and poignant in its intimations of the northern Protestant's profound insecurity, his hunger for the absolute assurance historical existence cannot secure for him and of the liberating dawn it perhaps could.

As I arose from prayer, six or eight persons, all at the same instant, pressed around me, crying, 'Oh, come and see (naming such a one) – and – and –' until I felt for a moment bewildered and the prayer went out from my heart, 'God guide me'. I passed from case to case for two or three hours, as did my brethren in the ministry, until, when the night was far spent, and the stricken ones began to be removed to the shelter of roofs, I turned my face homewards through one street, when I soon discovered that the work which had begun in the market square was now advancing with marvellous rapidity in the homes of the people. As I approached door after door, persons were watching for me and other ministers, to bring us to deal with some poor agonized stricken one; and when the morning dawned, and until the sun arose, I was wandering from street to street, and from house to house, on the most marvellous and solemn errand upon which I have ever been sent.

NOTES

1. See Oliver MacDonagh, 'Time's Revenges and Revenge's Time: A View of Anglo-Irish Relations', *Anglo-Irish Studies*, IV (1979), pp. 1-19. See also Mac-Donagh, *States of Mind: A Study of Anglo-Irish Conflict* (London 1983).
2. For an excellent discussion of some of these works, see Edna Longley, 'The Writer and Belfast', in *The Irish Writer And The City*, ed. M. Harmon (Gerrards Cross 1984), pp. 66-70.
3. *Challenge and Conflict: Essays in Irish Presbyterian History and Doctrine* (Antrim 1981).
4. For a study of the Presbyterian Church's political relationship with the British polity, see Peter Brooke, *Ulster Presbyterianism: the Historical Perspective, 1610-1970* (Dublin 1987).
5. In the nineteenth century W. D. Killen, who completed J. S. Reid's monumental *History of the Presbyterian Church in Ireland* (1833 & 1867), attempted to prove that Presbyterians had played only a small part in the Rebellion. Barkley accepts J. B. Woodburn's view (see *The Ulster Scot*, 1914) that they were considerably implicated in what Killen had termed 'the revolutionary mania'.
6. Barkley is a little disingenuous about this declaration of support for Emancipation. For a more cold-eyed account of Presbyterians and Emancipation see Finlay Holmes' painstaking biography *Henry Cooke* (Belfast 1981)), pp. 64-76.
7. This reading is hinted at in Killen's account of the Rebellion (in *The Presbyterian Church in Ireland*) and suggested by Woodburn in *The Ulster Scot*. Ian Adamson's *The Identity of Ulster* (Northern Ireland 1982) explicitly re-states this reading of the events of 1798.
8. No full-scale history of the Revival as yet exists. John T. Carson's *God's River*

in Spate (1959) is an evangelical's centenary celebration. Interestingly Ian Paisley has written on the Revival in one of his historical soundings. Peter Gibbon, in *The Origins of Ulster Unionism* (Manchester 1975), attempts a brief assessment of the phenomenon in Marxist terms while David Miller has examined it as a product of the process of modernization. See David W. Miller, 'Presbyterians, and "Modernization" in Ulster', *Past and Present*, No. 80 (August 1978), pp. 66-90. It would be fascinating to read a historical recreation of the events of 1859 in the manner of such a writer as Le Roy Ladurie. It is also a strange fact that the world of northern Protestant revivalism has scarcely been explored by Irish writers. Sam Thompson's play *The Evangelist* was a rare attempt to address the topic directly. And Stewart Parker's play *Pentecost* (1987) was informed by evangelical feeling.

9. Though individual writers can exploit this lack as liberal freedom, often in a highly engaging fashion, as in the poetry of James Simmons.

10. Quoted by Finlay Holmes, *op. cit.*

11. Quoted by Holmes, *op. cit.* The author of this attack on Cooke, accurately, if not fully consciously, caught that blend of boorishness and racism which often characterizes Unionism at its ugliest. The degree of support and sympathy for White South Africa which currently exists amongst Unionists would, I believe, be well worth study. One suspects that it is not inconsiderable.

12. The report is included in William Gibson, *The Year of Grace* (Edinburgh and London 1909).

17

AWAKENING FROM THE NIGHTMARE: HISTORY AND CONTEMPORARY LITERATURE

It was John Montague in his poem 'A New Siege', published in 1970 and subsequently made part of *The Rough Field* in 1972, who first gave eloquent expression to a sense of *déja vu* in relation to Ireland's contemporary troubles, which has dominated much literary and artistic responses to the dreadful events of the last twenty years.

> Once again, it happens.
> Under a barrage of stones
> and flaring petrol bombs
> the blunt, squat shape of
> an armoured car glides
> into the narrow street
> of the Catholic quarter
> leading a file of helmet-
> ed, shielded riot police;
> once again, it happens,
> like an old Troubles film,
> run for the last time.

The siege of the Bogside in Derry is just a re-run of something that has been happening for centuries, the re-iteration of historic event, a tragic inevitability. It was in 1972 that Seamus Heaney published his collection of poems *Wintering Out* which announced and inaugurated his obsessional exploration of mythic antiquity and of the strata of historic inevitability, as a mode of artistic comprehension of the earthquakes which were shaking his province. Poems such as 'The Tollund Man' and 'Bog Oak' juxtaposed pre-history and history, myth and

243

moment in ways which gave us to know an awesome, yet curiously religiose and therefore consolatory inevitability in the current troubles. In his essay of 1974, 'Feeling Into Words', Heaney himself has written of how his poetic response to the Northern crisis was governed in the 1970s by a pervading sense of historic repetitiveness:

To some extent the enmity can be viewed as a struggle between the cults and devotees of a god and a goddess. There is an indigenous territorial numen, a tutelar of the whole island, call her Mother Ireland, Kathleen Ni Houlihan, the poor old woman, the Shan Van Vocht, whatever; and her sovereignty has been temporarily usurped or infringed by a new male cult whose founding fathers were Cromwell, William of Orange and Edward Carson, and whose godhead is incarnate in a rex or caesar resident in a palace in London. What we have is the tail-end of a struggle in a province between territorial piety and imperial power.[1]

In other words the Ulster crisis is one more manifestation of a conflict between two almost metaphysical realities, the pattern of Irish history pre-determined in pre-history.

Heaney's volume *North* (1975) made further soundings in Ireland's and Europe's mythic and historic past, finding there intimations of primal pattern and 'befitting emblems of adversity' as he developed his elegiac, haunted vision of an island in thrall to predatory deities and to dark cults of blood, sex, revenge and power.

But Montague's and Heaney's variously complex awareness of historic repetition was, in the period, only a highly sophisticated variant of a fairly widespread popular perception. Patrick Galvin's play *We Do It for Love* (first presented by the Lyric Theatre in Belfast in 1975), at a more readily available and immediate level, gave expresson to this sense of things in the image of the troubles as a merry-go-round, from which his characters in a war-torn city cannot step down.

> I'm spinning round
> I'm spinning round
> I'm on a losing Merry-Go-Round
> I want to leave old Belfast City
> It's falling to the ground

sang the characters in the finale of the Belfast production. But the undertaker in Part One of the play has reminded them all of the city's repetitive fate:

> O happy days are here again
> Sectarian wars are on again
> . . . .
> There's shooting up in the Falls
> There's blood on Derry's Walls
> O Happy Days are here again
> And the skies are red with fear again
> Happy Days Are Here Again.

And in academic and journalistic circles, A. T. Q. Stewart's work of 1977, *The Narrow Ground*, did much to confirm a view of the present crisis as the re-emergence in modern times of an antique struggle rooted, as Stewart seemed to hint, in an almost Jungian collective unconsciousness which drives Ulstermen and women to deeds of desperation in generation after generation: 1641 is 1886 is 1912 is 1969, implies the structural organization of his deeply depressing book.

The view of history which underpins these several literary and academic interpretations of the recent Northern Irish past is an essentially static one. It presumes that the 'plot' of Irish history means that events at different periods are merely recurrent manifestations of an underlying theme. And, as such, these interpretations consolidate the historiographical awareness of most Irish people, an awareness which has remained constant since at least the beginning of the nineteenth century. For in the last two centuries nationalist Ireland has told itself an oft-repeated tale which emphasizes the recurrent nature of Ireland's historic dilemma as that of a subject people, and it is this vision of 'a most distressful nation' which governs popular historical consciousness despite recent social and political advances north and south, and despite the revisionism of modern Irish historiography. The northern Unionist, too, has preoccupied himself with a vision of his past and present which highlights the repetitive, static quality of his Irish experience. For a myth of an exacting and perennial siege cautions the Unionist against raising the gates to liberalism, fraternity and political trust. In both the Nationalist and Unionist versions of the Irish past there is therefore a profound sense of history as a given, as a nightmare from which it is impossible to awake.

It need not, of course, be so. The nationalist view of the past

245

could highlight the progressive developments of Irish life, the uneven but undeniable advancement of the people from feudalism to modern democratic government, but so profound have been the traumata endured by the Irish since the seventeenth century, and so painful is much contemporatry Irish experience, especially in the North, that such a revisionist interpretation would seem fanciful to most Irish nationalists, if not downright impertinent. The Unionist view of the past could highlight (and the attempt is sometimes made) the increasing social and libertarian advantages of incorporation in a modernizing, multi-racial British state, but so deep-rooted is popular awareness of and resistance to nationalist Ireland's claims on the six counties that the myth of siege overwhelms any more progressive self-understanding. So Unionist and Nationalist feels his present to be linked to a 'continuous past'. To be Irish is to endure the nightmare of historical stasis.

In the 1980s a number of highly successful literary works have appeared in Ireland which reckon with this predominant view of the Irish past, but which do not acquiesce in it: two plays, Stewart Parker's *Northern Star* (1984), Frank McGuinness's *Observe the Sons of Ulster Marching Towards the Somme* (1985), and a long poem, Brendan Kennelly's *Cromwell* (1983). The success of these works may be an indication of a developing openness to new interpretations of Ireland's past and present experience. What they unquestionably reveal is the vital energy of contemporary Irish art in its engagement at fundamental levels with crises of identity, violence and historical consciousness.

Stewart Parker's *Northern Star* offers as its setting 'Ireland, the Continuous Past'. The play dramatizes the night thoughts of the Presbyterian rebel, Henry Joy McCracken, as he awaits his fate following the collapse of the '98 Rising. Almost all of the work allows those thoughts to be overwhelmed by a terrible sense of inevitability. Indeed, much in Parker's theatrical technique confirms for his audience the profound awareness of an implacable historic condition which haunts the doomed man. McCracken, towards the end of the play, expresses the acute pain of his vision in a terrifying speech in which he recognizes his own impotence as one who had hoped to move history in a new direction:

So all we've done, you see, is to reinforce the locks, cram the cells fuller than ever of mangled bodies crawling round in their own shite and lunacy, and the cycle just goes on, playing out the same demented comedy of terrors from generation to generation, trapped in the same malignant legend, condemned to re-endure it as if the Anti-Christ who dreamed it up was driven astray in the wits by it and the entire pattern of depravity just goes spinning on out of control, on and on, round and round till the day the world itself is burst asunder. . .

Also, towards the play's conclusion McCracken comes to understand the basis of this interpretation of Ireland's past as cyclical nightmare. Catholic and Protestant are locked forever in a grim struggle for possession of the land. As he admits to Jemmy Hope, they had missed that obvious truth about their native country. It is 'A field, with two men fighting over it, Cain and Abel. The bitterest fight in the history of man on this earth. We were city boys. What did we know about two men fighting over a field.' Parker's play allows us to see McCracken arrive at this bleak truth and to watch him fall into the abyss of a terrible disillusionment. We see him live through seven stages of intellectual and personal awareness. And the slightly programmatic structure of the play's development consolidates the sense of historical determinism that pervades the work as a whole. McCracken must perforce live through seven distinct phases in his experience, like the seven ages of man in the familiar literary and dramatic trope. The trajectory of his experience must follow a predestinate curve. The awful givenness of Irish reality allows for almost no other possibility. So we see the youthful, naive good-fellowship of the Mudlers Club where conspiracy seems a youthful lark, a sauce to savour young manhood's pleasure – the Age of Innocence. Idealism follows when to stand for the United Irish is a dramatically charged thrill. Then the Age of Cleverness arrives in brilliant talk of cultural renewal. The Age of Dialectics brings acute definition and political theory; the Age of Heroism the possibility of defining action. But the Age of Compromise ensues when the rebels are forced to uncomfortable choices between the factions, which bring a devastating Age of Knowledge with its wretched intimations of failure.

Further to suggest the continuous present of Irish history Parker employs a daring dramatic technique: Each of the seven ages of the play has its appropriate dramatic style in striking pastiche of the playwrights of the Anglo-Irish tradition. The

Age of Innocence and bravado dramatizes conspiratorial good cheer in the style of Farquhar. The Idealism of the early age of the United Irish story has its satiric expression in the melodramatic excesses of Boucicault. In the Age of Cleverness, Wilde's epigrammatic mannerism determines the dialogue. Shaw is model for drama as argument in the Age of Dialectics. The Heroic Age of military aspiration finds expression in the Hiberno-English grandiloquence of Synge-song, while the Age of Compromise, in which McCracken recognizes that he must make common cause with the Catholic Defenders against the greater evils of Orangeism and militia, is realized in the evasive intimacies of O'Casey's Dublinese. The Age of Knowledge which dawns in prison at a hanging employs the sardonic realism of the Behan of *The Quare Fellow*, enforcing a mood of savage despair.*

So Parker's play is dominated by a sense of historical inevitability. The implacable quality of Irish experience emphasized throughout is most powerfully symbolized at the end of Act One when the ghostly figure of a woman (the cottage in which McCracken is living is apparently haunted) materializes as a phantom bride who weds the hero with a deathly kiss and a predatory embrace. She is simultaneously the death which awaits him, his tragic destiny, and the Shan Van Vocht whose blood-lust is insatiable. But doom and determinism are not Parker's final words on the Irish condition. And this renders his play a significant occasion. In his compelling portrait of the man McCracken, Parker suggests that personal deficiencies in his character may have contributed to an inadequate social and political analysis. The corollary of such an estimate of McCracken's career is that greater personal maturity might allow for a more truly ennobling and liberating approach to the Irish imbroglio. Parker's McCracken is a convincing, often very moving study of a political dreamer, tempted by a sense of destiny, even if it

---

* In the theatre the effect of this literary extravagance is hard to judge. One realizes the intention – that of suggesting how Irish history's continuum allows for surprising and illuminating anchronism. Wolfe Tone as Wilde is a witty parallelism, for example, identifying the dandy in the suave revolutionary. And, on reflection, it seems possible that the stylistic variety of Anglo-Irish drama to which *Northern Star* testifies is the correlative of the social instability that our history has involved. But in simpler terms the stratagem seems a slightly too well-worked means of avoiding the theatrical banality of the historical costume drama. Parker may have succeeded in writing a kind of theatrical quiz show. Spot the dramatist is fun, but that game tends to distract the audience from the sombre statement the work is making.

involves disaster and the Shan Van Vocht's deathly embrace. Mary Bodle, the Catholic woman who has borne him a child, lets him know the truth. It is not the killing he fears but living: 'It's living that you fear. That's the sore spot on your soul. Living the way I do, most people do. Humdrum, ordinary, soon enough forgotten. That's why you're in love with that rope more than you are with me and the child.' She knows he will choose death when he could be 'living a decent ordinary life in a new country'. McCracken's bitter riposte betrays his self-destructive hubris: 'Doing what? Can you honestly see me, in some Main Street in Massachussetts, behind the counter of a draper's shop?'

In the play the figure of Jemmy Hope hints at what a less self-indulgent and truly efficacious political philosophy in the Irish situation might be. A sense of the revolutionary possibilities of a socialist analysis of Irish history saves this play from quite abandoning us to the deterministic despair that the Beckettian final speeches of the play so powerfully realize:

. . . So then the plunge, the wrench, the plunge, the rough strangle, and so there an end. To finish. Unless only to begin anew, there is of course that. Only to glimmer on in the effigy of another time, other times, other effigies, never to know end's mercy, never to be let end, never to know mercy, so much for the rope's comfort. . .

This play leaves us with an image of a hanged man and of Ireland as a place 'brain-damaged and dangerous, continuously violating itself, a place of perpetual breakdown, incompatible voices screeching obscenely away through the smoky dark wet'. But we also remember that poignant conversation in which Hope, a ghost from the future, as he tells McCracken, suggests how the fateful power of the land to divide men into mutually destructive factions might be broken: 'It's not beyond resolution. If every man was awarded the equal fruits of his labour – from the land that he works.' His faith remains intact and sounds with the resonance of *hope* in what he calls, as he takes his final leave of McCracken, 'the long memory of this town, the long dream': 'Evil days. Never you fret. The moral force of the labouring class will prevail, whatsoever comes or goes.' Hope's conviction is that we shall not always be condemned to repeat the nightmare of the past. The past need not be continuous, though McCracken goes to the gallows.

In Frank McGuinness's *Observe the Sons of Ulster Marching Towards the Somme*, the descendants of McCracken and Jemmy Hope go to war and to death in battle.

A common belief among those trapped in the grotesque nightmare of trench warfare in the Great War (in which on a quietish sort of day 7000 British men and officers were killed and wounded as a matter of course) was that the thing would last forever. They were trapped, they sensed, in what was becoming a permanent state, a world that with the mail delivered, newspapers arriving only a day late, food hampers despatched for the officers from Harrods, and with its underground network of trenches, was developing as a surreal parody of what had once been thought to be the real world. One observer of the progress of events on the Somme wrote in August 1917 (quoted in Paul Fussell's brilliant and moving work, *The Great War and Modern Memory*): 'Both sides are too strong for a finish yet. God knows how long it will be at this rate. None of us will ever see its end and children still at school will have to take it over.'[2] As a metaphor of unending conflict, of entrapment in a historic disaster that cannot be transcended, the trenches of the Great War are unnervingly suggestive of contemporary Ulster's anguish. And the fact that Carson's volunteers were present at the Somme adds poignancy to the metaphoric correlation. Indeed, something of Protestant Ulster's modern historic experience may be seen in the events of those few days in July 1916 when so many of her loyal sons marched to their deaths. Two days of heroic sacrifice, in which they exceeded all expectation by driving a salient into the German lines which could not be sustained, found the survivors back almost at the point from which they had started. They had vindicated themselves but at great cost, their sacrifice only one more tragedy in the permanent theatre of war.

It is a measure of the imaginative power of Frank McGuinness's play (which opened in Dublin's Peacock Theatre on 18 February 1985) that he suggests how the Somme experience had implications for our understanding of the Ulster Protestant's contemporary dilemma. He sees in the Somme a metaphor of a society trapped in poignantly self-destructive heroics, where courage is absolutely real and absolutely uncreative.

The play is structured as three scenes imagined through the memories of a Somme survivor, the blind Kenneth Pyper, an

aged Anglo-Irish Unionist, whose opening monologue and concluding speech frame the work. In these two appearances we
are made to understand how the events of the Somme must be
read as bearing on contemporary reality. Pyper asks in haunted
pain, 'Why must this persist?' and insists: 'We claimed we would
die for each other in battle. To fulfil that claim we marched into
the battle that killed us all. That is not loyalty. That is not love.
That is hate. Deepest hate. Hate for oneself.' Pyper's awful personal fate is to have survived when he had in fact wished to
die. He must draw his breath in pain, if not to tell his comrades'
story, then to be true to the cruelly self-destructive vision of the
Ulster for which they died, which he knows in a blindness which
allows him a sight of the truth to be a monstrously inhuman
falsity.

The three scenes of Pyper's obsessional recollecton take us
from training camp, where eight volunteers meet and prepare
for action, to various parts of Ulster where on leave they attempt
to come to terms with what they know to be before them, to the
last scene in which at the front they gird themselves for the final
assault. In the first scene we learn that the volunteers hail from
different parts of the province and we watch them developing
relationships, while the second scene allows us to observe them
confronting in pairs their individual attitudes to their terrifying
situation. This scene, employing a split-stage technique, express-
ionism and a brilliantly designed set (for which in the Peacock
production director Patrick Mason and designer Frank Hallinan
Flood must take all due credit), inevitably reminds of O'Casey's
second act in *The Silver Tassie*. Indeed, McGuinness's play might
be seen as building on O'Casey's daring experimentalism, and
as an extension of it. At four Ulster locations individual destinies
are hammered out. A man near to shell-shock, driven on by his
ex-commander in Carson's army, conquers fear on Carrick-a-
Rede rope-bridge; another duologue in a church challenges
Ulster's puritan religion as a perverse nihilism; two Belfast
Orangemen at the Edenderry field swamp their awful terror in
a tribal drum-beat, while Pyper and a blacksmith, David Craig,
before the stone figure on Boa Island in County Fermanagh,
explore the meaning and potential of homosexual feeling in a
wary, tender reaching-out to one another. It is inevitable that
this relationship should seem the principal one of the play, for
we cannot forget that the events we witness are images in the

elder Pyper's memory. And his development is the most dwelt upon throughout. In the first scene he is the cynical aristocrat, failed husband, failed artist, whose distaste for his Ulster background is only exceeded by his almost decadent longing for oblivion. His love for David Craig is seen transforming a sardonic nihilist into an anxious interpreter of his comrade's experience as they march to battle. Love for one man is expressed in community of feeling with all of them as in the final scene he tries to make sense of their hell. They are fighting for their own places, their own rivers; the Somme is the Bann, the Foyle, even the Lagan: 'It's bringing us home. we're not in France. We're home. We're on our own territory. We're fighting for home. This river is ours.' So he utters the final battle cry of a prayer before the action, accepts the group's 'Badge of honour', the Orange sash. But the terrible irony is that his moment of personal salvation wrought through homosexual love, in which philosophic despair is redeemed by commitment to his lover and to his comrades, involves him in preparing them for slaughter. A sub-theme of the play is therefore the ways in which group male solidarity and the hells of circumstance can betray homosexual integrity. Kenneth Pyper is the most profoundly trapped of these loyal sons of Ulster since he is condemned to love, loyal to a cause he knows has destroyed David Craig and all the rest of those with whom he has come to feel at one.

McGuinness's play is as dominated by a sense of historical inevitability as Parker's *Northern Star*. But where Parker implies that there may be a way to escape the treadmill in a socialist and therefore political redefinition of the Irish conflict (though he also reflects on McCracken's personal immaturity), McGuinness's powerful work suggests that the roots of the problem are primarily psychological. For Pyper chooses to give in to the nightmare in a perverse homage to his dead companions. He fails to face the challenge of his own self-knowledge, preferring the intimate nightmare of his own memories to the psychological growth his encounter with Craig might have stimulated.

It is a measure of the success of Kennelly's *Cromwell* that the challenge of the Irish nightmare is addressed head on and the psychological ramifications of our appallingly oppressive past confronted with a liberating authenticity. *Cromwell* is a collage of speeches, letters, historical fragments, fantasies, legends, jokes, satires and personal poems, all directed to an exploration of the relationship between England and Ireland as between the Lord Protector and the work's 'little hero', M. P. G. M. Buffún Esq (full name Michael Patrick Gusty Mary Buffún). Kennelly advises 'The method of the poem is imagistic, not chronological. This seemed to be the most effective way to represent a "relationship" that has produced a singularly tragic mess.' A consequence of this imagistic method is to make it seem as if everything in the poem is happening at once. This allows for the perhaps rather too frequent satiric anachronisms of the work, as when:

> Oliver Cromwell's first season as
> Manager of Drogheda United was not
> Impressive A bit of a calamit-
> y, in fact. 'Get rid of Cromwell' howled
> The Drogheda fans, 'Send him to Home Farm
> Athlone, St Pats, Bohemians, U.C.D.
> The bastard has brought nothing but harm
> to our side. Fling him into the sea.'

But it also allows for the work's most compelling effect, that is to suggest how Irish history is the nightmare imagining of its principal victim, the work's protagonist Buffún – who is all of us. It is as if the dominating presence of Cromwell/England has created a condition of Irish being in which temporality has been drained of teleology and everything happens at once, to no purpose, to no end, except the black comedy of grotesque meaningless violence. One commentator has written penetratingly of this work's strange temporal vision:

Defleshing goes deep. It goes beyond politics, sociology, psychology, to the level of being. It is a reaching of 'time' at the quick of existence. Kennelly is, like Proust, à la recherche du temps perdu. This forgotten time is hidden under the new Irish time, the time of Cromwell. This time flows like some original sin at the base of our Irish psyche. Each one of us is at some moment or other appropriated in a personal way to this chronology.[3]

Accordingly, for this commentator a key moment in the work is where

> Friends beat me up on the way home from school.
> Suddenly a new time happened in me.

> It wasn't that I'd come the rough or acted the fool
> Too much for them to bear, it was more that they
> Needed a victim that June afternoon.

So was the schoolboy victim appropriated to the new Cromwellian time – the time of the Curse:

> The first time I heard the curse in sleep
> Was now and a thousand years ago
> It didn't assume a pig-shape or dog-shape
> Nor was it tarred and feathered like a crow
> It wasn't an old solider talking his wounds
> Nor a priest doing fifteen rounds with the Devil
> It wasn't the smell of blood in killing hands
> I'd hardly call it foul
>
> It was more like a small patient hiss
> The sound a wind might make trying to be born
> A kind of pleading.

In this time the Lord Protector rules, aided by a bizarre platoon of mythological, archetypal henchmen. The Giant, for example, is the implacable force of a repetitive Irish history:

> I threw a party for Oliver Cromwell
> at the Royal Yacht club in Dunleary.
> He was boring the arse off me with all
> His talk about that estate down in Kerry
> Where he planned to fish the Cashen and Feale
> Till the people would breathe his name in awe.
> Bored to my bones, I introduced Cromwell
> To the giant who was standing in the harbour,
> Cooling off. The giant is not at home in crowds.
> To-day, as ever he was very peckish.
>
> 'Pleased to meet you, Oliver' the giant said,
> 'It's not easy having one's head in the clouds
> And one's belly yearning. What do you suggest?'
>
> 'For starters', Cromwell smiled, 'try twenty-thousand dead.'

Cromwell himself is a figure of absolute self-confidence, absolute self-absorption, and absolute authority. He is all that Ireland lacks. In a long unpublished reflection on his poem that Kennelly wrote while he was working on it, the poet brooded on the image of Cromwell from which this poem derived:

There are other examples of English history, some serious, some extremely unserious, at work in the poem, but Cromwell is the chief one, the focus, the paradigm. The paradigm of what? Well, to start with the paradigm of power, of an egotism hard to understand and impossible to measure; of a compulsive need to possess and control; of an unquestionable value of his own being as a model for erring humanity. . . of a truly passionate sense of mission and purpose. . .

Yet in the face of such integrity of being Kennelly explores the inchoate psyche of Buffún, who he characterizes as

history's echo-chamber. . . some sort of man with many voices; not merely a man who speaks but one who is spoken through, a human wound through which history's blood seeps, congeals and then reworks itself into a new fluency.

Buffún wheedles, complains, boasts, blusters, mocks his enemy, excoriates the foe, relishes his discomfiture, provokes, entertains, but throughout is tortured by a corrosive sense of his own worthlessness and futility. Indeed images of vertiginous emptiness recur through the work as Buffún encounters his own multifarious identities. Buffún's fate is to possess no true selfhood, racked as he is by the 'terrible incestuous angers of Ireland':

> I thought I had died
> And was looking down on these mad absences
> And presences prowling cities; prowling minds
> To lash and smash them to smithereens
> Until all the living became shaken ghosts,
> The future a prison crammed
> With cowed nobodies and stammering haven't-beens.

Cromwell confronts the repetitive and quite unsparing nature of the Irish and English violence which this corrupting relationship has spawned. It's like a dangerously active infection:

> The bacteria enter the bloodstream through the lungs,
> Eyes, or tiny cuts in the skin.
> Quick as a tick, you're a victim.
> Also, you too infect your own lice.
> That is how the cycle begins again.

And the cycle has the atrocities of 1641 recurring as a farmer patrols his border land in the present troubles, a rifle at his shoulder.

Kennelly's work assumes the determinism of Irish history, but to portray this is not his primary purpose. Rather it is to allow the nightmare so full and complete an expression in a poetic imagining that Cromwell's time can be transcended. *Cromwell* attempts a shaman-like act of purgation, an imaginative exorcism of demonic possession, a breaking of the spell. It allows us to sup full of horrors; it allows the butcher to walk straight into our heads; it peers into the pit in an act of communal remembering and self-analysis which gives to its chastened and battered conclusion a note of hard-won grace:

> I peel the mushroom, moist flesh of earth and air,
> I taste ruined cities of man and God,
> I hear the makers calling (are the makers mad?)
> In the light of day and the light of night.

Such imaginative transcendence of an historical dilemma[4] may be the preserve of the artist. The state of consciousness to which it bears salutary witness, however, must compel attention as paradigm of that true freedom in history which it is the business of a liberating polity to serve.

NOTES

1. Seamus Heaney, *Preoccupations* (London 1980), p. 57.
2. Paul Fussell, *The Great War and Modern Memory* (London 1975), p. 72.
3. Mark Patrick Hederman, 'The Monster in the Irish Psyche', *Irish Literary Supplement*, Vol 3, No, 2 (Fall, 1984), p. 15.
4. Kennelly originally intended the title of the poem to be 'In the Light of Night'.

ACKNOWLEDGMENTS

'Saxon and Celt: The stereotypes' appeared in *Literary Interrelations: Ireland England and the World*, eds Wolfgang Zach and Heinz Kosok (Tübingen 1987), pp. 1-9.

'Tom Moore: A Reputation' appeared in *Gaeliana*, 8 (1986), pp. 39-50.

'The Church of Ireland and the Climax of the Ages' appeared in slightly different form as 'The Church of Ireland: Some Literary Perspectives' in *Search*, Vol. 3, No. 2 (Winter 1980), pp. 5-19.

'Canon Sheehan and the Catholic Intellectual' appeared in *Literature and the Art of Creation*, a festschrift for A. N. Jeffares published in 1988 by Colin Smythe Ltd.

'Yeats, Joyce and the Irish Critical Debate' appeared in a shorter form in a volume of essays on contemporary Irish writing published in 1988 by Colin Smythe Ltd.

'After the Revival: Seán O'Faoláin and Patrick Kavanagh' appeared as 'After the Revival: The Problem of Adequacy and Genre' in *Genre*, Vol. XII, No. 4 (Winter 1979), pp. 565-89 and in *The Genres of the Irish Literary Revival* (Pilgrim Books and Wolfhound Press, 1980) pp. 153-77.

'Some Young Doom: Beckett and the Child' appeared in *Hermathena*, No. CXLI (Winter 1986), pp. 56-64.

'Austin Clarke: Satirist' appeared in *The Poetry Ireland Review*, No. 22 (Spring/Summer 1988), pp. 111-21.

'Denis Donoghue and Us Irish' is part of an essay which appeared in *Krino*, No. 4 (Autumn 1987), pp. 88-95, as 'Forms of Critique'.

'Show Me a Sign: Brian Moore and Religious Faith' appeared as 'Show me a Sign: The Religious Imagination of Brian Moore' in *Irish University Review*, Vol. 18, No. 1 (Spring 1988), pp. 37-49.

'Poets and Patrimony: Richard Murphy and James Simmons' appeared in a shorter form in *Across a Roaring Hill: The Protestant Imagination in Modern Ireland*, eds G. Dawe and E. Longley (Belfast 1985), pp. 182-95.

A shorter and slightly different version of 'A Northern Renaissance: Poets from the North of Ireland 1965-1980' appeared as 'An Ulster Renaissance: Poets From the North of Ireland' in *Concerning Poetry*, Vol. 14, No. 2 (Fall 1981), pp. 5-23.

'Remembering Who We Are', first published under the title 'The Whole Protestant Community: The Making of a Historical Myth', was issued in slightly different form as a Field Day pamphlet in 1985.

'Awakening from the Nightmare: History and Contemporary Literature' combines and extends two essays in *Fortnight* No. 216 (March 1985), pp. 23-4 and *Theatre Ireland*, No. 13 (1987), pp. 40-41.

We are grateful to all the editors and publishers of the above.

For permission to include 'Gipsies Revisited' from *Lives*, and 'The Chair Squeaks' from *The Snow Party* by Derek Mahon, and to quote from the poems of Derek Mahon and of Frank Ormsby, we are grateful to the Oxford University

Press. All quotations from the poetry of Patrick Kavanagh are by kind permission of Katherine B. Kavanagh, c/o Peter Fallon, 19 Oakdown Road, Dublin 14. Quotations from Ciaran Carson's *The Irish For No* are by kind permission of the Gallery Press. All quotations from the poetry of Austin Clarke are by kind permission of R. Dardis Clarke. For permission to quote from Donald Davie's 'Helen Keller' we are grateful to the author. For permission to quote from Brendan Kennelly's *Cromwell* we are grateful to Beaver Row Press and to the author. Extracts from 'Bog Oak', from 'A New Song', from 'The Peninsula', and other quotations from the poetry of Seamus Heaney, are reprinted by permission of Faber and Faber Ltd from *Wintering Out* and *Door Into the Dark*. Extracts from 'Seals at High Island' and other quotations from the poetry of Richard Murphy are reprinted by permission of Faber and Faber Ltd from *High Island*, *The Battle of Augrim* and *The Price of Stone*. 'No More Sea', the extract from 'The Kingdom' by Louis MacNeice and other quotations from this poet are reprinted by permission of Faber and Faber Ltd from *Collected Poems*. The extract from 'After The Summit' by Tom Paulin is reprinted by permission of Faber and Faber Ltd from *Liberty Tree*. The quotations from 'The More a Man Has the More a Man Wants' by Paul Muldoon is reprinted by permission of Faber and Faber Ltd from *Quoof*. Quotations from the poetry of Geoffrey Taylor are by kind permission of Mrs Mary Taylor. The quotation from John Montague's *The Rough Field* is by kind permission of the author.

This book is published with the assistance of The Arts Council / An Chomhairle Ealaíon, Ireland.

INDEX

Adamson, Ian, 241n
AE – *see* Russell, George William
Allingham, William, 146, 147, 189
Anster, John, 32
Arnold, Matthew, 7-8, 9, 20, 35, 36, 41, 42, 47n, 180, 206
Auden, W. H., 137

Balzac, Honoré, 103
Barfield, Owen, 155
Barkley, John M., 230-3, 241n
Barnes, William, 207
Bayley, John, 168
Beckett, J. C., 228
Beckett, Samuel, 55-6, 117-26 *passim*, 143
Beckford, William, 27
Behan, Brendan, 248
Bennett, Arnold, 156
Bergson, Henri, 35
Berkeley, George, 3, 49, 63
Betjeman, John, 41, 55, 146
Birmingham, George, 51, 53, 56, 62-3
Blackmur, R. P., 169
Boucicault, Dion, 248
Boyd, Ernest, 91
Braidwood, John, 211
Brooke, Stopford A., 15
Brown, Stephen, 92
Browne, Valentine, 132
Butler, Samuel (bishop), 32
Butler, Theobald Richard Fitzwalter, 162
Byron, George Gordon, 19, 21-2

Canning, J. A., 240
Canny, Nicholas, 3, 4
Carleton, William, 51-2, 53, 56, 105
Carlyle, Thomas, 8, 67
Carpenter, Andrew, 60
Carson, Ciaran, 218-19, 220
Carson, Sir Edward, 250, 251
Carson, John T., 241-2n
Cecil, Lord David, 155
Chaucer, Geoffrey, 53
Chesterton, G. K., 163
Clare, John, 200
Clarke, Austin, 50, 93, 94, 96, 127-140 *passim*, 146, 169
Clerke, Mary – *see* Dowden, Mrs Edward

Collins, William, 21
Comte, Auguste, 35
Connolly, Cyril, 93
Cooke, Henry, 233, 234, 239-40, 241n, 242n
Corcoran, Austen, 76n
Conrad, Joseph, 193
Corkery, Daniel, vii, 17, 77-8, 82, 86, 92, 170
Cousins, James, 153
Crawford, R. G., 233-4
Cromwell, Oliver, 252, 255
Cronin, Anthony, 16
Cullen, Louis, vii
Curran, C. P., 78-9
Curran, Sarah, 25
Curtis, L. P. Jr, 12n, 13n
Cusack, Michael,, 123

Darby, John Nelson, 64n
Darwin, Charles, 37, 50, 60-1, 142, 145, 148, 208
Davie, Donald, 126, 201-02n, 209, 214
Davis, Thomas Osborne, 44, 73
Deane, Seamus, 20, 44-5, 85-8, 205, 211
Devane, James, 80
Devi, Ganesh, 27n
Dickstein, Morris, 169
Dillwyn, Mary – *see* Taylor, Mrs Mary
Donoghue, Denis, ix, 133, 139, 166-73 *passim*
Donegal, Lady, 24
Donne, John, 200
Dowden, Edward vii, 14, 27n, 29-48 *passim*, 59
Dowden, Mrs Edward, 33, 34
Dowden, John, 29, 33
Dowden, John Wheeler, 32
Dowden, Richard, 32-3
Drummond, W. H., 5-6, 7, 9

Edgeworth, Maria, 127
Edward VII, 9
Edwards, Philip, 47
Eglinton, John, 35
Eliot, George, 37-8, 41
Eliot, T. S., 199-200, 238
Emmet, Robert, 25

Faber, F. W., 35
Ferguson, Samuel, 7, 29, 44, 147

INDEX

Fiacc, Padraic, 227
Fielding, Henry, 53
Fletcher, Ian, 30
Flood, Frank Hallinan, 251
Ford, John (dramatist), 129
Foster, John Wilson, 165n
Foster, Roy, vii
Frederick William IV, 19
Froude, James Anthony, 8-9
Fulton, A. A., 234, 235
Furnivall, F. J., 35
Fussell, Paul, 250

Gallagher, Michael Paul, 184
Galvin, Patrick, 244
Garland, 200
Gibbon, Peter, 242n
Gibson, William, 242n
Geraldus Cambrensis, 3
Goethe, Johann Wolfgang von, 18, 29, 43
Gosse, Edmund, 15, 59
Greeves, Arthur, 156-64 passim
Gregory, Augusta Isabella, Lady, 57
Green, Roger Lancelyn, 156
Greene, Graham, 101, 174
Griffin, Edward Morgan, 54
Gwynn, Stephen, 16, 28n

Hall, Anna Maria, 65-6
Hall, Samuel Carter, 65-6
Hamilton (Calvinist minister), 239
Hamilton, Florence, 154
Hannay, James Owen, 53;
    see also Birmingham, George
Hardy, Thomas, 208, 213
Harris, Eoghan, 56
Hawthorne, Nathaniel, 99
Headley, F. W., 142
Heaney, Seamus, 10, 11, 12, 17, 192, 209, 210, 215-17, 243-4
Hederman, Mark Patrick, 253
Hewitt, John, 10-11, 12, 147, 189, 204
Higgins, F. R., 93
Hill, Geoffrey William, 51, 207
Holland, Lady, 14
Holmes, Finlay, 241n
Hooper, Walter, 156
Hope, Jemmy, 249
Hopkins, Gerard Manley, 192, 207, 208
Horace, 213
Hugo, Victor, 18-19
Hunt, Leigh, 18
Huxley, T. H., 142

Hyde, Douglas, 57, 129

Ibsen, Henrik, 35, 41
Ingram, John Kells, 32, 36

James, Henry, 99
Jarrell, Randall, 222
Jeffrey, Francis, 22-3, 28n
Jesus Christ, 35
Johnson, Samuel, 21, 155n
Johnston, Dennis, 128
Jones, T. Mason, 32
Jordan, John, 146
Joyce, James, viii, ix, 9, 16, 49, 51, 77-90 passim, 128, 171
'Jude the Obscure' (pseud.), 116n

Kavanagh, Patrick, 15-16, 50, 52, 103-16 passim
Kearney, Richard, 84-5
Keble, John, 35
Kelleher, John V., 7
Kennelly, Brendan, 246, 252-6
Kenner, Hugh, 168
Kiberd, Declan, 84-5, 122
Killen, W. D., 241
Kilroy, Thomas, 50
Kingsley, Charles, 20
Kinsella, Thomas, 82-3, 203-4
Kipling, 206

Larkin, Philip, 208-9, 213, 215
Lever, Charles, 32
Lewis, Albert James, 154
Lewis, Clive Staples, ix, 152-65 passim
Lewis, Warren, 156, 159, 161, 162
Longley, Edna, 168
Longley, Michael, 189, 214-15
Longman, Thomas, 18
Lynd, Robert, 80
Lyons, F. S. L., vii, 205

Mc Cormack, W. J., 58, 61
Mc Cracken, Henry Joy, 246
Mac Donagh, Oliver, 224-5, 226
Mac Donagh, Thomas, 16, 129
Mac Donald, George, 163
Mac Greevy, Thomas, 79-80, 84
Mc Guinness, Frank, 246, 250-2
Mc Guinness, Norah, 143
Maclise, Daniel, 19
Mac Neice, Elizabeth, 154
Mac Neice, John Frederick, 54, 154
Mac Neice, Louis, 54, 154, 164, 189,

INDEX

204, 213
Mac Neill, Eoin, 77, 92
Mahaffy, John Pentland, 34, 36, 41
Mahon, Derek, 56, 212-13, 217, 218
Malory, Sir Thomas, 157
Mangan, James Clarence, 79, 147
Marlowe, Christopher, 47n
Mason, Patrick, 251
Maunsell ('great-grandmother'), 142
Mauriac, François, 101
Maxwell, Desmond, 204
Medawar, Peter, 155n
Mercier, Vivian, 58, 118, 119, 127
Miller, David W., 242n
Mitchel, John, 73
Montague, John, 210, 217-18, 243, 244
Montague, Henry, 233
Moore, John, 25
Moore, Brian, ix, 174-88 *passim*
Moore, George, 50, 80
Moore, Thomas, viii, 14-28 *passim*, 79
Moran, D. P., 77, 92
Morris, William, 39, 157
Morton, Jelly Roll, 200
Mozart, Wolfgang Amadeus, 21
Muldoon, Paul, 218-21
Murphy, Richard, 189-97 *passim*, 200
Murphy, Thomas, 50

Newbolt, Sir Henry, 206
Newman, John Henry, 35, 124
Nicholson, Nancy, 144
Nicholson, Sir William, 144, 145, 151
Nietzsche, Friedrich, 35

O'Brien, Conor Cruise, vii, 172
O'Carolan, Turlough, 135
O'Casey, Sean, 54, 57, 85, 92-3, 128, 153, 248, 251
O'Connell, Daniel, 24, 33, 72, 83, 97-8, 99, 104
O'Connor, Frank, 81-2, 93, 94, 95-6, 98, 141, 151, 169
Ó Faoláin, Seán, 52-3, 72, 79, 81-2, 91-103 *passim*, 104, 111, 112-13, 114, 146
O'Flaherty, Liam, 92-3
O'Grady, Standish, 57
O'Higgins, Kevin, 206
O'Leary, John, 30
O'Neill-Crowley, Peter, 73
Ormsby, Frank, 203-4, 216, 217
Ormsby, Lucy Mary, 193
Owen, Wilfred, 152

Paisley, Ian Kirk, 235
Parker, Stewart, 242n, 246-50, 252
Parnell, Charles Stewart, 7, 74, 100, 101, 128, 207
Pater, Walter, 39, 41
Paulin, Tom, 16, 88, 223
Phibbs, Basil, 141
Phibbs, Geoffrey –
    see Taylor, Geoffrey
Pope, Alexander, 136
Power, Patrick, 50
Plunkett, Sir Horace, 143
Pynchon, Thomas, 182

Rabelais, François, 136
Reid, Forrest, 156
Reid, J. S., 239
Ricks, Christopher, 168
Robinson, Lennox, 143
Rodgers, W. B., 147, 204
Rogers, Pat, 127-8
Rossetti, Dante Gabriel, 39
Ruskin, John, 47, 59
Russell, George William, 78, 91, 92, 104, 143, 144, 153, 205

Said, Edward, 21
St Bernard, 187
St Paul, 3
Saintsbury, George, 17
Salmon, George, 36
Sarsfield, Patrick, 194, 202n
Sassoon, Siegfried, 152
Schubert, Franz, 55, 120
Schumann, Robert, 19
Scott, Sir Walter, 19
Shadwell, Thomas, 132
Shakespeare, William, 29, 35, 36, 39, 47n
Shaw, George Bernard, 9, 153, 165n, 248
Sheehan, Patrick Augustine, viii, 53-4, 65-76 *passim*
Shelley, Percy Bysshe, 36, 42
Sheridan, R. B., 47n
Sidney, Sir Philip, 157
Simmons, James, 189-90, 197-201 *passim*, 242n
Southwell, Sir Robert, 227
Spencer, Herbert, 35, 142
Spenser, Edmund, 3-4, 5, 6, 7, 8, 10, 11
Squire, Charles, 157
Stendhal, 18
Stephens, Edmund, 60

261

INDEX

Stephens, James (poet), 153, 157
Stewart, A. T. Q., 245
Strong, L. A. G., 16, 80-1
Swift, Jonathan,, 63, 136-9
Synge, Mrs Kathleen, 60, 64n
Synge, J. M., 57, 59-62, 64n, 81, 92, 103, 123-4, 170, 248

Taylor, Geoffrey, ix, 141-51 *passim*
Taylor, Mrs Geoffrey (Mary Dillwyn), 142n, 145
Taylor, Rebekah Wilbraham, 141
Tennyson, Alfred, 20, 47n, 206
Thomas, R. S., 51
Thompson, Sam, 242n
Todhunter, John, 34
Tolkien, J. R. R., 155, 163
Tone, Theobald Wolfe, 248 & n
Trench, Wilbraham Fitzsimon, 14-5, 18, 19
Trilling, Lionel, 169
Trollope, Anthony, 51, 53
Tyndall, John, 142

de Valera, Eamon, 94
Vendler, Helen, 168
de Vere, Aubrey, 29, 43-4

Wagner, Richard, 157
Wain, John, 155
Waugh, Evelyn, 174
Webb, David, 27n
Welch, Robert, 17, 26
West, Elizabeth Dickinson, 35, 40, 42, 47n
White, Agnes Romilly, 164
White, H. O., 40
White, Jack, 56
White, Terence de Vere, 16-17
Whitman, Walt, 38-9, 41, 45
Wilde, Oscar, 248
Williams, Charles, 155
Williams, Patrick, 227
Wilson, John, 22, 28n
Woodburn, James Barkley, 9-10, 241n
Wordsworth, William, 18, 145, 207

Yeats, John Butler, 29, 31, 33, 34, 44
Yeats, William Butler, vii, viii, ix, 9, 15, 16, 29-30, 31, 38, 41, 42, 44-6, 57, 59-60, 77-90 *passim*, 91, 92, 93, 95, 97, 103, 128, 132, 144, 153, 157-60, 163, 164, 170, 171, 180, 189, 200, 205, 206, 207, 226